Bill Mixer

— A —
BOY
— AT —
WAR

A Boy at War

Copyright © 2023 by William G. Maier

All rights reserved. No part of this publication may be reproduced, stored in a retrieval system, or transmitted, in any form or by any means, electronic, mechanical, photocopying, recording, or otherwise, without written permission of the publisher.

Book interior and cover design by Karl Moeller

ISBN-13
979-8-218-24937-3

Garamond typeface 12 pt.

Grateful acknowledgement is made to the following for previously published material:

Brothers: Black Soldiers in the Nam, Goff & Sanders
A Terrible Love of War, James Hillman
American Reckoning, Christian G. Appy
What it is like to Go War, Karl Marlantes
War is a Racket, Major General Smedley Butler
Armageddon In Retrospect, Kurt Vonnegut

A BOY AT WAR

Bill Maier

INTRODUCTION

My country's involvement in the Vietnam War intensified dramatically during the summer before my senior year of high school. I didn't like any of my options, but I especially did not want to be conscripted into the military. Two of my good female friends from high school were willing to legally marry me to keep me from having to go to Vietnam, so I wasn't worried about it until August 25, 1965, 10 months before I would graduate and be draft bait when marriage no longer counted as a draft deferment. You had to have a child and be married to get a deferment and I couldn't morally use a child that way, although the first person I hired as a combat veteran counselor was an excellent therapist who was born to keep her father from being drafted.

College would only give me a deferment until I got a Bachelor's degree, but not for graduate school. Then I would likely be drafted as an officer and I had no desire to give orders to others. I could see Canada from the kitchen window of my family home and could have dodged the draft by going there, but then I would have been a criminal in the United States for the rest of my life and I couldn't do that. So I joined the Marine Corps with a group of my friends, thinking I would be safer if I got the better training they provided. Instead, I found that very little of the training I received as a Marine ever helped me do my job in combat.

I was a rebellious kid in high school who chose not to be part of any of the typical social cliques. The popular kids might not have had me anyway, but as I walked down the hall I would be walking with a middling shy guy one day and a big boisterous athlete the next. Always an insomniac, I didn't need much sleep in high school and snuck out and back into my parent's house during the night a couple of times a week.

I got my first job and started smoking cigarettes at 15 1/2 years old. During school hours, I went to Tilly's, a little cafe/grocery store near the school, to smoke cigarettes and hang out. Every school term from 7th to 12th grade I was on the student council. The brainy nerds and I talked about books and played Pinochle. Mostly, I hung out with the regular students. I often got in trouble for talking to fellow students in class about the teacher's lecture. The teacher would say, "Bill, if you have something to share, say it to the whole class," which I was only too ready to do. I seldom did my homework, but I always participated in class discussions in a provocative way. I did throw a few spitwads at people too, still, most of my teachers seemed to enjoy having me in their classes.

My family went to church every Sunday and as a senior, I was the Vice President of the Methodist Youth Fellowship in charge of our weekly programs. I remember that during the first three weeks of that year, I presented my arguments for why it was sensible to be an agnostic. As a result of my persuasive arguments, two group members abandoned their childhood beliefs and joined me in my doubts.

During the first two months of my combat tour, I was a dumbfounded 18-year-old, relying on the hard-earned wisdom of those who had been in Nam longer. I was considered a "ground pounder" because most days we walked 5 to 15 miles in the sand or rice paddies of ankle-deep water.

Training had done little to prepare any of us for how quickly we needed to be flat on the ground when rifle fire came at us. "Eating dirt" was the way we referred to this violent reflexive action. I learned how fast I needed to "bite the dirt" by diving to the ground with the help of some great fellow Marines who were willing to stick their necks out to pull my ass down. The fourth time my unit of about 100 guys, Lima Company, was suddenly hit by the Vietcong fire, I was standing slack-jawed as bullets ripped by me when Mo reached up a powerful black hand and slammed me to the ground. He came to the Marine Corps from the slums of inner-city Los Angeles, where he had learned the survival skills of getting away from gunfire as a younger child, plus he had two months of combat before I got there. My transition from nonchalant teen to exhausted, hungry, thirsty, and hyper-alert teen soldier is probably familiar to many veterans of past brutal wars, but hard for today's Tik-Tok youth to fathom. We were thrown out there into the immediacy of life-and-death situations, the USA, we called "the world," nothing else seemed real. Combat felt surreal, like I was on a different planet.

Ten months into my tour, on December 1, 1967, my battalion, 1500 men, was assigned to Special Landing

Force Bravo. Bravo included one other battalion of Marines, a fleet of helicopters, and many mobile artillery vehicles that traveled on wheels or tracks. We worked from the ships of the Navy's Seventh Fleet which were floating just offshore of all of our landings. Special Landing Force Bravo, after training in amphibious assaults for three weeks in Subic Bay, the Philippines, returned to almost constant intense engagements with the North Vietnamese Army who were well-disciplined and heavily armed. We operated within sight of the Demilitarized Zone between North and South Vietnam. This type of fighting against forces that usually outnumbered us began to change me in many ways.

I invite you to sit in judgment of the choices I made in Vietnam. Should I be condemned for my behavior or is war the cause of the change in my values? You might decide that my tender conscience has been tortured enough for the things I did. Each American combatant had a different approach to staying alive. I leave it up to you to determine if the character I developed should be condemned or thanked, or just left alone. I have included the horrific and praiseworthy things I did and will fully support your final judgment of me.

As Kurt Vonnegut said in *Armageddon In Retrospect*,

"If, on Judgment Day, God were to ask Paul (me) which of the two should rightly be his eternal residence, Heaven or Hell, Paul (me) would likely suggest that, by his own and by Cosmic standards, Hell was his destiny—recalling the wretched thing he had done."

CHAPTER ONE
A LIFETIME OF TRAUMA IN THE FIRST WEEK
FEBRUARY 23, 1967

"To write of war is to reach as close as possible to that which can't be lived through"
                                              James Hillman, 2004.

I twinkle a flirtatious, "Goodbye" to the redheaded stewardess, then stumble and bump into a seat back. Embarrassed now, I turn and flash her a cockeyed grin. She smiles back at me and says, "Good luck to you, Marine." I have a spring in my step from our friendly exchange and trip on the door outside. One moment I am in the Boeing 707's cool interior, the next I am hit by the humid blast furnace heat of Da Nang Airfield. The line of GIs exits the plane ahead of Ken Boyd and me and heads toward a cluster of tents. Contrary to yesterday's staging at Okinawa, Japan's airfield which was a regular military base with solid buildings and paved roads, everything I see at Da Nang airfield, except for the tarmac runways, is made of dirt and tents.

The steamy air smells of what I will later find out is rotting fish and human feces used for fertilizer. Like any airfield, this one is surrounded by flat terrain. Immersed as I am in the smells and the deafening noise from planes, helicopters, and jeeps buzzing around, terror takes me over and I forget about the attractive girl I left on the plane. Nobody tells us what to do or where to go, and I'm afraid that bullets will start flying at any moment. Though I'd spent my grade school years in the desert heat of Yakima, Washington where I was used to vigorous play outdoors all day in the summer with my younger brother, Brad, it was no preparation for the heat now enveloping me in Vietnam.

Dutifully I follow the guy in front of me. We are used to following orders from the 16 weeks of boot camp and training. Maybe the first guys off the plane received orders, but Ken and I just follow along. Ken is the only guy I know on this commercial 707. Our whole line of 18-year-olds moves at a half crouch, hurriedly snaking in single file across the tarmac. Boyd, Ben Elliott, Mike Clark, and I from Port Angeles High School Class of 1966 had joined the Marines on the Buddy System on September 9, 1966. Looking around nervously, I wonder if we are already in danger and worry that we should be in a low crawl as we cross the tarmac.

Ken and I file into the dispersing tent on the edge of the airfield. He is acting calm, but he adjusts his glasses on his nose and stutters, "I wo-wo-wonder what unit we will be assigned to?" I scan the situation to determine how I can take advantage of it, then answer in my usual cocky-sounding voice, "We'll soon find out."

Inside the tent, I see that the side facing the airfield is rolled up for ventilation in the sweltering heat. Ken and I are sitting next to each other on gray metal folding chairs, silently waiting to see what will happen next. One of the three 19-year-olds in the front of the tent speaks loudly through a bullhorn, "PFCs Avril Johnson, Greg Carpenter, and Marcus Williams go to the truck outside. You are going to Charlie Company of the First Battalion of First Marine Regiment (1/1)." It appears we are being assigned to units. Five minutes later, when half the guys are out of the tent, the same booming voice rings out, "PFCs William Maier, Jack Brown, Steven McCormick and Thomas Heller, you're going to Lima Company of the Third Battalion, Seventh Marines of the First Marine Division (3/7)." He lists six other guys and then yells, "Pile in the 6X truck outside."

As soon as our group is all in the back of the big green military truck, it starts driving west. I wave goodbye to Ken. He disappears behind me, I'm evermore aware that this is the end of anything familiar. No one I went through training with is here. I have no idea how to protect myself, and I don't yet know how comforting the firepower of a rifle will feel. Before boot camp, I had never fired a gun. Riding with these equally young and scared-looking strangers, I am struck by the magnitude of the change in my life. I'm a small-town boy who is used to always being around people I knew, except doing my early morning paper route, bicycling across town to work as a Little League umpire, or being the Sunday janitor in the empty McGlenn's Thriftway grocery store. Before this moment, it was rare for me to not be around either family or friends for more than a few hours.

As we bang along in the back of the big truck, I get my first view of a third-world country. It is odd, but I feel like a tourist as I watch the black-pajamaed, heavily burdened peasants walking purposefully or pushing or pulling carts along the road. As they stagger along, most of the people I see have haggard faces and recessed eyes. Shacks made of cardboard, corrugated metal, tar paper, plywood, burlap sacks, plastic, rags and bamboo fronds line the dirt road. We are making our way inland from the airfield. I note several hills, rice paddies, and featureless rolling white sand stretching on both sides of us. Then ahead appears a mountain-sized block of granite called Marble Mountain.

As we start driving right alongside it, the truck slows due to the crowds of people on the road. Marble Mountain has rocky cliff-like walls with a few scraggly trees growing out of cracks in the rock face. On the top, I can see well-established bushes and trees. Looking around I find the jumble of American military installations mixed with Vietnamese squalor difficult to understand. I have no idea how important this location will become in my life and my ability to form friendships.

As we drive south and west through vast rice paddies, the makeshift shacks become increasingly further apart. The sun appears in a gap in the clouds and reflects off the bright white sand. We leave the rice paddies about two kilometers further southwest on a well-traveled road through open sand. We are on our way to a ten-foot-high sand berm that encircles a Marine base. This has to be 3/7 base camp area. Before we can see anything inside the base, the dirt road passes through the base's garbage area. People are scrounging around the dump for anything useful. Now I understand where some of the shack materials came from. The base's entrance is guarded by a stout metal pole that swings open to let our truck through.

We leap off the back of the truck in front of a tent with the words "3/7 Battalion Headquarters" stenciled in black paint above the door. A business-like Marine approaches and examines our orders. "Maier, Brown, McCormick, and Heller you guys follow Cpl. Nixon to Lima Company," he says, pointing at the four of us and Nixon. We walk for a couple of minutes to the Lima Company tents. Lance Corporal Ron Fox, the clerk at the Lima Company command tent, points at McCormick and me and says, "You two big guys are assigned to 60mm mortars to hump ammo." Brown and Heller are assigned to the first platoon. I know from training that an infantry company is supposed to consist of 120 men who carry rifles, machine guns, rockets, grenade launchers, and mortars. All of us are called infantry, nicknamed "grunts, ground pounders, or legs." Cpl. Fox says, "The company is out in the field now, so I will take you to your tents and come get you for chow in three hours."

Four older Marines are standing outside the company tent. "Hey, do any of you guys want to play poker after chow?" asks the shortest member of the group. I am a competent poker player, so I naively say yes. I return to their tent after eating for the game.

By the end of the evening the high-level noncommissioned officers, or NCOs, have cheated me out of $150. As I exit the tent, I realize I have been suckered by a strategy they use to take new recruits' money. This is how it operates. The man to my right bets into me, and when I call his bet the guy to my left raises the bet. This way if any of them get a good hand, my money has helped build a bigger pot for them. They probably split the profits they make any time they get a pigeon in their trap. This practice of cheating recruits means that if they were out in the field they would be vulnerable to being shot at by their own men. I never saw any of these E-7s or E-8s out in the field. I will need to watch my step in this world.

I realize that my bumbling youth better change. I am a good athlete, but I tend to run into things or rush through physically demanding activities. Trusting my athleticism has shaped me into a long skinny, aggressive defensive lineman in football. Despite a lanky build with my stubborn nature, I can hold my ground against much heavier boys. Elliott, my high school friend was also a defensive lineman. Like me, he is tall and lean, but he is faster and stronger, so he could force his way through blockers to make the tackle on the ball carrier. Barging into things isn't a good idea here.

It rained during the night, so this morning the sand is wet until we return from the chow hall. I've been hearing gunshots in the near and far distances all morning. Fox, the company clerk, shows us the ropes. Our first stop is battalion supply. McCormick and I each receive packboards, as well as a rucksack, cartridge belt, M-14 rifle, two ammo pouches, nine-7.62 caliber magazines with 20 rounds each, a flak jacket, a steel helmet, two metal canteens, a knife (known as a K-bar), a rubber poncho and an entrenching tool. The total weight of our gear is 35 pounds. Additionally, McCormick and I are given seven mortar rounds weighing 27 pounds, which we are instructed to strap onto the flat of the pack-board.

I trudge back to the mortar tent with my heavy burden, when sharp rifle fire snaps close to me. In my mind's eye, I imagine someone hiding in the bushes shooting just over the top of the berm, hoping to startle us. Well, it sure frightens me! My eyes dart around in search of cover, but I remain frozen in place. This is the first time my body experiences the completely foreign feeling of being shot at. A fast-moving bullet has no chance of getting down low enough to hit me, but I don't know that yet. I shake myself out of my stupor and continue walking back to our tent.

Six hours pass with the four of us having no idea what is going on. If I had been stuck with nothing to do like this in high school, I would have started up a conversation with anyone around. Here, the others are quiet and wary.

Following dinner, the four of us FNGs (Fucking New Guys) are led to a group of Marines meeting in the soft sand at the foot of the berm for instructions on how to stand guard duty in the bunkers which are spaced around the perimeter. We all have M-14s, cartridge belts with ammunition, flak jackets, helmets, K-bars, and two canteens. McCormick and I accompany two Marines to a bunker.

"You take third watch after him," one of the combat soldiers says, pointing at me and then at McCormick. "No more talking," he calmly states. The bunker has four sandbag walls, each five feet high. Inside the bunker, a second row of sandbags faces out toward the landscape, where we are to keep an eye out for an attack. Only the head of the person on watch sticks above the top sandbags. The rest of us can be out of harm's way because the floor of the bunker is dug down. Unlike me, the other two guys in our bunker don't seem nervous at all, but they are not joking or talking. They seem focused on their task of remaining alert. We all take turns being awake through the night while the other three Marines sleep. The clouds lift during my watch, but the sky is still overcast. The hidden moon allows me to see that in front of me are trees, bushes, and three hooches that look like they belong in a primitive African jungle.

The next night, Fox informs McCormick and me that we have been assigned to patrol outside the berm. It's getting dark, which is a slow process here. The sky gradually begins to explode into the greatest light show I have ever seen. It reminds me of the Port Angeles city-sponsored Fourth of July fireworks displays. Seven months ago, my girlfriend Mary Dyar and I watched the fireworks with other people from the community, all of us saying, "Wows" and, "Oohs." That show appeared to be a speck on the horizon when compared to this colorful sky. As we gather (stage) near the berm for a ten-man patrol outside the perimeter, the bright, slowly changing colors fill the whole sky. Pink, orange, and purple puffs of smoke from air-burst explosions reflect the setting sun, reminding me of my hometown's fireworks.

After the first three guys move out toward two overlapping rolls of barbed, concertina wire, the squad leader signals me to leave with a silent motion of his left hand. We space out because we have been trained to keep enough distance between us so a hand grenade won't get more than one of us at a time. If we are bunched up, we would become "an attractive target." Each step gets scarier.

The sand is wet from today's rain and it's an eerie off-white color, as I walk out over the top of the berm in the fading light. My dramatic sunset of 20 minutes ago has lost its colors. I hear sporadic gunfire and explosions in the distance. I am now much more afraid than I was last night on guard duty or when I got off the 707 at the airfield two days ago. This is real danger! I can't fathom that I'll have 13 more months of this kind of fear. We did no training for the feeling of this type of patrol, and even if we had, it wouldn't have held the intense danger I am now feeling. My senses are much more alert than when I was inside the berm. I make awkward jerky turning and scanning motions, trying to get as much information as I can from my five senses. My fear is urging me to shoot my M-14 at the bushes that look like moving Vietcong. I don't know what to do. I'm scared, so I follow the barely visible guy in front of me.

I'm on the path between the zigzagging between the ends of the internal and external roles of waist-high, hooped concertina wire. This wired route stretches around the battalion area, 50 feet beyond the berm. My cartridge belt cuts into my hips as I walk in a crouch to the open end of the outside coil. The helmet feels like I'm holding a bag of sugar on my head. Everything feels awkward and strange and my fear of the unknown keeps building. The memory of my fear, when the bullets passed harmlessly overhead, has become less intense. Out here walking around in the open is a whole different thing. It all seems surreal, and I feel like I am inside a bizarre scene designed by

Salvador Dali. I don't know what it is I'm looking for, but I know that I want to see it before it hurts me.

I scan side to side searching for danger. Every bush seems like it could be hiding a VC. We pass through a treeline with bushes on uneven ground and I realize I can no longer see the base. The crescendo of fear has reached terrifying proportions. I can see the footprints in the sand of the three guys in front of me, but the soldiers aren't visible. I feel completely alone in a dangerous situation. I begin to swivel more frantically to look for danger. Other than walking, I am not sure what we are doing. After two hours, we return to the safety of the berm, retracing our steps back through the opening in the waist-high barbed wire.

In the tent, I collapse on my cot and can't believe how much safer I feel.

The next morning the four of us FNGs are ordered to get on top of one of two massive track vehicles, called Amtraks. They are 10 feet tall, 20 feet long, and 10 feet wide, and are much like a big travel trailer with one-inch thick double steel walls and a hinged door that drops down to become a ramp in the back. The heavy door is tapered and opens the entire back for ease of loading supplies or troops. The ramp is wide enough for a jeep to drive in. There is a 60-caliber light machine gun mounted on top. We are sitting on a double row of sandbags around the top edge.

In addition to the standard gear that I was issued three days ago, my rucksack now holds four C-ration meals adding another 22 pounds to my cumbersome packboard. When I am naked, I weigh 145 pounds and stand 6'2" tall, so not much meat on my bones. The waist strap of my packboard digs into my hips, and my shoulders are being rubbed raw by the straps. Every time I move, I overstretch and readjust the pack. Our two Amtraks pass through the gate and I notice the football field-sized garbage pile once more. As we continue on, we turn west, the opposite way we came from Da Nang airfield. We drive off the road and proceed through various landscapes, including sand and the ubiquitous rice paddies. I see four Vietnamese hooches to the north of us and notice some children and elderly people moving around them. This is a typical domestic scene in this territory, but I am feeling on high alert for any possible attacks because it's all so new to me.

As we drive down a slope next to a dry rice paddy, I see the grotesque scene of two naked bodies, a Vietnamese man and a woman around 20 years old. The man's dick has been severed and is stuck in the woman's mouth. The ace of spades, a playing card, protrudes from her vagina. "That card is the Alpha Company, 1/7, marker," the machine gunner says. "They want the Vietcong (VC, or Charlie) to know they killed these people." My stomach churns with disgust, and I wonder what horrendous things must have happened to that unit to cause them to behave in such a dehumanizing manner. Could I ever pull something like this off, I ponder? We continue forward. A few kilometers later, we arrive in the midst of the Lima Company's 80 Marines.

Brown and Heller, two grunts (Infantry: Military Occupational Specialty, MOS code=0311), descend. With our pack boards and the extra pounds of mortar rounds, McCormick and I awkwardly haul our heavy asses down the ladder on the side of the Trak. Marines from Lima Company have gathered around the open back ends of the two Amtraks. "This is Del Malinowska, who you will be the ammo humper for," Butch Austin, the mortar squad leader, says to me as he leads us over to two of the three mortar pits. I see that Del is a couple of inches taller and 70 pounds of muscle heavier than I am. "This is your gunner, Mo," Butch says to McCormick. Mo is a black-skinned, broad-shouldered athletic-looking guy who is a few inches shorter than me. He reminds me of a shorter, thicker Clarence Coleman, a school friend from the only black family living in Port Angeles. I bring a box of C-rations over to Del's gun so they can split them up. My company and I finish unloading food, ordnance, and water from the Amtraks. Everyone fills their cartridge belts with bullets, their canteens with water, and their packs with supplies. Then 15 minutes after the four of us new guys arrived at the Lima Company bivouac, the Amtraks leave with our garbage.

"McCormick and Maier, tail-end Charlie, you will be the furthest back people covering our rear," Butch says as our company departs. A sniper behind McCormick and me begins shooting at us the moment the company's last men in front of us walk over a rise and disappear. He and I stare at each other, unsure of what to do. Do we return fire from such a vulnerable position? We could look for cover, but the rest of the crew is probably leaving. Instead, we take off running to catch up with them, stumbling under the weight. We make our way up to the rest of the company and adjust our spacing. "Proper spacing" means maintaining visual contact with the men in front and behind you while remaining as far apart as possible. For the next five hours, we patrol for no apparent reason.

We set up our perimeter for the night as the first hints of dusk appear in the gray skies. We mortarmen excavate three mortar pits. It's good dirt, not rock-hard dry rice paddy or sloughing sand, so we dig circular pits six feet across and 18 inches deep in just 15 minutes. Del has the gun set up. Bud Jones, our team leader, uses his compass to determine the direction of the two visible tree lines. "Shoot a round at both treelines to set the exact distance and scare anyone who might want to use them for cover to shoot at us," Bud says quietly to Del.

McCormick and I snap our ponchos together and find two three-foot-long sticks to hold up the center of our tent. We tighten it up and stake the sides into the ground. After preparing and eating our C-rations, Del goes into the mortar pit for first watch at 10:00

p.m. I lie on the ground trying to sleep, but my mind's racing with all the ways I could be killed. No one says anything about being afraid of death, but our facial expressions are filled with terror and anger. "Wake Bud up at 3:00," Del reminds me at 12:30. With only my clothes to keep me warm, the nighttime temperature of 65 degrees begins to feel cold. I'm terrified I'll fall asleep and have my throat cut.

At 3 a.m., I wake Bud up, get in the tent, and then fall fast asleep for two and a half hours. I had no idea this was such a luxurious amount of sleep. During the rest of my 13-month tour, being able to split watch three ways was rare in "The Bush"; the norm was two people.

It's strange to wake up in the dark, lying on the ground in a place I'm only just getting to know. It rained during the night, so the sand is wet. I decide on the ham and eggs meal for breakfast. My C-ration can opener is a 2-inch by 1/2-inch strip of thin stainless steel with a hooked, fold-out stub of a blade. I cut four slits in the bottom of a small empty can from last night's dinner and bend the sides in to let air flow into my makeshift stove. I rip open the sealed plastic utensil packet and remove the 3-inch square of heavy brown foil containing one heat tab. I light the blue tab inside the can stove and place the opened can of ham on top of the blue flame until it begins to bubble. After eating, we dismantle our tent and begin stowing our belongings. Then we fill in the mortar pits and we leave by 6:45 a.m.

During the morning we walk through rolling hills and flat areas with rice paddies. I'm not sure where we're going or what we're doing. We move as quietly as possible while remaining on high alert. After hours of moving, Butch, leading the mortarmen, motions with his hand for us to stop. Our group of 12 guys, along with the rest of the command post, CP group, are in the center of Lima's 84-man double-column movement that spans a half mile. We all find cover and appear to have come to a halt on a well-worn path through bushes and trees that leads to an open area. Someone yells, "Engineer up!" I stay put and looking around, and wonder what an "engineer" is. A man with a lot of equipment hanging off his pack walks past us; he must be the engineer. He walks in a low crouch to the front of the company to the pointman. 15 minutes later, someone else yells, "Fire in the hole." I try to hide my long body by getting even more intimate with the dirt. A muffled explosion occurs. I come to the conclusion that an engineer must be someone who blows things up.

After several hours and a few more miles of walking, just as we take off our packs, we are surprised as three bullets whiz by from a tree line 500 meters away. Everyone around me falls to the ground, rifles pointing out in all directions around us. The Marines facing the tree line fire four-to-five round bursts. Finally, I too get down and fire my entire 20-round magazine at the tree line. Then I struggle to get the buckle on my magazine pouch open. It's the same type of stiff canvas strap and metal buckle as on a pair of rubber galoshes, which is also the same strap and buckle that secures the bipod legs to the mortar tube. Unbuckling that strap will determine how quickly one can hit the enemy with mortar fire. By the time I change magazines, all shooting ceases. The other Marines used two or three magazines, while I only used one.

I get off the ground along with everyone else a few minutes later and begin setting up a perimeter for the night. The same routine as the night before: dig the mortar pit, pitch the tent, cook, and eat a meal. While we eat Del explains what happened earlier, "Fuckin'-A, man, they found a booby trap and blew the fuckin' thing up." Del tells me I'll be first on the watch in an hour. Because the moon isn't up, the transition from twilight to darkness is quite frightening. Later, by the time I wake Bud for second watch, there is faint moonlight that is obscured by the overcast skies.

As we eat breakfast and pack our belongings, it begins to rain. I walk behind Del, as Lima Company leaves, my poncho covers me and my packboard. Again, I have no idea what we are doing, except walking around in the bush. The rain stops two hours later. We remain in this location long enough for our ponchos to dry. Mo is two feet to my right, when a bullet whizzes between us, sounding like an angry bee two inches away from my ear. A fraction of a second later, many more rifles fire at us. The bullets from across the rice paddy pepper the ground nearby. I freeze in place and my jaw drops. As he dives for the dirt, Mo grabs my shirt by the right shoulder and slams me down with him. My body's natural reflexes and sense of balance keep me from getting hurt. I am grateful for my body's memory of the dance-like javelin-throwing movement I used to win ribbons for my high school track team the year before. I will need to use all of that coordination, plus some over here.

We open fire on the tree line two football fields away. None of us is hit, and the firefight is over in seconds. The second platoon of riflemen is then sent across the paddy to investigate the source of the firing. The rest of the company prepares to leave when the second platoon returns. As they pass us, Bud asks one of the returning grunts if they found anything. "Nothing; no blood trails, bodies, or any sign they were ever there." For the rest of the morning, we walk and stop. I'm trying to imagine how the enemy could simply vanish, or how did they survive our onslaught of 7.62mm rounds and machine gun fire?

Around mid-afternoon, we set up our field perimeter for the night out in a dry rice paddy and into the trees. The third platoon is dispersed among the trees. Mo and Del's mortars are manning two positions of our perimeter out in the paddy so that it is possible to fire each gun without hitting the trees. As part of the perimeter defense, both pits are located on the outside edge of the company's position. With no infantry between our mortar pit and what is known as "No-man's Land," which is anywhere that isn't controlled by Americans and is considered enemy territory. Duty watch that night has a very different feel. I can hear heavy-track vehicles moving in the distance, then two Amtrak arrive in the middle of our perimeter.

Some of us are tasked with unloading the C-rations, ammunition, and other supplies. All of our garbage is returned to the trak. "Anything you leave out in the bush will be used to make booby traps," Jackson says. Bud, Del, and I shared a cardboard C-ration box of 12 meals. They let me choose one meal first, then they each chose one, and so on until we each have four meals to carry. Del ends up with ham and lima beans. The "ham and motherfuckers" are always the last one chosen. Butch, the mortar squad leader, goes over to Capt. Marks' tent that evening, and with his dark features, confidence, and size he reminds me of my high school friend Mark Pesola who was the lead actor in most of the school plays. Butch returns to us and explains that we will be using a new strategy of keeping the mortars together in an attempt to bracket the enemy with mortars rounds in front of their movement and behind them when we see them running.

That night, after we sight-in our mortars, the forward observer, or FO, orders artillery rounds to prep-fire two additional areas from which the enemy could attack. Two rounds per volley scream over our heads and explode in the treelines. An Antos unit arrives an hour before dark. It's zooming across the paddy and I think it must be going 40mph. This powerful tracked vehicle, with its six 106mm recoilless rocket tubes and a 50 caliber spotter rifle, will occupy one of our perimeter positions with nothing behind it because the back blast when it shoots would fry you at eight paces.

I wake up after an uneventful night to overcast skies and no rain. At the first sign of daylight, however, a sniper fires two shots at us and we retaliate. The Antos fires a 50-caliber spotting round directly at the sniper's position, followed by a 106-caliber round. What an amazing sight! As the round screams out of one of the six barrels and blasts into the tree line where the sniper was, a burst of flame shoots 20 feet behind the Antos. But once again, when the third platoon investigates the results of this onslaught of our firepower, they discover nothing.

Today, the Antos joins us on patrol. It's reassuring to know that an ambush will be met with so many rounds as quickly as that thing maneuvers and fires. We're doing more stopping than walking today. We walk slowly for about two hours through various landscapes before stopping for an hour. After three more long stops, we set up in a loose perimeter with fields of fire all around us. Then we just sit around until it's time to patrol again in an hour. Finally, we come to a halt for the night. We haven't seen a single Vietnamese person all day. Before I begin first watch, Bud instructs me to close my right eye as soon as it begins to darken, so that my eye will have full night vision when it is completely dark. It's been scary to wait 15 minutes for night vision to start working the last two nights and I'm grateful for Bud's instructions.

In training, I'd learned that I could see much better in the dark if I didn't look directly at something. Employing these two skills, I'm getting better at spotting danger in the limited light of dusk or dawn.

After a breakfast of beef steak, apple sauce, crackers, and peanut butter, our 60mm mortar team is heading out on a search-and-destroy mission with the third platoon. The rest of Lima Company stays in position and keeps our knapsacks. So we are only carrying our weapons and cartridge belts, which means we have our pack boards with 27 lbs of ammo. The 28 of us sweep through the village where we were sniped from the night before.

First squad's eight members spread out in front, each 20 feet apart. We four mortarmen trail first squad, with the platoon commander, a second lieutenant with his radio operator, a forward observer (FO), and a corpsman. Del, the mortar gunner, carries only a 45 pistol, our heavy mortar tube, and his two full canteens. Second and third squads are slightly behind first squad on either side. Bud and I are in charge of protecting our backside. We perform full-body pivots in order to cover the front, the sides, and behind us. Despite the fact that my finger is always on the trigger of my M-14 with the safety off, the muzzle points at the ground as it passes in line with Jackson walking in front of me. When I concentrate on the rear, where there is no one from my unit, my rifle is raised to scan for the most likely targets.

We sweep four villages, carefully searching each as we pass through. As we leave the fourth village a barrage of bullets comes from a cluster of Vietnamese hooches behind us and whiz by our heads. In my terror, I fire all 20 rounds in my magazine in one burst. I pull the second magazine from my ammunition pouch and fire shorter bursts until that magazine too is empty, then replace it with a new one. When we return to the village and we only see women, children, and elderly people. They appear scared but innocent. Back when I was at the battalion area base camp, I'd overheard grunts at the mess hall complaining about being shot at by elderly villagers and children. I wonder just how innocent these Vietnamese standing before me are. Is it possible that they are our enemies?

CHAPTER TWO
FRIENDSHIPS

"It (war) is conducted for the benefit of the very few, at the expense of the very many"

Major General Smedley Butler,
two time Medal of Honor recipient, 1935.

Last night's watch was uneventful, but as usual, I was terrified. This morning the fog is thick. The final meal in my pack final is a B-3 Unit with boned chicken, canned bread, cocoa, cookies, and berry jam. Bud and I are in the mortar pit to cook and eat our breakfast and he shows me how to heat up the canned bread by using the C-ration opener to cut slits into the top of the bread can, drizzle some water onto the top of the can, and then to heat it up you place the can over the flame. While I mill around with the guys and enjoy my warm bread and jam, I begin to notice a growing sense of connection to those around me. Jackson sits casually on the edge of the mortar pit, his handsome face is relaxed. He is a quiet, dignified boy who appears to be more like a man than the rest of us. His 13-month tour in Vietnam is coming to an end in four months. Del is cleaning his pistol a few feet away from Jackson. I wonder if we'll spend the entire day just sitting around. Despite only knowing these guys for six days, it already feels much like I am hanging out in the plaza of my high school,l chewing the fat with a group of my friends.

After six hours of doing nothing but staying alert and being fearful, we finally pack up and arrange ourselves for the usual double-column traveling formation and begin the daily move. No one tells us what to do. The guys around me don't seem to care who is giving orders or what those orders are. This movement appears more purposeful than usual, so perhaps we're on our way somewhere specific. We do stop a few times, but the stops are brief. During the second stop, somebody from first squad yells, "Engineer up!" The engineer then walks to the front of our line to disarm a booby trap. After three more hours of walking, the fog begins to clear. We leave a tree line and then see the berm of our battalion area, "The Rear," and walk back into the main gate.

Once inside the mortar squad tent, we clear the center of the floor of cots and dump all the dirty, damp gear on the floor in a spread-out pile. We hang our rifles, cartridge belts, and packboards on the wooden 2X4 tent frame, then we make our way over to the mess hall for dinner. Without my heavy gear on, I feel light enough to float off the ground. The mess hall is identical to every other Marine mess hall I've ever visited. Still, there is something different about me this time.

My new status as a combat Marine is now revealed by the fact that I am covered in dirt and looking as grubby and hostile as the infantry grunts, not like the clean guys that are serving us our food. I line up with a stainless steel tray and get served macaroni and cheese with canned string beans, corn, and white bread. We mortarmen are seated quietly around two long tables with benches, only attending to our eating. I eat every crumb and on my way to take my empty tray to the guys washing dishes, I snag a piece of white beard from the guy behind me. Then I stand off to the side of the guys giving their trays to the kitchen patrol people (KP), and three more guys give slices of bread from their trays. Now, I am feeling almost full. I'm a skinny, tall teenager with a big appetite and thus begins another coping mechanism for staying alive during my tour of duty in Vietnam.

With clear sunny skies, a breeze picks up in the late afternoon. We spend a few hours straightening out our gear before I go to the PX. I purchase three packs of Winston cigarettes as well as some comic books. I haven't read a comic book in years, and I'm not sure why I'm doing it now, but I need something to keep me entertained. As evening falls, a group of us heads over to the outdoor movie theatre. I watch Madame X for the first of many times. The movie begins at dusk, and a burst of rifle fire whizzes over our heads from outside the berm. Several rounds are "tracers," which produce a bright red line along their path to help the shooter see where their bullets are going in the dark. I can see how high they had to climb and the angle they had to take to clear the 10-foot-high berm that surrounds the rear and protects us from rifle fire. Back at our tent after the movie, I decide to readjust my cot by taking off the wooden brace at the end so my ankles don't press into the wood while I sleep. Because none of us have to stand watch, I gratefully get a full six hours of sleep.

Sunday's breakfast is a little more upscale than the others: bacon, choice of eggs (over-easy for me), pancakes, juice, and milk. Several of the guys leave for church services. I go knife-throwing with Igor, a short ammo humper on Stan's mortar team. Stan is the third gunner. Igor and I begin attacking a telephone pole near the battalion supply with our knives. After the terror of The Bush, it's easier for me to imagine launching my K-bar at a VC, with the point striking his or her heart before the handle. Brad, my brother, and I used to go out in the backyard and throw our pocket knives in the grass to see who could stick it the best, but this has a more desperate feel to it.

I received no training in knife throwing, but it feels like it could easily be necessary for close-quarters fighting. And, I'd rather stick my K-bar in a guy 10 feet away than stab him close up. After an hour of throwing, I figure out the distance for two flips-about 10 feet-ending with the knife sticking in the pole. I can also throw underhand and keep the blade forward for about eight feet if I am closer. Igor, a kid from a small town in upstate New York, who I don't know much about, is frequently on his cot on the back left side of our tent, just oddly holding his head up off his cot for hours and doing nothing. I'm at the same skill level as Igor after an hour of practice. Later in the morning, I hang out in the tent and read Dr. Strange and The Avengers comic books.

Because the thirty of us will be leaving with the second platoon, we, Del's gun team, are told to arrive early for dinner. We board two Amtraks after dinner and travel out the front gate, and motor through vast expanses of sandy, brush-covered hills, and pass by hedgerows, tree lines, and the occasional hamlet surrounded by rice paddies and cultivated plots. The traks drop us off, and we walk for two more hours before setting up our night perimeter. At dusk, a sniper shoots at us, but I easily fall asleep a few minutes later. It is just as though the sound of bullets is playing me a lullaby.

When I wake, the wind is blowing gently, and the rain is bothersome. We spend the majority of the morning milling about. Being out in the field with only thirty other guys feels more dangerous. If we get attacked, I wonder if we'll have enough firepower to hold off the enemy until the helicopters arrive. I eat ham slices, fruit cocktail, crackers, peanut butter, and a piece of chocolate for my meal. Otherwise, we just clean weapons and do nothing until we have to leave around noon.

Eventually, we move through an area with narrow trails with the mortars in the "Tail-End Charlie" position of our single line. Everyone clears brush with their machetes. I notice that walking in the last position makes me feel a little safer because I try to step exactly where the guy in front of me did. Those footprints are much wider in the back. Suddenly an explosion occurs in the front of the line. The point man, Harry, has tripped a Chicom hand grenade, which has half the explosive power of an American hand grenade. There was also no "pling" as there is when the spoon flies free to arm an American grenade. A Chicom is frequently an empty C-ration can filled with explosives and nails. The opening is soldered shut and holds a four-inch wooden plug that has been bored out to allow a blasting cap to be inserted.

A narrow trail is an ideal location for a Chicom, which has an almost invisible tripwire a few inches above the ground attached to the blasting cap. As I listen to Harry scream, I picture his boot giving the taut string just enough wiggle to set off the grenade. The explosion has the potential to be lethal. He keeps screaming until the corpsman probably injects him with morphine and he calms down. Because we set up defensive positions to create a Landing Zone (LZ), I assume he has a serious wound and requires hospital treatment. The medevac helicopter, a CH-34 with a single rotor, flies in and then out almost instantly. A Huey gunship circles above, escorting it.

The rain returns in force in the mid-afternoon and I'm amazed to see how well the poncho protects all of my gear. We stop several times for about an hour.

These stops are both boring and terrifying times. Each time we come to a halt, I sit there, staying alert to my fields of fire, and I'm not sure why we've stopped. One disadvantage of walking tail-end Charlie is that I don't know what is going on at the front of the movement. Then we walk for two more hours and set up a perimeter a half-hour before dusk, with one side along a tree line and the mortar pit as one of the line positions, therefore no grunt positions between us and no-man's-land. For dinner, I try beans and wieners. I don't eat beans, so I toss them. As the night progresses, I get hungrier and hungrier. My mother's face flashes before my eyes. She isn't angry at me in the image, but she is concerned. I would have had lunch with Marjorie or Mary at the school cafeteria a year ago. The cooks all kept an eye on me because they knew I could eat like a horse and would want extra servings.

Before the first light of morning, we pack up and leave without eating. It's windy and cloudy. Before it's full light, we begin walking, now I'm really hungry. I'm also upset that we move without eating. After walking for an hour, we form an online sweep through a village. The air is cool, but I am drenched in sweat from the forced march. Ten minutes later, as we begin to move, the sweat evaporates and my body heat dries my clothes.

It takes an hour to complete the sweep of the hamlet, and we discover nothing. There are six hooches in a large area, that are constructed with bamboo supports, woven bamboo slats for wall coverings, and bamboo fronds for roofing. Three young mothers dressed in black pajamas are in a hooch; the rest of the villagers that are milling around are stooped and wrinkled elderly people or children. The people appear friendly and trustworthy, and the stop has given us time to wander around the village. I sit in the hooch with the three women. One mother is nursing her one-year-old son while she is sifting rice in a two-foot-diameter flat woven tray. She gracefully arcs the dry rice into the air. The kernels all fall into the tray neatly. In the light breeze, some of the chaff blows away. The mom ignores the boy's pee running down his leg into the rice.

The break finally allows us to eat. I heat a can of meatloaf and bread with grape jam from a B-3 unit and save the cocoa for later. Each meal's accessory pack contains a foil-wrapped heat tab, a plastic spoon, pepper, salt, instant coffee (which I never see anyone use), creamer, two Chicklets, a box of four cigarettes, toilet paper, and waterproof matches all sealed in a plastic bag.

The cloud cover lifts in the late afternoon, but not enough to allow the sun to shine through. As we move out, once more I am in tail-end Charlie. We stop five times for 10-40 minutes each. The lead squad must be finding a lot of booby traps. During the pauses, there is little to do. My area of responsibility is to scan behind us, and we have just walked through that area and would have seen any danger, so

I feel safe. Walking in the hard dirt we're patrolling through, it's difficult to tell where Igor who is in front of me has stepped. If we get ambushed, the guys in the front or middle of our line are the most likely to be hit. But, I might also get sniped at back here.

We set up camp in a tree line for the night. As we dig the mortar pit, it begins to rain, and we quickly stretch our poncho tents to cover our gear. I eat spaghetti and meatballs from a B-2 unit, which includes cheese spread, crackers, and a pecan roll. While we are eating, we come under attack. I dive for dirt, then notice that the more experienced guys just keep eating. They seem to know that the bullets aren't very close to us.

We've run out of food this morning. It's cool and overcast, with a few gusts of wind. I savor the cocoa I saved. As we wait for the choppers to arrive, we gather our belongings and take defensive positions. After Lt. Varner receives word that the CH-46s are on their way. The last thing we do is fill in the mortar pit. The two double-rotor choppers cause quite a windstorm as they land and lower their rear cargo doors, allowing us to board. We take off before I've even gotten into my seat. The safety protocol is to be a loud, large target for as little time as possible. As the bird struggles to lift off with the weight of 15 fully loaded Marines, it drifts toward the opening in the trees to our right. This forward momentum allows the pilot to pull back on the controls and get us moving up without stalling. I am aware my body is tense with the fear of the immediate danger of crashing, then I relax when we get high enough to be safe from rifle fire.

The next day after morning chow at the battalion area, Lima Company is ordered to go to the firing range to try the new Stoner Weapons System. We are the test subjects to see if this weapons system can withstand the conditions in Vietnam. We are the only unit that will use them. The base weapon is made of plastic and metal and can be fed through magazines or belt-fed like a machine gun. We turn in our reliable M-14s, M-60 machine guns, and 45 pistols in order to test this futuristic weapon that looks more like a toy to me. In fact, Mattel Toys did make the plastic stock, which has its logo imprinted on it. The Stoner is much lighter than the M-14, and the muzzle velocity of the smaller bullets is fast enough that if the bullet hits a bone the shock waves will kill a man. Instead of the nine bulkier M-14 magazines, we'll now carry 11 magazines with 20 rounds each. I'm not sure, however, if the added firepower and lower weight are worth the loss of my trusty old rifle's dependability.

We have only been testing these new Stoners for a day now, but they are already jamming on us. The problem seems to be that the bolt is completely exposed to the elements. The bolt has to slide back to chamber a new round, but sand and dust keep it from sliding. We experiment with different amounts of rifle oil to see if we can solve the problem. I wonder what will it be like in the filth of the bush, and what about the sand that blows in the wind? Worse, what will happen when we dive for cover in the mud? Eventually, after a second day of firing, the Stoners appear to have relaxed from the hundreds of rounds we've fired through them, but I'm not sure they'll be able to protect us in the bush tomorrow.

While we are eating the next morning out in the field, we receive carbine fire from across the rice paddy. From that side of the perimeter, twenty Marines fire back, and five rifles jam. Nobody is hurt, and life continues as usual. We embark on a company movement, and head in the direction of the carbine fire. A carbine is a 22-caliber rifle that is significantly smaller and lighter than the enemy's other rifle, the AK-47. A carbine sounds more like a mosquito buzzing by your ear than the angry bumble bee sound from an AK.

Despite the magnitude of our Western resources, the Communists and Vietnamese appear to be better suited to this type of guerrilla warfare. They take advantage of opportunities. Our ammunition fits in their weapons, but theirs doesn't fit in ours. For example, they use a 61mm mortar, so our 60mm ammo drops down their tubes, but their larger 61mm round does not drop into our 60mm tubes. When we get to where they fired from, we find no evidence of Viet Cong or NVA.

Over the last three days, we've had two firefights, and the Stoners jammed frequently. This morning is cool and foggy, and not a single leaf moves. Last night the company established a listening post (LP) with three riflemen 100 meters outside our perimeter. The three Marines moved quietly in the near complete darkness to the pre-determined hiding spot near a brushy area where the enemy might approach us. If the LP hears an enemy move through the expected area, they could sneak back on their pre-determined route to get inside the overlapping fields of fire that form our defensive perimeter without us shooting them. Alternatively, the LP could remain hidden, radio us about the enemy, and we could shoot them without hitting the Marines. Standard Operating Procedure (SOP) calls for radio checks from the command post to the platoons and LPs every hour during the night watches.

On all the radios, the volume is almost completely turned down. The company radio watch person quietly calls out each platoon, whispering, "Lima 1," and in response, Lima 1, the first platoon, presses their squelch button once to confirm everything is fine, or twice if they have spotted an enemy. Tonight, the guys in the LP let us know they're coming in by hitting the squelch button three times in the first light of the morning.

The next day, as we approach a tree line, eighty of the company's members keep moving, leaving twelve of us to set up an ambush. Our twelve consists of Igor and me from mortars; Andy, an M60 machine gunner, and Mike, his ammo humper, Kevin; an M-79 guy; two squads of riflemen; and the radioman, Harry, from the third platoon. The fear of being discovered in our ambush position grows as each hour passes. I try hard not to make a sound, but I'm convinced that any movement my body makes can be heard from a long distance. Although no one approaches our position, my growing terror of "what ifs" has made me acutely aware of the sound of my breathing. While we hide, the fear I feel in my body dramatically fluctuates. At my most terrified, it feels like the enemy is only a few feet away and I can hear the loud bass drum of my heartbeat. I'm not sure how much this high-level anticipatory fear is useful. When I played defensive lineman in high school, I always wanted the running back to attack me in my position. It was a chance to make a move and be a hero. Here in Vietnam, even though I am prepared to fight, I would rather not be tested.

In the late afternoon, we return to the battalion area. Butch comes from the officers' tent and says, "The brass says the Stoners are challenged due to getting sand in the tight moving parts, having poor ammunition, and letting bullets rust in the chamber overnight. They've figured out that we need to shoot at least 1000 rounds through every Stoner to get them working effectively." Throughout the foggy morning, we fire magazine after magazine through the various configurations of our weapons at the firing range.

After breakfast in the mess hall, we get a holler from the company command tent for all ninety-two Lima Company guys to mount up. We put on our packs and secure our weapons. I know we're going to the bush, but I have no idea where or why. Rather than exiting through the front gate, we proceed south through the wire. To begin with, the weather is cloudy and cool. We walk and stop for several hours until it rains in the late afternoon. We cross a slow-moving creek. I carefully and quietly wade into the water, my rifle over my head. I'd have a hard time protecting myself if the enemy decided now was the time to kill a Marine.

In the middle of the 20-foot-wide creek, the brackish water is up to my chest. As I come up the far bank, still in waist-deep water, a two-foot-long green snake moves rapidly toward me. I recognize it as one of the "Two-Steps," so named because its venom is supposed to kill you two steps after being bitten. With my Stoner, I take a single shot. The high-velocity bullet hits the water just inches from the snake, but the shock wave instantly kills it, and the dead snake floats harmlessly passed where I am shaking in the stream. I wish the VC were this simple to dispatch.

As it has been every day since I arrived, gunfire can be heard in the distance all day and night. Every few hours, artillery barrages, bombings, and other explosions occur.

I'd like to say a few words about combat infantry marines and the word "fuck." In combat, the F-word appears in nearly every sentence a marine uses. When I was in high school, my guy friends and I said fuck when we were angry or frustrated. The girls didn't seem to say it at all, except for Marjorie, who swore like a trooper. Here in Vietnam, there is rarely a sentence that doesn't include it because fuck is used to emphasize the disgust, anger, or hopelessness we feel. Without higher-ups supervising us, we teenage combat marines use the word fuck two or three times per sentence. Fuck escapes the mouth or enters the ears like it's the air. It also matches everyone's mood in this type of combat. Most of us were tough enough to get through high school, but now we have to be even tougher and meaner, and the frequent use of the word fuck appears to fit this persona.

Chapter Three
After Vietnam
You Can't Talk About That Here

The first night back in Port Angeles, I tried to sleep knowing there would be no more Vietnam in my future, but it was a lost cause. For the 5 hours I was in bed, I tossed and turned, dozing off a few times with one eye open. Although I have no recollection of being upset when I returned home, my big sister, Barbara, claims that most nights I screamed and cried in my sleep. That first night, I remembered the night before in the barracks at Camp Altaire, where most of us returning from the war, we were all on high alert. Nobody in my family understands, and even my father, who served in WWII in Ketchikan, Alaska saw no enemy action.

Because the next morning was Saturday, the entire family, with the exception of Barb, was upstairs for breakfast together. Mom had gone above and beyond, preparing French toast, sausage, milk, and orange juice. Despite the lack of sleep, I felt fully functional because at least I had rested in a comfortable bed for six hours. Over breakfast, my brother Brad, who had been the starting quarterback for the undefeated Port Angeles High School football team, told me a few stories about their season. Brad, and our friend, Bernie Fryer, who was the team's wide receiver and a High School All-American, had defeated East Bremerton when Brad threw Bernie a last-second touchdown pass.

That evening, my friend, Donna Reed, knocked on the family room door at 6:15 p.m. She had come to offer to give me a ride to a party at the duplex that Wiley Duckett and Don Corning were renting on Front Street, Highway 101East. After sponging clean the counters and table, I finished my part of the dishes by sweeping the floor. Chris, my younger sister, washed the pots and pans while Brad unloaded and loaded the dishwasher. Donna and my family had always had a good relationship because they made each other laugh. Donna and I said our goodbyes and made our way to the party.

As we approached the apartment, I saw Greg Revitt and Larry Ranta smoking cigarettes on the steps outside. Elliott and Boyd were with their families, which left me alone with my old peers who knew nothing about combat. Donna and I found Harriette Covington, Candy Cotton, and Steve Colvin drinking beer and conversing with Wiley and Don inside. I gave Don $5 and went in to get beers for Donna and me. Two hours later, we, again, all chipped in to help Wiley get his older brother, Bill, to buy another case.

I was becoming increasingly inebriated when Greg asked me what had happened in Vietnam. The first thing that came to my mind was the heap of dead Vietnamese bodies I'd seen and I blurted out. "On New Year's Eve, there was a pile of about 100 North Vietnamese soldiers that we had killed the day before. One Vietnamese guy was burnt to a crisp, and he was lying on the side of that pile in a crawling position." Now, writing this 51 years later, I can imagine the horror on my friends' faces. To me, it seemed like a simple story. I obviously didn't want to scare them with stories about bullets flying by or enemy artillery raining dirt on me.

That's when Donna gently took my hand in hers and led me to the sidewalk. We sat on the Front Street curb, and she cautioned me, "Bill, you can't talk about things like that here." I remember that I looked at her, but I didn't feel anything. Over the course of several weeks, I noticed that people approached me tentatively to ask about my experiences in Vietnam like you would approach an injured animal. When they did, my mind would race with ideas for what to say. The battle stories I told became more distinct, and my role in each scene became more defined than it had actually been. I worked to recall which version I had given to which person. Couldn't be too much gore. My stories contained a lot of bravery and a lot of effort. The strain of telling fabricated stories was becoming too much for me by the end of that first summer, and I vowed to tell what actually happened, or more often, say nothing at all.

Chapter Four
Firing the 60mm Mortar

"For a great many years, as a soldier, I had a suspicion that war was a racket"
　　　　　　　　　Major General Smedley Butler,
　　　　two time Medal of Honor recipient, 1935.

My younger brother Brad turns 16 today, March 10, 1967. I've only been in Vietnam 15 days, but it already feels like it's been a year. After breakfast, it's a clear morning with no breeze, when Butch Austin, the mortar squad leader, walks us and our mortars over to the firing range area, and we practice using the mortar. I carry the 47-pound mortar tube by the two-inch-wide strap, which digs into my shoulder. The end of the shoulder strap is attached to the canvas cup that holds the top of the mortar tube. The other end of the strap clips to the sealed bottom of the tube. A little canvas strap secures the bipod legs and is held tight with a brass buckle that must be released to spread out the legs so the barrel will be at the proper angle.

The target is a block away from me, and I want to get the mortar on the ground and fire as quickly as I can. I easily remove the cap as I lower the gun to the ground on its baseplate. I struggle to get the thin canvas belt off to expand the bipod. The metal tip of the belt gets caught in the buckle. I try to loosen the strap just enough to pull the metal end straight out of the clasp without getting the tip caught. Finally, I get the gun set up and look over my right shoulder to set the bipod out in front of me, putting one hand on the bottom of each leg.

The sleeve that holds the legs slides up and down the barrel, it has a hand crank to loosen or tighten it. Once in position, I adjust the slide to a possible correct height. First, I loosen the sleeve to allow it to slide down the barrel far enough to approximate the -73°- angle. Then I turn the sight's crank until the target is in the sight, and set the elevation gauge to the angle Del reads off the range finding chart. When the bubble is almost perfectly centered. I tighten the slide crank. I'm off to the right of the target when I look through the peep sight, again. I turn the traverse wheel until the target reappears. Back to the level where I need to turn the bottom support between the two legs to raise the barrel high enough for the bubble to sit level at 73°. I just need to make one more adjustment to the traverse and I'll be ready to fire.

Bud is ready with a high explosive (HE) round. The round has a shotgun shell in the base of the tail with four explosives plastic-wrapped wafers, called increments, clipped between the wings of the tail. To shoot 500 meters requires one increment. To shoot a mile requires the power of all four increments at an angle of 45°. To shoot the distance of one football field requires only the shotgun shell with the gun at an angle of 82°, or almost straight up and down. By the end of that day, I have practiced setting up the mortar many times, and though I'd only fired two more rounds. I have reduced my time for setting up the gun to half a minute.

The whole time that the mortar team has practiced, Lima Company Marines have been breaking in their Stoners. After we return the mortar guns to the tent, we head over to work on our Stoners too. Another day in the rear without getting shot at seems too good to be true.

After dinner, I find a poker game. These players are a lot of fun to play with, but clearly, they haven't played much poker. For example, they often keep drawing in 7-card-stud with nothing but a gut-shot straight possibility in their hand, even when someone else has a big pair showing. The odds of hitting a gut shot are 12 to 1, so I know they will tend to end up with nothing nine out of ten times they try this. Four cards in succession are called an "open-ended" straight possibility, which has 5 to 1 odds of making a straight, or five cards in succession. I develop a poker strategy so that I can keep the suckers putting money in the pot whenever I have a good hand. The technique I choose is to randomly raise the first bet when all we have is two hidden-down cards and one face-up that everyone can see. This is different from what I think of as bluffing. When I have good hole (down) cards, I always raise the bet, but I also raise whenever I have a "3" showing and other undetermined times. I picked "3" randomly because it isn't a good card. Most of these players stay in the betting until the last card or two in hopes of hitting a good hand, no matter what they have in their hand. When they don't get their hand on the last card they fold, even after investing all that money in the pot. That's when I bluff as if I have a good hand to be sure they fold.

When I get back to our tent with my $70 of winnings, McCormick is packing up his gear to move to the battalion's bigger mortars, the 81mm. McCormick and I have spent very little time around each other, but we have developed mutual respect. I feel happy for him. He is a nice, calm guy, who always works efficiently. The battery of bigger guns almost always stays within the battalion area. If they carry it to the field, it requires three guys to carry each gun, one carries the tube, another the legs, and another the baseplate. I reckon, McCormick's odds of dying just dropped dramatically.

The next day, Lima Company prepares for three different patrols. The first platoon travels with Del, Bud, Jackson, Mark, Larry, and me. Hopefully, our Stoners will perform better than they did last time. As we approach the tank area, it is foggy. Because we mortar and rocket men carry such heavy loads, we ride on the two tanks. When I'm walking, I always try to make myself as small as possible, usually walking at a half crouch, and constantly looking for the best place to "eat dirt." This is the polar opposite of how it feels to ride up here on this noisy tank, where we mortarmen, with our heavy packboards, are exposed high up, and have nowhere to hide.

The rocket and mortar gunners still carry pistols because their big weapons are slung over their shoulders and even the pistol grip Stoner would require them to have on a second sling. The grunts are spread out around the tanks with good spacing. I have mixed feelings about being on the tank because it makes so much noise that we know for sure that every enemy within a mile can hear us coming. I doubt, however, that they'd dare to snipe at us when we can send a 90mm projectile at them in seconds? With the tank's outer surface sloped, we are exposed from whatever side we are on.

While we plow right through a thick-stemmed bamboo grove, we receive incoming fire from the right. We jump off the tank in a "New York Minute," and set up our gun at the rear of the tank. The tank's turret slowly turns towards the target, and they get off two rounds before we fire the mortar. I imagine a well-dug-in VC freaking out as the ground around him heaves and pitches from the big explosions. The grunts patrol where the fire came from and find nothing. The platoon radioman calls in a medevac for a squad leader. I don't know who it is, but someone got shot in the arm. We pile back onto the tanks, head out, and travel another two kilometers, stopping twice to clear booby traps. The grunts discover an anti-tank mine. It is a three-inch thick round plate with a stiff wire sticking just above the ground. If you bend the wire with your foot, it will arm. Then, when it snaps back up, you're dead, even if you are a tank. We do not have an engineer with us, so one of the grunts who is carrying C-4, carefully sets up an explosive charge. We and the tanks move a safe distance away, which is a good thing because the explosion is much bigger than when the engineers blew up a mine two weeks ago.

The food and supplies have not been distributed yet, so we aren't having to carry that weight until the tanks start heading back. In the heat of the afternoon, we divide up the C-rations and get more water and ammo. Then the tanks head back to the battalion area, leaving the thirty of us on our own. When we can no longer hear the tanks, we start walking, but we haven't gone far when we get shot at from a tree line a half mile away. It's been a typical day in the bush, and thankfully no one has gotten hit.

The fog rolls in as we are cooking our breakfasts. I try a new way to boil water more quickly for the cocoa. One of the grunts gives me a piece of C-4 plastic explosive, which I roll into a marble-sized ball. I drop it into my stove and light it, placing my canteen cup over the stove. It makes a roaring little fire with flames over the top of the cup. Less than a minute later the water is boiling. I cook my spiced beef over the flame by pulling it off and on until the flame starts to die down. I decide to enjoy my hot cocoa and cookies before I dig into the real food.

After the fog clears and before we get mounted up, we get shot at. The radioman calls in artillery, "Arty." Del pumps four HE rounds and a white phosphorous (Willy Pete) into the area the muzzle flashes are coming from. A minute later our big "Arty" overshoots the area, and I hear the radioman tell them so, by saying, "Drop 50 meters and fire for effect." Half a minute later a salvo of three, 155mm artillery rounds tears into the enemy area.

A Huey gunship arrives a few minutes later, escorting a CH-34 medevac chopper. As the medevac lands to pick up an injured grunt on a stretcher, the Huey strafes the enemy area. While the medevac heads to base, the Huey patrols overhead, and we break camp and mount up to sweep over the area of incoming fire. We discover nothing. We find neither spent rifle cartridges nor other VC evidence. We travel through rice paddies, villages, and sandy, rolling hills for the rest of the day. When the first signs of dusk appear, I close my right eye to prepare to be able to aim with it in the dark, and we come to a halt for the night. The mortar pit we dig resembles a cone rather than a flat-bottomed hole. We have to scoop the sand out with the outer shell of our helmets. The helmet liner, made entirely of plastic and webbing, has been set aside. Each time I scoop sand out with my full helmet, more sand pours back into the hole. Finally, we have a deep and wide enough hole to set the gun and spread the legs at a 45 angle for maximum distance shooting in any direction.

An hour after sunrise, we begin a double-column movement with mortars at the back. The heat and sun drive the clouds away. This is my fifth patrol as tail-end Charlie, and I realize that in this position my wide-set eyes are an advantage. I have wider peripheral vision, so I can scan the area behind me without turning as far as other guys need to. Bud is 50 feet ahead of me. I keep track of where he steps while also keeping my senses alert and ready for a rear attack.

Midday, we gather on a hillside for another potentially dull day of combat. Today, we remain vigilant after an eventful and terrifying day yesterday, but nothing happens. In this setting, talking is minimal, and this contrasts with my outgoing high school personality. I made it through yesterday's firefight, but if high school Bill had been plucked from Mr. Renee's Civics class and dropped into that firefight, surely he would have collapsed in terror. In fact, I'm not sure if any of my high school buddies could have handled it. During boot camp, I discovered that even the tough bully types were among the first to crumble under real pressure. I sit for hours, aware of feeling afraid that the small dirt depression I'm in only protects me in one direction.

We arrive at our night position near the outskirts of a village of three hooches. The soil is quite hard. My E-tool is set to 90°, similar to a pick. I swing hard, but only getting three inches in, and pry out a small chunk of dirt. In these conditions, it takes about 30 minutes to dig a safe place to fire the mortar. We are all drenched in sweat. The second platoon lieutenant advises us to remain wary, and not begin night watches until later. All thirty of us are nervous. In the pitch-black sky, we suddenly hear the whistle of an artillery round, followed by a pop and clank of a brilliant illumination shell that brightens the area around us and it looks like someone just lit up a giant birthday cake with the equivalent of a thousand candles. Despite my terror, I can't help but chuckle at the chaos this kind of light show would insight at a drive-in theater full of teenagers making out in their cars back in "the world."

Our 105mm artillery round puts out five times more light than the 60mm illumination round. Del fires HE rounds at three different preset targets, and the rest of us keep an eye out for any VC this might roust out of hiding and cause to run. The machine gunner sprays the same areas, and the 3.5-inch rocket man (bazooka) fires into the center target. Another whistle, pop, and clank produces instant daylight as the first parachuted fiery candle approaches the ground. We can't see any enemy, but it's reassuring to know that the artillery and illumination will make them think twice about harassing us tonight.

Chapter Five
Childhood Development
"Shoot First and Ask Questions Later"

After the birth of each of her children, my mother suffered from severe postpartum depression. I was 2 years old, when my brother, Brad, was recently born. My sister, Barb, was at that time 4 years old, but she still remembers me sitting on the kitchen floor taking apart an alarm clock. As she did for hours most weekdays, our mother was sitting blank-faced at the kitchen table. When she became aware of me and the alarm clock, she started screaming swear words at me. This became a common pattern in my life. I remember that my youth was filled with examples of behaviors that would get this reaction from my mother. I quickly learned that I had a choice of either having an anxious, depressed mother yelling at me or not having a mother at all.

I recall, however, that there was a rare vivid moment of connection with her at five years old when I had the flu and she lovingly put a cool washcloth on my forehead. That moment stands out because it was the only time I felt a response from my mother that was attuned to my needs.

In the social life of my childhood, I developed more acceptable outlets for these trouble-making skills. But when I was 18 years old, those early developed trouble-making skills helped me decide "to shoot first and ask questions later." I experienced hundreds of life-threatening situations near the DMZ of Vietnam between February 1967 to March 1968 that required instant reactions, to kill or be killed. I might get in big trouble, but at least I would be alive. I might get in trouble, but at least my mother would pay attention to me. In fact, there were several firefights where my lack of concern for the moral consequences of my behavior probably saved my life. I learned to not weigh the reflected sense of who I was in the world. Untethered from moral principles, combat taught me to not trust delay. Now, friendships have since taught me to wait for that reflected image to help guide my behavior.

Chapter Six
Operation Canyon

"More self-righteous killing, more gut-wrenching fear, more earth despoiled in the name of the nation, the leader, the cause, the god"

James Hillman, 2004.

Our day begins before the end of last watch when a sniper fires three rounds into our perimeter. In seconds, we retaliate and launch an HE round while all of the facing weapons fire bullets at the incoming shooter. And that's the end of it because, of course, that VC vanishes. There's just enough light so we start preparing breakfast.

This first month of my tour has felt like a regular gathering of guys. Everyone is about my age, and we spend every waking moment together. I imagine Ken Boyd is now somewhere in this same forest, but closer to the mountains to the west, and Ben Elliott is further north and closer to the ocean to the east. Today reminds me of last August when I hiked up to Boulder Lake in Olympic National Park with Ken, his brother Bob, and Ben for two nights. This now, in the Vietnam jungle, has some of the feel of that experience, minus the grab-assing kid stuff.

If you dropped in on this scene, you'd have no idea we'd been shot at earlier, except that the guys watching the perimeter appear alert, we who are cooking breakfast are doing everything closer to the ground, and no one stands unless it's absolutely necessary. None of this is like walking through the halls of high school, that's for sure, and shit, that was only a year ago. For sure, back then I had never considered killing another human being. But now, the strange sense of intimacy I feel with guys I've just met, combined with the fact that I don't know anyone else for miles around me, leaves me all alone with the horrible decision of who and when to kill. Geez, how the fuck do I know, but the sick part is that knowing when to kill someone could save my life.

Just as we begin to move out, we are suddenly hit from the same location where the sniper shot this morning. Second squad is positioned in front of the mortars. They start doing "recon by fire." This is done by scouting the area with rifle rounds and M-79 grenades before approaching it. The enemy stops firing and I feel safer walking through the area now that all those bullets have flown in here, but I'm also more vulnerable from behind with so many brazen enemies around. When we set up for the night, a listening post (LP) is stationed in a draw, not far away from my position.

At the first signs of dawn, in the breezeless morning, the LP clicks three times with their radio to announce their return. We meet up with Captain Marks and the rest of the company at noon. They have captured a Viet Cong soldier who is approximately 25 years old. He is blindfolded and his hands are tied behind his back. He's dressed like all the Vietnamese, whether they're attempting to kill us or seeking our protection, in black pajamas and a black conical hat. It's strange having him around for the two hours before resupply arrives. I feel the urge to punish him for the casualties we've suffered, even though I know he's a human being.

The wind picks up and blows dust and sand around, as two Amtraks arrive. The captured VC is in the squat position that these people are accustomed to. He has lowered himself all the way down to his haunches, and his buttock is just barely off the ground. A ChuHoy interrogator comes out of one of the Amtrak. This is my first encounter with these interrogators. I've heard that they were VCs who defected to join the Army of the Republic of Vietnam (ARVN). When he approaches the prisoner, the ChuHoy immediately strikes him in the face with the barrel of his rifle. Then he begins to torture and question the VC, while one of the grunts points a rifle at the prisoner. I couldn't care less. The part of me that has forgotten he is a human being believes that this is necessary to obtain the information needed to keep us safe. It's hard to believe that a year ago, in Civics class, I argued against capital punishment with

John Doherty because I thought it was inhumane. John was a devout Catholic, and his belief in killing people for punishment seemed contradictory to his faith to me at the time. Now I am willing to be a judge, a jury, and an eager executioner.

Two hours later, we have our supply of ammo, our canteens are full, our meals are packed, and our garbage is loaded onto the Trak. The ChuHoy climbs to the top of the Trak, while the VC is tied tightly to the inside of the vehicle for transport to the POW camp at the base of Marble Mountain,

As we trudge along, the clouds move in and the wind picks up, swirling dust and providing some relief from the heat. Out of nowhere I hear a faint swishing sound a fraction of a second before a 61mm mortar round, the same power as the rounds I carry, throws sand up in the air ten steps from me. If that round had been closer, no matter how quickly my body reacted, I would not have made it to the ground. We have no idea where to return fire, but it makes me appreciate the weapon that I use.

It begins to get dark and we prepare for the night. The weak light from the crescent moon behind the clouds will not provide any illumination until just before dawn. During my watch, the bushes seem to be moving and I am on high alert for any rustling or visible movement. It's the thickness of a silhouette that distinguishes a bush from a VC. I've learned to look into a tree and focus on any dense area in the foliage that may be a person. 'Birders' know this well, when they are looking for a photo-op in dense foliage. However, any dense area may harbor death, here. At the age of 18, I know nothing about bird watching. The last watch begins two hours after the moon rises to quell the intense darkness. It's been raining during the night, but now that the wind is blowing everything is dry. The moon appears behind the clouds and all the bushes I was afraid of turn out to be just that: bushes. The persistent mosquitos start to dwindle, and I hear the first buzzing of a single fly.

As the sun rises at 5:42 a.m., I do the last few minutes of my watch, and the rest of the guys mill around getting their breakfasts together. We hang out after breakfast with the gun still set up. We stow our garbage in our packs but, because we're not moving, the flies get worse. We're good and filthy, and they don't pay as much attention to us as they do when we are clean. The captain must have received an order from the battalion, as we finally leave in the mid-afternoon. The front of the column is hit as soon as we get stretched out into our double columns. The VC anticipated our path and planned an ambush. The mortars are near the front of the columns, and I hear someone yell, "Corpsman up!" Fear grips me. I scan my fields of fire through a scraggly brush, nerve-rackingly looking for an enemy to shoot at. I find nothing to vent my fear on and minutes later, everything is quiet, as we wait for the medevac.

Off to our left is a dry paddy. As the Huey patrols overhead, we stretch out into a perimeter to provide cover for the incoming medevac chopper. After the birds have flown away, we sweep through the area where the ambush occurred. A tunnel is discovered by the pointman from the lead platoon. They call up a short and skinny new guy. He vanishes into a small opening in a brush-covered hillock. A few minutes later he reappears and yells, "Engineer up." After the 'tunnel rat' gets to cover, we cover our heads when the engineer yells, "Fire in the hole." Then, the C-4 explodes and there is a secondary explosion. The tunnel rat clearly discovered munitions. After a double-check of the area, he yells, "All clear." It feels good to know that we've taken out some of the VC's options for blowing us up and that one less tunnel is available to them.

During my youth, I'd been able to figure out how to have fun in most situations. This ability has most likely allowed me to survive this long in the madness of the warfare around me. Torture and murder were never things I considered using for entertainment. Today, for pleasure, I combine the peaches from the turkey loaf meal, with the pound cake from the meatballs and beans, and I enjoy the delicacy of the 'bush,' with a cup of cocoa on the side. The morning seems to drag on indefinitely, and we don't know what the day will bring. When I finish my morning snack, I notice that the three platoon commanders have been meeting with the command group. They haven't informed us grunts of anything. Despite the fact that our officers are friendly and respectful to us, they are all college graduates, which means they are at least four years older than we are.

It has been cloudy all morning, but when we finally put on our gear and head out, the clouds break up and allow the punishing sun to quickly heat things up. It goes from 73° to 85° by 1:00 p.m. Blessedly, at 4:00 p.m., the wind slowly increases to its peak of 11 mph, which seems to thin out the flies.

At 5:00 p.m., we set up a perimeter and hear two Amtraks approaching with resupply. The traks take off as soon as the supplies have been unloaded and the garbage has been stowed. Harry, one of the two company radio operators hollers, "Mail call." The captain then calls out a name, and that guy appears and grabs a letter. My parents have sent me two letters. I get one from Mary Dyar and one from my friend Marjorie Bell. Marjorie, of course, is extremely irreverent and makes me laugh. It's strange to read about the intimacies of 'the world' while sitting on the sand with a group of guys I've spent every minute of my life with for 40 days. Mary is attending the University of Puget Sound in Tacoma and is most likely at ease in a private college setting. Marjorie has not yet completed high school. She'd be partying, having intellectual conversations with friends and teachers, flirting with boys, and getting into mischief. What and who am I? Will I ever talk about esoteric things like philosophy, again?

I see the tracers from a VC a half-mile away, shooting at the Freedom Bird, as it rapidly gains elevation from the Da Nang airfield. The 707 is clearly to high for the small, low-velocity bullets to get to it, but it brings a smile to my face to think of this nearby farmer having a hidden rifle to believe he can stop the imperialists with his dangerous, futile effort. It is all so surreal, and with equal futility, I imagine I could set a sky hook onto that plane and get towed out of this bazaar situation while the tendrils of my real life remain.

My flak jacket feels heavier than usual on this foggy morning. It weighs ten pounds, and won't even stop a carbine round, but it might save my life in the event of a mortar or grenade explosion. The flak jacket is intended to shield me from shrapnel. It's a cotton vest with steel plates covering my chest and back. The helmet has the same feeling of being heavy and unlikely to protect me. In fact, when I patrol along on a typical day and think about the real dangers I am in, I realize that the most likely way I will be hit is by an explosion from the ground by a booby trap or mortar. As a result, the concussion will be trapped inside this seven-pound pot, causing additional damage to my brain.

Again the next morning, an eerie fog hangs in the air for several hours. It is easy to imagine phantoms appearing as enemies. Visibility is blurry and fluctuates from a short toss away to as far as I can throw. As we head out after mounting up, the rest of the company slowly dissolves into the fog in front of me. The mortars are again at the tail end of the double column. Our spacing is a little closer together to assure staying in visual contact with the guy in front and behind us in the fog. Around 10:00 a.m., the fog lifts, but there is no breeze and it is heavily overcast.

In the afternoon the sun comes out and it's quite hot. Today's constant state of affairs has been wet, either from fog or sweat. We patrol alongside a rice field that's at least two miles long. As we near a village, there is an explosion in the middle of our line that is about half the size of an American hand grenade, indicating that it is a ChiCom grenade. Incoming small arms fire is then directed at that area of our line. From where I am, I can see several muzzle flashes from the enemy, so I fire two magazines into the flashes before removing my packboard to get a round ready for Del, as he sets up the gun. My heart is racing as I drop a round with two increments down the 75°-angled tube to travel 1000 meters. The round explodes several meters short of the target, causing no reduction in the incoming fire. Del makes the necessary adjustments, and we fire three more rounds into the area around the muzzle flashes. There's a yell, "Corpsman up!" The VC triggered the ambush by detonating that grenade. We form a wide circle around the injured person, who I never get close enough to see, and wait for the medevac. Our adversaries are silent and most likely have vanished. I can see the village from across the rice paddies but it appears to be peaceful.

Two resupply Amtraks arrive a few hours after the medevac chopper departs. We quickly transfer everything from the Traks to our packs and climb on the heavy amphibious vehicles and head past the village for a five-mile journey. Three feet away from me, a carbine round slams into the row of sandbags stacked two high around the edge of the top of the Amtrak. On this Trak, all 15 of us lie as flat as we can on the top and return massive firepower. The platoon's light machine gun, combined with the Traks' two heavier machine guns, fire a lot of bullets, but at what we don't know. The Traks drop us off and head back to base. We hike another mile and set up for the night.

The next morning begins with us rapidly dismantling last night's position and putting our gear on in dense fog. We pass through several villages and travel a mile, finally stopping for breakfast in an area where there are no hooches. The fog clears, and the sun shines brightly. We can hear that a major battle is taking place a few miles west of us. There is a lot of Stoner, AK-47, machine gun, and carbine fire, as well as mortar, hand grenade, and artillery explosions. Two Huey gunships fly by, 50 feet above our heads, heading for the battle. The AK and carbine fire stops as gunships' firepower is added to the cacophony of sound. We only hear the occasional Stoner or M-79 firing for a few minutes before the Hueys fly back over our heads. A piper cub spotter plane patrols above the battle zone and the area around us.

As we continue to move toward the south, not toward the rest of our company, the temperature rises dramatically due to the clear skies. Walking is always done in a semi-crouch, scanning every direction, attempting to step in the footprint of the guy in front of me, while I listen for bushes being rubbed, with my finger on the trigger, safety off, muzzle dipping to the ground as it passes my comrades so I won't shoot them if my Stoner accidentally fires. We have increased our level of alertness this morning, knowing the enemy we encountered have to go somewhere, and they might run into us. Our daily walking ends with no further action, however.

We can see Puff-The Magic Dragon firing in the distance tonight during first watch. 'Puff' is a small prop plane with a 40mm cannon. Every fifth round it shoots is a bright red tracer, which allows the pilot to see where his bullets are going. We can't see any gaps between the rounds from our vantage point a mile away, so it looks like a long red line in the sky that connects the plane to the ground. After witnessing the explosion of a 40mm round from the M-79, I can easily imagine the saturation that occurs in the field being attacked. Within seconds, a football field-sized area is engulfed in explosions on every inch of the field.

Footnote

+*Operation Canyon included these last four days of combat, with more bullets flying at me than in the previous month. This is now confirmed by my records. To me at the time, it was just more days in paradise. In ten months, I'll be wishing for such light battles. A year ago, I was playing an April Fool's joke on my classmates. Now I'm becoming more aware of a snarling sensation inside me that's increasing in intensity, frequency, and duration.*

We move out before the sun comes up in a company online sweep toward the expanse 'Puff' prep fired last night. After clearing several booby traps, we approach rolling sand hills with bushes, clumps of trees, and open spaces. Then the buzz and hiss of small arms fire fills the air. Del has the mortar up and running in 12 seconds, and I've dropped an HE round down the barrel. "Hundred meters long and right 50 meters," the grunts radio back. Except for his size, Del is a regular nice guy. He and I go about our business with mutual admiration. I can picture him effortlessly chucking hay bales. I don't think I ever heard him complain during our ten months together. We pump mortar round after mortar round. Mo's gun is doing the same thing somewhere on the other side of the tree line to our right. The enemy's fire doesn't stop.

Minutes later, two Huey gunships can be heard beating against the air in a rhythmic pattern. As they pass over our heads, they fire their forward guns. They circle back up and begin firing their heavier medium machine guns from above the enemy, making passes perpendicular to our line of fire. They use rockets in the third pass. Two violent 'swishes' emerge from the first bird's side, followed by two explosions a fraction of a second apart. Despite the fact that the enemy has stopped firing, the choppers make one more machine gun pass. The Hueys continue to fly overhead as a medevac CH-34 arrives to pick up three members of the third platoon. Nobody is killed on our side.

We continue our sweep into the enemy zone, establishing a large circular perimeter. We ammo humpers form part of the perimeter, while Del and Bud remain in the center of the circle of Marines with our gun. We hear "Engineers up" and "Fire in the hole" for the rest of the day, followed by varying levels of C-4 explosions and a few secondary explosions that must be enemy munitions. The usual 11 mph wind provides cooling with our loose-fitting utilities.

After dark, we travel another mile in the same direction we did this morning. We can only be separated by a few paces to maintain visual contact in the dark and establish our perimeter in the total darkness of the new moon. Cooking dinner is done with caution, as it is clear from today's action that there are many enemies here in this area. Jackson and I take turns keeping watch on the perimeter, each getting about an hour and a half of sleep. Everyone is roused to leave before the sun rises.

The first three hours of the morning are spent slowly walking a few hundred yards in a double column and then stopping to clear booby traps. During the first two hours of daylight, "Puff" patrols above us and fires heavily. The daily mid-morning Freedom Bird is shot at from afar. That gives me a sense of where our battalion area is located. We're not heading toward it, but we're also not heading away from it. For the past two weeks, each of us has gotten an average of two and a half hours of sleep per night. Tiredness is a low-level constant that becomes much more intense on night watch, and my growing hunger is unlike anything I've ever known. Within an hour after eating despite the help of a C-ration meal, I'm hungrier than I've ever been. Today is a prime example of how bad things can get, even after resupply. We ate breakfast in the dark 16 hours ago and walked all day with a fully loaded backboard and no food. What is the point of this mindless walking? In the pit of my stomach, I am becoming increasingly enraged.

Again we don't stop until after full dark. It is 9:00 p.m. when we finally cook one or two small cans of food after we dig in and set up our shelter. Although the food feels good for a few hours, by the middle of the night the gnawing hunger starts its growing dominance of my awareness. Again, I debate if I need to hold the point of my K-bar under my chin so I don't fall asleep, with the mosquitoes in my ears and the sky so dark that the bushes are not even visible to be afraid of. I decide I am too hyper-alert to fall asleep in this dangerous territory, so my knife stays in its sheath. The mosquitoes begin to lessen and the soldier-looking clumps transform into the bushes they are. Within a few minutes, the first of the flies come swooping around. The day of constant flies, hunger, and tiredness begins.

We break camp and leave in heavy fog. As usual, I trudge along in my tail-end Charlie position, unsure of where we're going. Adrenaline keeps any dragging-ass tendencies at bay. The sensation is more like hyper-alert. Terror is probably more accurate. I cannot allow the lazy teenager inside me to have even a single second of my time.

A Viet Cong sniper fires a few rounds at our position. I bite the dirt, remove my pack-board, pull out an HE round, and wait a few seconds for my buddy, Del, to be ready for me to drop in a round. His first shot grazes the muzzle flashes, so we fire for effect. Will I ever be able to fire a shell that quickly? Nobody is hurt, and the enemy only fires for a few seconds. We continue our reconnaissance patrol to the point where we were hit from, find nothing, and after walking several hours more, we set up camp for the night.

This morning has a different feel. The fog clears for once. The heavy overcast and clouds remain but the heat gets quickly up into the high 80s, despite the sun being hidden. As we patrol at mid-afternoon, the sky is clear, and the daily breeze makes it bearable because the day doesn't get any hotter. I have never been this dirty in my life, except the one day Brad, my brother, and I played tackle football in the deep mud of a rain-soaked playfield just east of the YMCA back in "the world." That sticky mud had been a one-day thing my mother was disgusted with. We left our clothes outside. The dirt now, less than two years later, is deeply ground into my skin.

In the late afternoon, we stop walking to eat the last meal in our packs. After all these days in the bush, it's amazing how good a can of beef steak can taste. The can is two inches tall (about the size of half a Campbell's soup can). Another small can is fruit cocktail. A taller can includes four crackers, a container of peanut butter and a chocolate bar. It alleviates my constant hunger. To think I was ever hungry as a child is a farce. We move through a territory I recognize as being near the battalion's base in the early evening. We march through the main gate in the dead of night, pile our belongings in our tent, and retire to sleep. There is almost no feeling of 'being home.'

Despite the heavy overcast, we wake up to 80° heat. I'm relieved that I'm not carrying anything today. I go to breakfast with two of my friends, Mo and Del. I consume as much food as possible. On my way back to our tents, I notice that the PX will be closed until 10:00 a.m. Several guys with towels are lining up to use the shower. I clean and oil my Stoner, sharpen my K-bar and machete, and straighten out my gear.

An hour later, "We Gotta Get Out Of This Place" by The Animals is blaring on the radio at the PX, which seems appropriate. Except for the clerk, a short Lance Corporal, E-3, I am the only guy here. There is a new supply of comic books. I get The Fantastic Four, Dr. Strange, and The Avengers. Are we men or boys? Should I be playing with toy soldiers under the blanket with a hidden reading light? The comic book display predominates the PX, clarifying how little we know about being men. My high school cartoon reading was Mad Magazine. Cigarettes are the second biggest display. They do not have any Winston cigarettes, so I buy a carton of Parliaments with a recessed filter. This decision may have saved me from problems related to smoking in the decades to come, because, although not advertised that way, Parliaments were a low tar and nicotine cigarette. Later in "The Nam", I kept buying them because that recess kept the filter from getting soggy when rain or sweat was dripping down my face.

The third platoon tent has a poker game in the afternoon. Harwell is there with his record player playing "Respect," by Aretha Franklin. Again it is amazing how bad these card players are. Holding on to terrible hands until the last card and being able to be bluffed out even when they have good hands at the end. Thunder has me thinking that a bombing mission must be happening. The rain starts at about 8:30 p.m., and they cancel the movie because of it.

It is raining as we are rousted out of our cots to mount up. We head over to breakfast. The mess hall is full, with a line to get food. I grab the stainless steel tray with the five depressions to keep the food separated and head through the line. I know I will get no extras today. On the walk back to the tent the rain lets up. We get all packed and then mill around for four hours before the operation starts, and by that time the rain starts again. We walk over to the helicopter pad at about noon. Del's gun team and 26 guys from Lima company's second platoon, fit into two CH-46s. We fly south and toward the mountains to the east. We land and rapidly spread out into a perimeter. The birds take off as soon as the last guy jumps out. We hold our perimeter until the choppers come back two more times with the rest of the company. On the third drop-off, we receive incoming fire as the skids hit the ground from a tree line to the north. It is the distinctive rat-tat-tat of an AK-47. Compared with the lightweight 22 caliber carbine bursts the VC also use, it is a heavy sound, the same caliber as our old M-14s, at a slower rate of fire. By now my ear is intimately aware of the differences in their sounds and how much more dangerous the bigger bullets are.

We are in a wide perimeter around a low rise as night falls. Del and I are stationed in the mortar pit to the right of Igor and Stan. To our left, two grunts from the second platoon are splitting the watch. On first watch at 9:00 p.m., we rely on hearing to notice if any enemy attempts to pass between us because it's dark enough that I can't see the hand in front of my face. Several US artillery barrages pepper the area where we were hit from when we arrived here in the early hours of the night. Puff's long red line is far enough distance that we can't hear its exploding rounds. Starting around 12:30, the crescent moon, though obscured by clouds, begins to provide enough light to see the positions on either side of me.

Two F-14 fighter jets bomb the enemy position in the middle of the night. They fly away after dropping 12 bombs in three runs, proving that I am in more danger than I thought. Small arms fire can be heard nearby all night, but we are never shot at.

We fill the mortar pit and begin humping after a quick breakfast, heading toward the mountains. A spotter plane patrols the skies above. Its motor suddenly coughs, and it slowly spirals toward the ground east of us. The engines cut in when the bird is almost to the ground, and resumes its patrol above us. I'm sure the pilots were laughing their asses off at how much they scared us. Much like rebounding in basketball, sensing what they are seeing and receiving reports from our aerial observer's (AO) radio informs us of what may happen to us. All of the Marine assault components protect each other from an enemy breaking through our line and alert us to where to go. When rebounding, you aggressively go after the ball as it hits the rim, but you also have to keep the man you're covering away from the basket by sensing the space between your nearest teammates so that no one else can sneak between you. I can tell those flyboys are keeping us safe, and I respect them despite the fact that they are obviously smart-asses.

With all of the buildup in the night and morning, we spend the day walking 10 miles, clearing five booby traps, and otherwise doing nothing. We come to a halt shortly before dark near a village surrounded by dry rice paddies. We are instructed to dig our mortar pit in a paddy just outside the village. The soil is hard clay. We experiment with various methods for digging the pit. The shovel head's pick end sinks two inches, but we can only pry out the dirt stuck to the pick. Swinging the short handle with the shovel at a right angle results in less depth but a wider chunk of dirt.

Most of us use our straightened shovels and stamp hard with our steel-plated boot soles. Even with the dirt piled around the edge and me lying at the bottom of the hole, my body is barely protected, so the muzzle flash of the mortar will be visible above the pit's sides.

The rainy morning is splashing big drops off the hard-pan dirt. Our berm around the mortar pit has kept the river-lets from draining into the pit. As we finish breakfast, the rain lets up and we pack up. We start a sweep, as two Antos come zooming across the paddies to meet us. Now our online sweep has six 106mm recoilless rockets in the center of each half of the line. The six rocket launching barrels are on a swiveling turret that can spin all the way around in two seconds.

The river on our left flank is greenish brown with swirls that can allow me to see that it is moving, otherwise, the surface is undisturbed, moving at a speed faster than we are walking. If I broke into a fast jog, I would be able to stay abreast of the occasional twig that passes us on its way to the ocean. All hell breaks loose as we are heading into a hilly treeline. Both Antos fire six rounds toward the hillside the enemy assaults are coming from. The whole hill explodes into the air in a million pieces. As they rush forward with the Antos, the grunts radio us the coordinates of the enemy. Having shot all our mortar ammo, we pack back up and scurry to the moving grunt assault. The entire reinforced platoon rushes to pursue the routed enemy. With no grunts blocking my opportunity, I squeeze off my diagonal 4-5 round bursts that arrive at the four areas of enemy muzzle flashes. My bullets arrive chest high in a tight diagonal strip and the muzzle flashes stop. It's a satisfaction not dissimilar to hitting a tennis shot just out of my opponent's reach and just inside the boundary of the court. Ten seconds later the firefight is over and we go back to walking. I'm conscious that it's possible I just killed my first person and somehow feel the efficiency of this act of war.

After a while, the rain comes back with a vengeance, and the temperature drops rapidly. For the next hour, we move through paddies and treelines with no resistance. When the rain stops, it gets hotter than it was before the rain. I hear the slow, loud clanking of approaching Amtraks. Resupply is greatly appreciated. It has been unsettling to feel unprotected with only two rifle magazines and no mortar rounds. A wall of fire, our most common cover, would have only lasted a few seconds. We reload our magazines, sort the food, restock our canteens, and load mortar rounds onto our packboards. Then, we put on our packs and make a double column, and head to the foothills.

We set up our nighttime perimeter and prepare our dinner with heat tabs. Dirt, sand, and mud are in everything. The early night is filled with air strikes and artillery barrages. We have dug a two-foot-deep pit, which feels much safer to man during watch, but sleeping on the ground outside the pit is scary in this hostile territory. For the first time, I sleep wrapped around my rifle, with my trigger finger on the trigger guard rather than the trigger. I'm on my right side, my left hand on the muzzle near my face. My head is nestled in my helmet which acts like a pillow and protects my skull from shrapnel. If I was at home I would be trying to sleep while I was pondering how I could best explain The Allegory of the Cave to my friends. Again, I wonder if I will ever get excited about something as esoteric as philosophy.

When we wake up, we can hear heavy aircraft flying high above us. A few minutes later, the ground buckles and heaves in waves that toss me into the air, and are followed by the thundering sound of 500-pound bombs exploding nearby. The morning is clear and cool, and smoke traces decorate the glorious sunrise. We eat and start an online movement in the direction the bombs landed. After clearing two booby traps, we continue to move through several clusters of three or four hooches situated in tree lines surrounding a never-ending rice paddy.

We walk right by two of the bomb craters from earlier. They have an exact cone shape and are as deep as a three-story house. At the bottom is an eight-foot-deep pool of water. We keep moving, and surprisingly, when we are at the edge of the rifle range, we get hit hard from the bombed-out area. Then, I hear a quarter-second swishing sound and a mortar round explodes in front of me. I dive for the dirt, rip my packboard off to get at the mortar rounds, and expend a magazine. I can hear the radioman from the second platoon saying, "Lima 6, Lima 6, this is Lima 2. medevac. Over." "Lima 2, this is 6, medevac inbound," he says. This is followed by the two Antos launching volleys of rockets at the enemy.

The firefight lasts until the battalion's artillery barrage hits the area where we had fired our mortars and where the grunts have been firing at. I hear one Marine screaming, and another moaning. A minute later, the screaming Marine is quieted; I assume the corpsman has given him a shot of morphine, maybe two, whatever it takes. I hear two Hueys thumping in the distance, and they suddenly roar over our heads, firing repeated rockets in the direction of the enemy. Five minutes later, the medevac arrives. Two stretchers are being loaded, and one man with a field dressing on his shoulder is being assisted onto the bird. From where I am it appears that the guy with the shoulder wound is Johnson from the second platoon, but I'm not sure. He probably won't be playing poker for at least a few weeks.

We re-sweep the bombed area, angrily destroying the hooches. Several hooches are burning, as we set up a tight perimeter. The first platoon's corpsman comes over to where I am lying on a three-foot-high berm, looking out on an open area in front of us. He set his shotgun down, aiming out in front of us and tells me that he has been with Lima 6 and a ChuHoy interrupter questioning a captured enemy. When they were done interrogating the prisoner, the corpsman shot four morphine vials into the prisoner's neck to kill him. A strange feeling of righteousness and murderous rage coexists with the "looking-over-my-shoulder" feeling that although we make the laws here, we might be in trouble for murder.

Chapter Seven
To Kill or Not To Kill

"We can never prevent war or speak sensibly of peace and disarmament unless we enter this love of war"
James Hillman, 2004.

I was in my individual poncho tent while it rained during the night. The tent acts to block the rain so I can light a heat tab and a Parliament cigarette. It is a struggle to smoke in this rain but the recessed filter keeps it dry and the burning tobacco evaporates some of the drips. We eat and get our gear packed up.

As we leave in the middle of the morning, the rain stops. The Antos take off in a blur. We continue to toil. We follow a small, brownish-green-hued river in the rain. The river snakes broadly, much like the others I've seen here from helicopters. It formed its route long ago, meandering more to the side than it does toward the ocean. Our path is between the rises and parallel to the river. We travel through a variety of terrain, including sandy hills with bushes and hedgerows, rice paddies, and villages.

The Freedom Bird takes off only a few miles away, so I know we must be close to "the rear." A carbine fires three rounds in the distance, and a smile cracks through the grimace that is becoming a constant feature on my face.

So much has happened these last three weeks. One of my card-playing buddies, Maak Warren, is dead. Another, Mike Johnson is wounded badly enough that we may never see him again. We have killed, captured, and tortured so many of the enemy. A feeling of simmering rage looks out from inside me, fueled by an image of leaving a supposed friendly village and then my friend being killed from it. It is a feeling that I almost want to be shot at or see a VC running, so I can squeeze the trigger for which my right index finger has been itching. I have less and less awareness of any feeling except this itching. Every cell of my body seems involved. Pushing out from my gut to all my extremities with a desire to exact revenge and protect myself. I can sense those of my fellows who are seething like I am.

Even Jackson seems angry. His mild manner is scarred by a look of hostility. Searching with the muzzle of the Stoner for something, anything, to take his revenge on. There is a large explosion ahead of me. Someone has stepped on a landmine. Because of our good spacing, the medevac is only taking out one more dead Marine. There is no one to shoot at. My barely bottled-up rage has me moving in a herky-jerky manner, pivoting around looking for anything to squeeze the trigger at. Anger is not always a good thing. This kind of body language makes me stand out as vulnerable. The day goes on, waiting for the next invisible death to strike. My destructive urges feel all-powerful and at the same time, I feel impotent to find anyone to pay back for my losses. I used to get angry with my Mother often, but even with her, I never had the urge to hurt her. We struggle into the battalion area.

I'm exhausted and filthy, so I don't bother going to the mess hall. There is no one in line for the shower, so I grab my soap and towel and walk out into the warm rain. Washing is a different sensation than wanting to hurt or destroy someone. The dripping mud draws the dirt and grime off me, but it barely dampens my rage. As I'm drying off, a firefight breaks out a half-mile away from the base. Our large battalion mortars and the artillery fire barrages. I hope the devastation falls on the heads of some Vietcong and their villager allies. As the sun sets, I collapse exhaustedly onto my cot. Jackson is snoring two cots from me. In his sleep, he jerks violently.

Like clockwork at 7:00 a.m. on these non-rainy, cloudy days, the temperature starts climbing from 70° to 86° by 1:00 p.m. Stan and I head over to the mess hall. He arrived a month before Del and Mo and is going to Japan for five days of R&R (Rest & Recuperation). He is another mild-mannered guy, like Jackson. As he is imagining R & R, you can see the change in the amount of hostility etched on his face as it eases, with a smile of anticipation that is developing in the more relaxed state of his jaw. When we get back to the hooch, Stan packs up a ditty bag and puts it into his pack to carry to the airport. After taking a shower, he heads for the battalion office to get his paperwork. He looks naked walking away without any weapons.

I grab my towel and walk over to the gate, where I wait for any vehicle to hitch a ride with. The beach helps to alleviate some of my rage. I swim out into the warm water, then let an eight-foot, gentle wave wash me up on the beach. The natural calming gradually erodes the edge of my viciousness. Even when I'm at my most relaxed, the image of spinning around and stitching an enemy through the chest with a diagonal burst from right hip to left shoulder is becoming more and more ingrained in how I move through the world. I would have been a terror if I could have played football with this much zeal.

Would I have been this calm back in the States? Here, no one dares have an opinion about what I am doing. What I have seen and lived through are on my terms. Before these two months of combat, I was acutely aware of people's thoughts and feelings about me. Right now, I could care less what they think. What my peers might be thinking about me right now doesn't even occur to me.

Jackson, Igor, and Bud show up at the beach at noon, and at mid-afternoon, all of us hitch a ride on an empty 6-By to the USO club and the Da Nang PX. I get a Spiderman comic and several others that were not available in our tiny PX. The Freedom Bird takes off right over our heads. Is Stan up there, safe and sound? It seems impossible one of us could be safe without a wall of bullets. We, four, head back to 3/7.

I eat dinner, find a card game, win $50 of NPC, and watch Madame X at the movie. When I am heading back to the hooch, the darkness becomes daylight for five minutes, as the sky lights up from an aerial-dropped illumination round, which parachutes slowly down just outside the berm. One of the guard bunkers fires a five-round burst.

We wake to a dead, calm morning, not even the slightest breeze. After breakfast, we mount up and head over to the motor pool where the tanks are. The mortar and machine gun teams climb onto the sloped sides of two tanks. As we noisily head out the gate, the three platoons spread out around us. A strong wind picks up two hours into our trek. It's strange to have the power of a 90mm cannon to provide return fire while being so completely exposed. Where an Antos can turn and fire in one or two seconds, the attention-drawing tank seems to rotate its turret in slow motion. The VC could shoot a lot of rounds before it fires. We are so clean and showered that we are drawing the attention of the bugs. To the bugs or bullets, we are like magnets for their attacks.

The gusty wind is whipping around by mid-afternoon. Lima Company sets up on a raised area of bushes that overlooks a paddy. The tanks are inside our perimeter, so they are not exposed to zapper attacks. Zappers are VCs that come running in with a satchel charge, throw it at their target, and run away. The tanks are too slow to stop this, so we grunts hold the perimeter to keep the zappers out.

Before dark, each tank blasts a round into the most likely area we would be hit from. Both the blast and the round exploding at the target are impressive, and I feel a bit more invincible. The night proceeds with nothing happening but terror and a desire for destruction.

My favorite breakfast of ham and eggs tastes pretty good amongst the waning aggressive mosquitoes and the waxing flies. There is more than the usual gunfire happening near us, but we have nothing to shoot at, as we pack up after breakfast. The first day of clean skin is no fun. The flies, in particular, sound like they are mad that I showered. The buzzing noise increases the closer they get, seeming to burrow into my ears. The stillness of this overcast morning is broken by the tanks starting their diesel engines. The smell of the fumes permeates our territory. That smell mixes with the residual smell of gunpowder remaining from our pre-fire planning last night. 20 years later this smell would take me over when it felt like the Devil was after my soul.

The first platoon's first, second, and third squads walk to the sides and slightly in front of the two tanks. The tanks are 100 meters apart and have open fields of fire in front of them. Following the tanks, the other two platoons are spread out in double, staggered columns. The CP group, along with our mortars, follows the tanks. Our rear is covered by the second squad of the third platoon, which includes a machine gun and rocket team.

I am walking with my fully loaded pack just 50 feet behind the smell of dirty grease and diesel from the right-hand tank. We scan the area around us with the full knowledge that every enemy within miles knows we are here. Are they running scared, or preparing to attack a tank? I feel a lot safer than riding on the exposed side of the tank. It is comforting that we have that firepower to dissuade the enemy from seeing us as attractive targets.

Before we leave, the engineers detonate an anti-tank mine to add the odor of gunpowder. The sounds of gunfire have become more audible. We reassemble in an online assault formation. The tanks, as they were yesterday, are in the center of each half of the seventy-man line. The twenty of us in the CP group are responsible for covering an attack from behind. The increased exposure caused by the tank's noise, combined with our increased potency, results in gleeful terror and hyper-alertness.

The usual wind picks up in mid-afternoon as the temperature reaches 88°. Suddenly the world is full of bullets. We have our mortar down and firing just a fraction of a second before we hear the thump of Mo's mortar firing. The slow rotation of the tank turret finishes and they begin to blast at the incoming fire. The bullets are still flying everywhere. Then, everything is abruptly quiet. We hurriedly mount up and double-time toward the enemy position, leaving two squads to protect the corpsman who is with the four wounded Marines.

Grunts are randomly firing as they spot black pajamaed Vietcong running away from their ambush positions. It is clear from all the firepower that there are more Marine units to each side of us, but we never see them, nor do our bullets ever cross each other. We set up a perimeter around both our wounded and the dead VC they did not have time to hide. Two Hueys have joined the fight, as a double-propped CH-46 lands to haul out the wounded and the VC body.

We re-form and continue sweeping with the tanks for several more miles before we stop just before sunset. After digging the mortar pit, we ammo humpers are assigned to the outside perimeter. Jackson and I clip our ponchos together and attach them to two three-foot-tall sticks with the seam on the downside of the taut ridge of the top, which allows rain and dew to run off and down the lower poncho. We heat our C-rations while being mindful of our light exposure. A nearly full gibbous moon illuminates the night. I sleep for two hours before Jackson wakes me up for the last half of our sleep time. I'm getting tired as the moon sets and it gets darker. It's difficult to stay awake in the dead of night. More than fear of being attacked, the fear of exposing my unit if I am not awake to cover my section of the perimeter, keeps me from succumbing to the seduction of sleep. I'm sitting next to a tree, my finger on the trigger, confident that I can defend myself instantly if someone tries to sneak in, but the distance between Igor and Pops on either side of me is too great to hear if someone tries to sneak in.

After not nearly enough sleep, the tanks rumble away. We maintain our perimeter, eat breakfast and stay alert. I use C-4 to quickly boil my water for hot cocoa. I hear the clanging and engine noises of two Amtraks bringing resupply, after a few hours of tedium. A 6' tall, thin, clean-looking guy, climbs down off the top. He meets with the captain, then reports to Butch to be our new ammo humper, Greg Glenn. The look of confusion on his face feels familiar to me. You can tell that no one has explained anything to him. It's easy to imagine his expression as he stepped off the 707, expecting to be greeted by a hail of bullets. He'd been preparing for three or four days, but no one will have explained what was ahead of him. He doesn't have the appearance of a poker player, so the NCOs probably couldn't con him as they did me. He has little idea what he is afraid of. His eyes rapidly scan his surroundings. It seems like he could shoot at anything or would freeze if there was actually something to shoot at. Now I know the "why" of the nomenclature of FNG. If we have a firefight right now, it is not just that he would not contribute; he'll be an attractive target for standing up or being too close to other Marines. At this stage, he is a definite liability rather than an asset. I ain't no Fuckin' New Guy any longer. He is looking for someone or something to help him make sense of what to do. I am solidifying a lack of concern with the consequences of my choices as long as I survive and protect my able comrades. Greg will live or die by how quickly he learns the basic skills of staying separate, eating dirt, firing instantly, and walking exuding viciousness. Gone are the tendrils of imagining what my friends and family back home might think about my behavior. Nothing is fully formed inside me as to when to shoot and when not to, but I now know I am alone with that decision. The universe of Port Angeles is completely separate from the universe of combat.

The Amtraks leave and we head out in a double-column movement. As soon as we are completely stretched out in our two long snakes of men, sniper fire comes in from our right, wounding a guy in the arm at the front of the line. The corpsman patches him up enough for us to keep moving. The first platoon, at the front of our movement, comes under heavy fire from an ambush in the late afternoon. They radio back their coordinates and the azimuth and distance the fire is coming from. Bud yells to Del "Three increments, at 78°," and points to a tree in front of us for Del to shoot over. Bud had been able to use his folded-up, plastic bag-covered quadrant map, and compass to determine where the grunts are being hit from. He figured all of this out before Del got his gun ready for me to drop in a spotter round. The grunts radio back that we are right on the money. Del traverses with the small wheel on the aiming arm and adjusts the elevation to compensate for the concussion pushing the base plate into the ground. We "fire for effect."

By this time, Greg has prepared a round for me. We fire four HE rounds and two white phosphorous rounds before the gunfire stops. Then we set up a perimeter to get the medevac in before dark for the three wounded Lima Company Marines. Paul Fuchs, one of my poker buddies, is being carried on a stretcher with a big smile on his face. "Hey Stick, I got shot in the butt," he yells to me. This is the type of wound that we all hope for. Several days in a clean, safe hospital with no permanent damage to your body's structure, and if you get two such wounds that require 48 or more hours in the hospital, you don't get sent back to combat ever again. I give him my approval with a thumbs up.

Chapter Eight
Embedded Reporters

"The vicious passions aroused by discussions of gun control show how aggressively devoted much of today's citizenry is to keeping and staying armed"
James Hillman, 2004.

It rained most of the night and everything is wet. As always, all through every day and night, I hear gunfire and explosions off in the distance. The nearby shooting and artillery are heavier than usual. Greg comes over to look at my C-ration stove and fashions his own. He returns to his gear and cooks breakfast. Everyone stays away from him, as he fends for himself. He'll figure out what to do when we're being shot at, or he'll die.

The terrain we are now in has more sand and hills than we are used to. Dense vegetation clogs areas in the low spots. We move out with everyone using their machetes. We chop through the brush in a sweep formation. The stems of some of the bushes are an inch thick, requiring a perfect 45° hit with plenty of force. There is a feeling of safety to be traveling through virgin territory without walking on the booby-trapped trails.

The rain falls for a few hours after the peak heat of the late afternoon. At 6:00 p.m. in the pouring rain, we are attacked from the far left side of our line. There is no place to set up the mortars, so we act as grunts, responsible for overlapping fields of fire that cover 360°. No one in Lima Company is hurt. Our attack shifts to the left. Then we thoroughly sweep the area from which the enemy fired. As is customary, no evidence of their presence is discovered.

We stop on a hillside overlooking large rice paddies with more sand hills in the distance. There is a lull in the rain while we dig in and eat dinner. Mortars are set up inside the perimeter, so we will get to rest with 2/3rds of the time allotted for sleep. I'm first watch. Lying in the mortar pit, keeping an eye on all the areas around us, gets much harder as the full moon gets even more obscured by heavier rain. When we get back to battalion area, I am going to get an air mattress, rubber lady, to keep my body off this wet ground.

The next night, on last watch, the full moon shines through the clouds until dawn lightens the area around me. A firefight begins the day with the 'swishing' sound of a 61 mortar, followed by an explosion. Three more rounds landed inside our defenses. I hear the thump of the mortar being fired, followed by the agonizing wait to see if it will land on my head. We, the mortars, are not on the firing line, so we attempt to fire mortars at the enemy mortar.

Two Hueys roar over our heads, and fire rockets as they approach the enemy. The two birds then begin making individual passes over the enemy perpendicular to our firing direction. As each bird passes the enemy, it quickly climbs to an elevation out of range, circles around, and approaches from the same spot in the sky again. They charge straight down, machine guns blazing (each bird has two-50 caliber machine guns mounted in the nose). On their fifth pass, they fire machine guns as they descend, then switch to rockets just before they get to the enemy.

We don't take any casualties. We mount up without breakfast and head out on a search-and-destroy sweep through the enemy position. The grunts find a few spent cartridges (brass) and a blood trail that is partially obliterated. We set up in this area to do a more thorough search. Although we don't dig in, we set up the mortars, aiming at the two most likely areas we would be hit from. The grunts carefully search and dig out booby traps. An hour later we finally get to eat. Units of five or six Marines keep poking around in the village. Around noon a tunnel entrance is discovered by a few guys to the left of our mortar.

A short and skinny Marine, our tunnel rat, is stripped down to a tee shirt and pants. With a K-bar in his teeth and a 45 pistol in one hand, he stands in what looked like a sniper hole. His upper chest is visible out of the hole. He wiggles himself down and disappears. 20 minutes later he reappears, quite a bit dirtier. The captain talks with him and the engineers. He is sent back down the tunnel with several packs of C-4, blasting caps, and a 30' length of primer cord. When he resurfaces, we all find cover, a good distance from the hole. The engineers both yell, "Fire in the hole." A series of deep explosions probably collapse the tunnel. Two larger, secondary explosions let us know the tunnel rat discovered munitions.

The next morning there is heavy action happening near us. We mount up as a strong wind drives rain in the overbearing heat. With ponchos on, we head into the rain, which makes wearing glasses impossible. It gets cold in a hurry, dropping around 10° in 30 minutes. At 5:00 p.m., we engage a large enemy force that is well dug in. Our firing of rifles, machine guns, and rockets does nothing to diminish their AK-47 and carbine rounds. The Hueys come back and make their passes over our heads. They feel like an extension of my rifle, expanding my viciousness, as I try to spot where the fire is coming from. The helicopters are doing the same thing. They fire their door guns from above and behind us, then they make aggressive runs at the enemy position with their heavier nose guns.
The Hueys remain to provide support while resupply is flown in with two CH-46s, which transport out the three wounded Marines. The rain stops, but the cold wind lasts until the evening. We settle in for the night,

confident that visibility will be good due to the moon rising before full dusk.

While eating breakfast, the jets do several bombing runs near us. Then artillery sends in barrage after barrage on the same spot. We pack up and move to the south of all this bombardment. About noon, we arrange ourselves for an online sweep back towards the enemy-held area. The day starts to heat up and I hear small arms fire a few miles in front of us. Coming through a treeline, the right side of Lima Company opens fire and calls in the coordinates of the enemy to the captain. We shoot a couple of mortar rounds in the hope of catching the VC above ground.

There is no sign of an enemy presence when we move through their area. More gunfire can be heard in the distance. We come to a halt twice to allow the engineers to clear booby traps. We dig in on a slope in the afternoon heat, as the wind blows sand around. We form a long line, with our defensive positions facing the valley and rice paddies ahead of us. We have many targets of opportunity throughout the late afternoon and evening as the enemy abandons the area of US heavy fire in front of us. We're at the end of our range, but we try to shoot them as they flee to new hiding places. The second platoon grunts call in with the coordinates of several well-defended enemies with whom they are engaged. Del's three rounds of effective fire land directly on top of them. "You got those fuckers," one grunt yells over the radio.

Finally, I am dirty enough that the constant bugs are not bothering with me. In the slow-moving morning, we take the time to thoroughly clean our weapons and gear, then saddle up and head out into the bush. A long, boring day transpires with no booby traps or enemy encountered.

The rain is falling, as we stop for the night inside a tree line with a village of ten hooches east of us. It starts to get dark, the rain stops and I close my right eye. In full darkness, I have enough night vision to keep an eye out for any solid shapes and movement. Our mortar is set up next to the company radio operator. Radio checks take place every hour through the night.

Above the clouds, the moon begins to lighten the sky about the time we start watch. By 11:00, it is easy to make out the bushes. We make it through a night with no action, and because the mortars are inside the perimeter we split the watch three ways and each of us gets three hours of sleep.

It is a dead-still, foggy morning. Marines begin to appear out of the glum, as the sun takes over from the moonlight. Everyone is milling around getting food together. The familiar tedium of sitting around in the tension of high alert gets stronger as the morning rolls on. The fog lifts and it slowly heats up. By noon, it is blazing hot, but mercifully the wind starts blowing hard enough to provide some relief.

Resupply comes in on two CH-34s, blowing sand everywhere. Two reporters disembark along with our supplies. They are dressed like us, except carrying pistols, instead of rifles. As we break camp, the reporters are moving with us in the CP group. Their spacing is horrible. As we walk, I realize how likely the two of them are to draw fire. They walk completely upright, not scanning the area, and therefore provide no threat to the enemy. Clearly terrified, they don't look at all vicious. This means there is a section of the right-hand column where the field of fire is not covered. The whole company is vulnerable to being split apart there. Although they are not talking, they make a tremendous amount of noise. The quieter, the more experienced you are, the less fire you drew. Keeping proper spacing and exuding aggression, keep the enemy at bay. This is different than dealing with bullies in Junior High who used to gang up on us and force us to give them our lunch money. Aggression won't have worked with them, so I learned to keep a low profile and avoid them. It's deadly when you get attention here.

The CP group has just moved into a tree line looking out over a large paddy, when the company comes to a halt. I look out on the paddy from a three-foot-deep dry ditch. I can see how dangerous the reporters are to us. We must choose between two risky options. Ignore spacing and make sure our fields of fire overlap on both sides of the reporters, resulting in a very appealing clumps of four people in their part of the line; or leave a large gap in our ability to protect ourselves.

Bud is standing between me and the journalists. He's only five feet away from them. They're huddled together, seeing enemies everywhere. Igor is five feet from the other side of the reporters. In the bush, you never see that many Marines so close together. We must get rid of them because they have the potential to get us killed. I have no idea what they could be reporting because they appear to be either unaware of our surroundings or fixated on trivial details.

When the rain starts to make life more uncomfortable, I feel it serves them right for putting us in danger to get a story. When we set up for the night they are thankfully invisible inside our perimeter. It is amazing how much of a burden two people who are not naturally pulling their own weight are to an increased feeling of danger. This is true with FNGs also, however, they seem to almost automatically understand spacing. New guys all scan the environment with their rifles while making their bodies as small a target as possible. A new guy is all alone moving through our environments. He is much more of a target than a guy with a few firefights under his belt, but he is not like these reporters who have no idea how to keep from endangering themselves and everyone else.

On my first day back in Port Angeles after the War, Walter Cronkite came on the evening news as we were waiting for dinner at my folks' house. I was curious to see how the War would be portrayed. I couldn't imagine a news team being able to handle the real situations of that environment. I have heard a hundred times since then from people in the States, "I know all about that war, I watched it on TV." Walter rattled off a slew of body count figures. I'm curious about the dependability of totals and who reported them. The numbers would be made up if it was the Rear-Echelon Mother Fuckers, REMFs, reporting them to look good on their unit reports. If it was grunt units reporting, it was all guesswork, just like the "kills" you'll hear me claim.

The scene on the TV changed to a bizarre reenactment of an alleged event in Vietnam. American soldiers were arrayed going up a hillside. No bullets were coming toward them or the camera crew, but they were shooting as they went uphill, as if they were being shot at. Without saying a word, I walked over to the TV set and turned it off. This was obviously a staged production to satisfy the American appetite to know what was happening to 400,000 of their citizens on the other side of the world.

Chapter Nine
Happy Birthday

"Behavior sets standards, not ideals"
Karl Marlantes, 2011.

I am 19 years old and all of my birthdays have been celebrations before today.

Last year on April 28, 1966, my birthday was a big affair at my parent's house. Ken, Ben, Mark, four guys from my church group, and even Barb came back from the University of Washington for the cake and ice cream festivities. My folks gave me $500 toward buying an old VW. At that time, my whole world was steadily opening up before me. I would be able to drive home from work in the dark, instead of riding my bike at 9:00 p.m. None of us had any idea that I would be in Vietnam next birthday.

Here, in the Nam, my only present of the day is the cocoa Del gives me and the tremendous relief as I watch the two reporters get into a CH-34 to fly away. We, in the command group, will be able to trust everyone to do their part to assure our safety. The mortar guys wish me a happy birthday.

I do feel more mature. The reporters' terror made them behave in self-protective ways that were constantly increasing their noticeability. With them gone, the sense of order in the chaos is restored. The new guy, Greg Glenn, still has some of this sense of estrangement, but his behaviors fit in with the orchestrated movements of the rest of us. No extra motions, always alert, relaxed cocky attitude, aware of every possible danger and areas from which we could be shot.

There is no wind the next morning. It is overcast. As we mount up at 8:00 a.m. the temperature quickly rises to sweltering. The vicious attitude has returned to my face as we walk, we scan for danger. My mind is filled with conflicting ideas. If someone appeared in my field of fire would I have time to identify them before they shot me? What if I killed a kid? I want so much to stop someone who is trying to hurt us. What is my duty? Having always been rebellious, do I need to be controlled by my duty? These thoughts weave around the constant, dominant thoughts of where the threats would come from. The edge of bitterness will probably impel my reactions, but I am still debating the honorableness of it. Would I feel ashamed of myself if I shot someone who was innocent?

As is most common, I have no chance to act on these thoughts. The day passes with no enemy contact, no booby traps, and a long march to another unknown area in a strange country. As we set up for the night the end of my birthday has no relevance. I take a watch like everyone else. The juxtaposition of the childish idea of birthday celebrations comes up against the vivid awareness that our behavior is only about staying alive. The rain pours down for my whole first watch and seems a fitting end to a birthday that never was.

We finally leave the following afternoon, and arrive at an abandoned village after a slow journey. The soil is rich and deep here. The mortars set up in a basketball court-sized garden. Long rows of furrows run through the earth. I dig a deep sleeping hole between the furrows after the easy digging of the mortar pits. Each furrow is a foot taller than the troughs, with just enough space for me to sleep completely underground comfortably. My poncho is neatly stretched the length of my grave-looking hole, which even has a zigzag entryway, so a hand grenade blowing up in the step down would not hit me with shrapnel and a bullet whizzing in the open end would not hit me. I've gathered three bamboo mats for the sides and floor of my Taj Ma Hall of sleeping quarters. Along the southern edge of the garden, there is a 4' high, 6' wide causeway. The grunts' perimeter extends beyond that barrier. The CP group is to our north. The rest of the company has encircled us. This is the most secure I've ever felt in the wilderness of Vietnam.

I am over by my fancy hole. The rest of the mortar guys are milling around in the relative safety of the invisible grunts surrounding us. Del, John, and Jackson are sitting around the mortar pits about 20 feet from me. Greg has his shirt off. Jackson is fully dressed with his cover (hat) on. Del is bareheaded and fully dressed while he cleans his 45-pistol. They are all three sitting on a woven bamboo mat from a nearby hooch. Jackson is looking over at me with his friendly smile. Greg is holding his chin with his left hand, elbow resting on his slightly raised knee. He looks like a scholar contemplating a philosophical question.

An earnest look dominates Del's careful work on his pistol. Mo comes sauntering toward them, his muscled body almost seeming to roll. Out of the corner of my eye, I see Mo suddenly throw the 6'4" Del to the ground. Mo has him in a violent chokehold, saying, "Don't ever point a weapon at someone unless you're going to use it. I don't care if you know it's empty!" Mo grew up on the streets of East Los Angeles around guns and knew the danger. I believe this demonstration helped Lima Company only have one accidental, self-inflicted wound during my tour, when, two months from now an FNG machine gunner will accidentally shoot a hole in his foot with his pistol.

I am on first watch starting at midnight when the sky clears for the first time in many days. The waning gibbous moon of 61% illumination rises at 1:50 a.m., which changes the land and starry sky to a bluish hue with only the brightest stars visible. By the time I wake Greg for his watch at 2:30, the usual high clouds have returned.

I crawl into my sleeping trough, exhausted by my world. When I wake up at first light, there is a lot of activity around our two gun pits. Rather than being a wide causeway, the 4' high dike is made up of two parallel dikes two feet apart and closed off at each end. During the night, an enemy soldier ran right up inside our perimeter and lobbed three hand grenades at our mortars. A foot-deep hole has been blown in the furrow trough next to my tent. Shrapnel holes abound in my poncho tent. Del tells me that they decided to let me sleep once they confirmed that I was breathing. Perhaps I am immortal. Many new factors needed to align perfectly for me to survive within the kill radius of that American hand grenade. That grenade probably bounced off my poncho tent and landed inches away in the next trough. Who knows what would have happened if I hadn't been looking for the perfect sleeping spot? In war, it's one lucky minute after another until you get out. You either have it or you don't. The "luck of the draw" is important in games like poker. Remembering this event in 1986, 19 years later, I thought I was saved to become a combat veteran readjustment therapist.

After a quick meal, we patrol all around the two parallel dikes, stopping ten times to clear booby traps. As this pathway opens out into an area near a river, we fan out into an online assault formation. We trudge through the sand, then pass into a tree line, carefully searching several villages consisting of a few hooches each. I have a strong desire to hurt someone coming from the terror of waking to the near miss of dying.

The early morning fog lifts as the sun shines through the overcast, cloudy skies. We pack our belongings and leave in a double, staggered column, without breakfast. We haven't had resupply in a few days. We move quickly and never stop for booby traps. The sounds of US artillery being fired alerts us that we are close to the battalion area. Hunger and thirst propel us to the mess hall after we drag into our company area and drop our gear. My food seems to vanish as soon as I sit down. I decide to go to China Beach as soon as possible, but first I stop by battalion supply and get an air mattress and half a wool blanket and I pack my belongings. I walk over to the gate with my rifle, cartridge belt, and Kbar and talk to the guards while I wait for a ride. Then I'm holding onto the side of a dump truck as we bump along.

There are already a lot of GIs strewn about the beach. I find an area that no one is using, strip down to my skivvies, set my rifle on my towel, and walk out into the waves. The grime of being in the bush is awaiting the cleansing power of salt water on my face and body. The waves are gently crashing over my head. Each wave washes away another layer of dirt. Then I go swimming.

I ride a few waves and take the last one to shore. I drop exhausted onto my towel in the 90-degree heat of midday and feel refreshed. After three more body surfing stints, I dry off, dress and head back to get my gear in order. The highway is really crowded with trucks, buses, livestock, carts, children, and, like my ride, jeeps. There are many people carrying big bundles of sticks strapped on each end to eight-foot-long bamboo poles. They all have the same rhythm, bouncing in time to their shuffling steps.

I get all my gear outside the tent and shake the sand out of it. After I hang everything up, I find a card game in the first platoon's tent. "Hey Stick, get your fuckin' ass over here and play," Harry says. We play until it's time for dinner. I go into the club after eating and get a beer. The club is located in half of a tent, with five small tables scattered about. The beer and sodas are in garbage cans filled with ice. That evening is the movie Portrait In Black. Harwell and I get together to play Tonk for a few hours and are two of the last people to hit the rack.

I go over to Puff Fitzgibbons' supply tent after chow to get a new poncho. He sends me over to battalion supply because he is out. He appears to be a nice guy, but he treats me the same way the rest of the 'Short-Timers' do. They don't talk to me or are business-like. They appear to be insulated. They enjoy being with the other Short-Timers. This has the feel of cliques in high school, but their disregard for me is devoid of disdain. Maybe they've figured out how to interact with each other and have no desire to meet anyone else. They seem to be afraid to interact with me in the same way that the popular crowd would. These guys are also aloof, but I'm not sure why they're 'cooler' than me. Maybe interacting with me binds them to this place, which is the last thing a short-timer wants. Will I end up like them?

The day moves along with nothing to do. Igor and I play Mumbly Peg and practice knife throwing, then I sharpen my machete to a razor's edge. For the first time, I attempt to flip it up in the air and catch it on the handle. If I cannot see a clear, safe catch I let it fall to the sand. It is easier to track its progress with two rotations in the air than with one. The sharp blade goes up in front of me and the small handle lands right back in my hand.

We have a poker game in the mortar tent. Harwell joins us. He acts as if his cards aren't very good and then uncovers a great hand. Even I can never tell if he is bluffing unless he is forced to show his cards when someone calls his bluff. The game breaks up as we are told to head to chow early and get ready to move out. We head out of the eastern break in the wire past the mess hall. Two hours later, as the night darkens, we get closer together to be able to see the guy in front of us. It is pitch black an hour after sunset. Moving in the dark is scary because there is no way to see exactly where the guy in front of me stepped. We dig in and set up the perimeter. Three guys from recon have traveled with us. They leave the CP group before we start digging in, and stealthily disappear into the darkness.

We break camp early after eating breakfast. Then we walk in an area with dense bushes and trees for two hours and set up. This is an ambush. The first platoon and the mortars are stretched out in hiding places near a trail. I am well concealed, six feet from the trail. The noise of even my slightest twitch seems as if it could be heard by anyone on the trail. I know the VC can move silently. As the hours wear on, my breathing becomes rhythmic and under control so it makes no sound entering or leaving. My heartbeat is a steady disquieting sound. Then I hear Vietnamese voices and my heart beats faster and louder. It seems impossible that they can't hear it. They get closer and closer. My heart thumps even louder. The male voices pass my position on the trail.

They fade into the background. My heartbeat is still audible. I now know it is not audible, even to someone that close. Why didn't we set off the ambush by killing them? We break the ambush an hour later, and my ears are still acutely aware of my thumping heart.
In mid-afternoon, we join the rest of the company. They have been on a search-and-destroy sweep, attempting to push any enemy toward our ambush. The Vietnamese I heard must not have been worth triggering the ambush. Maybe they had no weapons, or we were waiting for a larger force.

We travel another few hours and set a perimeter well before dark. The mortar pit is one of the perimeter positions. We shoot an HE round into a bushy hillside across a rice paddy to gauge our range. At dusk, three carbine sniper rounds buzz through our position. We return fire with rifles, Bazooka, machine guns, and mortar rounds. The itch in my trigger finger feels sated as I effectively squeeze off 5 round bursts. I feel confident the bullets will arrive at the area of the muzzle flashes close to the ground, stitching diagonally left to right.

An hour later, Greg and I hold a position between the two mortar pits, with Igor and Stan to our right and their gun pit another 30 feet past them. Del and Bud are standing watch in our pit to my left, Jackson and Butch 30 feet past them. We all listen intently, as the enemy clearly knows we are here and it is can't-see-your-hand-in-front-of-your-face dark. The night, with its two hours of sleep, passes without incident.

Just as daylight begins to break, we trudge off after breakfast in a sweep of the area where the sniper fired last night. We don't expect to find anything despite being on high alert. On the backside of the bushy hillside, there are five hooches. The women and elderly men appear terrified. We're leaving when someone Zippos a hooch. Simply touching the dry thatch with a Zippo cigarette lighter ignites the fire. I feel a sense of accomplishment as the desire to destroy something grows within me. Could I burn hooches? I had the most fun at Methodist Church summer camp when I was 10 years old and got to help tear apart a cabin. That planned destruction just seemed to make sense to me. I was turned loose to safely strategize prying things loose and smashing them. This temptation holds the same desire. We search for two hours, then move out in a double staggered line, with mortars in the rear. I walk tail-end Charlie and we get shot at from the village behind us. The carbine rounds go by well over our heads and we speed up.

The day proceeds with traveling through rice paddies and sandy hills until we come across a small river with trees and bushes along its banks. The only evidence it is moving is the twigs and swirls that move smoothly along its surface. Holding our rifles over our heads we cross one at a time. The bank drops off sharply to a depth of three feet. At the center, the river comes up to my chest.

Our line of movement stops when I am out of the river. The grunts have discovered a tunnel entrance. A tunnel rat must be doing his job because we set up a temporary perimeter. An hour later we hear "Fire in the hole," followed by three large, muffled explosions. I feel a stronger sense of satisfaction, yet my desire to shoot someone keeps growing.

Five miles later, we halt for the night, and it begins to rain. I cut two poles for Greg and my tent with my razor-sharp machete. We drive the 45° point into the hard ground, tie a cord to a stake at each end of our clipped-together ponchos, and stake the edges to the ground tightly. Because the hard dirt is not clay-like, digging the mortar pit is relatively simple. The accommodating earth welcomes the open shovel. After a sniper fires one round through our perimeter, we respond with small arms fire.

Today will be another day that we are out of food until the resupply arrives. The mosquito corps is out in force pestering our Yankee skin before the sun comes up. The first fly comes burrowing in before I get up. As the flies multiply and the mosquitoes disappear, our listening post returns to the perimeter. With nothing else to do, the desire to kill the pestering flies is strong. Mosquitoes and flies both remind me of the VC. They make their presence uncomfortably known, while they stay away from retribution. Our most common type of resupply finally shows up a few hours later, a CH-34, escorted by a Huey lands in a flurry of dust. We load quickly, as the CH-34 keeps its rotor going. The Huey patrols overhead. Five minutes after landing they fly away, leaving us to pass out all the supplies.

I do some thinking about my sister Barb's birthday, which is today, May 6th. She is 21 and old enough to vote and drink alcohol in the USA. All through Grade School we would get together and talk after we were supposed to be in bed. I'd snapped my fingers to let Barb know I wanted to talk. If she snapped three times, it meant she didn't want to talk that night. Usually, she snapped back twice and I snuck over to her room to talk about our parents being too strict. One time she asked, "Are you thinking of dating Diane Klein?" I responded, "Yes, what do you think about that?" Barb said, "I think her reputation might not be good for you." That time, like many others, I took her advice and didn't date Diane.

Writing her a letter this morning, I'm torn between the type of letters I send to my mother and Mary Dyar, which sound like I'm in a tropical paradise and the type of letters I send to my friend Marjorie Bell. Marjorie's letters don't go into the most terrifying and gruesome details, but they do explain my current way of life. Barb could handle my terror nearly as well as Marjorie, but I end up with a letter that is closer to what Mom receives because I mail it to our house. Barb is a Junior at the University of Washington, so she'll get it when she returns home for the summer, and I don't want to put her in a position where she can't read it to the family. So I write a letter about my trip to China Beach and how the shower felt. I inform her of Del and Mo. I tell Marjorie about starving to death, barely sleeping, bugs, and mostly jokes. My friends and family have a variety of life events that they consider important, such as proms, school, dating, community events, sports, and hanging out together. It's all about blood and guts here, while I'm terrified, alone, and filthy.

We put our gear on, with its full weight resupplied, and head off on the daily grind. It truly is a tropical paradise. Every day, like today, or as I explained two months ago is similar; foliage, sand, striking skies, tranquil rice paddy scenes, and lazy rivers. The mornings are calm or a slight breeze, the heat builds quickly behind the clouds, and the wind, at almost the same pace every day, cools off the blistering heat of the afternoon. Even the anomalies like rain and clear skies happen in a random, repeating pattern.

We travel several miles with no resistance. The brush is thick and I have my rifle ready to fire with my left hand because I am hacking the brush with my machete. The brush thins and I casually walk along flipping my machete up like a circus juggler. Up it goes two rotations and lands safely in my right palm. It's not like anybody is watching me, except maybe the VC.

Eight years ago, back on May 7, 1957, I was at my desk toward the back of the Fourth Grade classroom and was the first to complete a math test. Mrs. Jeffrey, looking down at her desk in the right front corner, seemed preoccupied. The other students were still working on the test. For five minutes I watched a tractor out the window plowing the field beyond the playground. Just last year when I had been in this same classroom for third grade with Miss Smith, there had been apple trees covering that field. I loved to watch the slow-changing orchard-life drift by. This spring all the fruit trees had been pulled out and hauled away. The area was being plowed to plant grass for a bigger playground.

Feeling antsy and wanting to show off that I had already finished the test, I strolled up to the pencil sharpener attached to the wall between the teacher's desk and the blackboard. I turned the crank until the cone-shaped pencil lead tip was perfectly sharpened. Always pushing the envelope between drawing attention to myself and staying out of trouble, I flipped my pencil up in the air. By this age, I had developed the skill of flipping a hammer, stick, spatula, or tennis racket and catching it on the handle. Showing off, I flipped the pencil up above my head. I acted as nonchalantly as I could as it descended toward my palm. Like a tennis racket, I expected to be able to have it land horizontally in my right hand. Instead, the point came straight down and embedded in the soft flesh in the area below the pad of my right thumb. The lead broke off. 60 years later, as I write this I'm still able to see the black spot of graphite under my skin. That feeling of nonchalance and competence has gotten me in trouble throughout my life but it is also part of the character I became to survive in combat.

Every moment in Vietnam requires quick, precise reactions with no regard for social consequences, like perfecting the art of catching my machete on the handle as I walk in full combat gear. As I walked along, the razor-sharp blade descended to the handle in my right hand. This motion's rhythm reminds me of that mistake I made in fourth grade. A blunder here would sever my fingers. Today, any traces of 'The World' are completely obscured by the ground-in dirt on my palms. But my hand remembers the minor repercussions of a lapse in concentration back then, and I easily maintain the circus act. Nothing is ever said about my feat.

We only clear one booby trap in the five miles we walk. Setting up for the night, the rain starts coming down in buckets. Digging the mortar pit is a little easier than usual because the wet sand does not fall back into the pit as easily after the soaking rain. Bud has his quadrant map in its plastic bag out and sets aiming stakes on three spots around the pit. By the time the sun is setting the wind has stopped, and it has cooled to the low 80s. The rain keeps up for another hour after dark.

A sniper shoots in at our position, as full darkness takes hold. The middle aiming stake is right on the azimuth Bud had guessed as a likely place to receive fire. I drop an HE into the barrel with one increment angled at 70°, and the grunts radio back to raise 50' and fire for effect. We drop two more rounds in that area and then light it up with an illumination round, but none of the other grunts see anyone running away. Everything is quiet, and the rain stops a few minutes later. Inside me, impotence is at odds with a desire for vengeance.

CHAPTER TEN
AFTER VIETNAM
SUICIDE

I was sitting at my desk at the Lower Elwha Tribal Center when the receptionist buzzed me to say, "Marjorie Jones is on the phone for you crying and hysterical." I was renting a business office from the tribe for my Vietnam combat veteran Readjustment Counseling service.

"Thanks, Virginia," I replied, "put her through."

It was only one year into my federal contract to provide support services for Vietnam combat veterans and their families. Already, ten of 100 veterans who had called, choose the telephone over the loaded gun they were ready to use on themselves. Ed Jones was probably another suicidal Vietnam veteran, but in the three months of his weekly Tuesday afternoon counseling sessions with me, he had yet to disclose his level of desperation. Like a lot of my VA clients back then, Ed was a gruff, suspicious guy. In spite of being 6 feet tall with big shoulders, a barrel chest, and a slightly bigger gut, I saw him as a man who was more scared than intimidating.

Whenever a combat veteran came for his first session with me I would stand by the door to the office, gesture toward the interior, and say, "Go on in and sit in whichever easy chair you want and I will sit opposite you." My open-ended offer to pick any chair sometimes confused new guys who clearly expected me, as a well-dressed person of authority to sit behind the protective armor of my standard military-issue metal desk. Because it had taken me eight years of post-Vietnam therapy to notice that in public I always picked a seat with the best view of any potential attacks and easy escape routes, I knew that most of these guys would take the chair against the wall facing the door. I'd only made the mistake once of having the first meeting with a defensive combat veteran while I sat at my desk and he faced me on the other side. That vet went through all kinds of contortions trying to use body language to appear tougher than me. He settled on having his heavy right boot up on his left knee high enough to be visible between us. To learn to feel safe with each other we needed to have nothing between us and be close enough together to feel intimate. I modeled this from my parent's living room. It felt important for these fellows to know that even a well-dressed man could handle being around a surly man who was angry at the world.

Ed Jones was my hundredth combat veteran client. He had a rear-echelon job in Vietnam with the Army.

His area got hit with rockets twice and four times with small mortars like the one I carried in Nam. He deserved to be understood as to how scary it was to live in that environment, even though he felt undeserving of care and respect. Most of my clients felt like this. They considered someone else to have really been in combat, not them. I always thought the same thing about my combat experience. Because I never walked point or was a tunnel rat, I wasn't in combat. Because I didn't get wounded or killed, I wasn't in combat. The reality of my counseling job was that an estimated 150,000 Vietnam vets had already successfully suicided by this time.

This call had me scrambling for what to do even more than the time I heard the firing pin hit the bullet twice with one guy before he was willing to have me come to his house to talk to him.

Ed always accepted a cup of coffee to start our sessions. I wanted these combat soldiers to feel at home and pampered. He put cream and sugar in it, which seemed to match the incongruence of the big testy look on his awkward, almost shy face. He worked sporadically at one of the 200 shake mills west of Port Angeles. Although a dangerous and physically taxing job, it wasn't nearly as macho or well-paying as logging. The disgusting environment of the two big pulp mills in town provided a family wage job for many of the local guys who survived Vietnam. Ed didn't have much of a chance to get a job at either one of those mills because he didn't have a relative employed by them. He, like many of my clients, had moved further west and north eight times in the 15 years since he got out of the Army. If you keep moving in those directions, Port Angeles is the last place you can go in the US. He grew up in the South and was looking for a place he could fit in.

His treatment to this point was limited to him getting used to me asking him how some current-life situation felt to him. It was as if these guys had never been asked how they felt. His only hope for recovery from the overwhelming anxiety that he felt was to get enough familiarity with his emotions, which often took a year of weekly sessions, to be able to tolerate a combat group therapy setting. He had the disadvantage of still drowning his fears in alcohol. 96 of those first 100 clients had at least some history of problems with drugs or alcohol. Now I have treated 1300 combat veterans and the percentages of substance abuse are still the same. Alcohol is a frontal lobe depressant, the frontal lobe is how we modulate impulses like anxiety, so it compromises our ability to calm down, even though the euphoric effect of booze covers up the rising anxiety in the short run.

So, Majorie Jones' desperate phone call didn't come as a surprise to me.

Through the tears and sobbing, she said, "Ed is waving his pistol around and threatening me, the kids, and himself. He isn't making any sense. Please help us."

To help her focus I said, "Take a couple of slow, deep breaths. Where is he now?"

"He went out in the trees to take a pee."

"I'll be at your place in 15 minutes."

I drove west and south toward the Olympic Mountains. Like most of the roads heading up into the foothills, each turn got more remote. Just like the five acres I lived on, the Jones had a long dirt driveway off a dirt road that had turned off a graveled road five miles above Highway 101. The roads that went up into the woods had these isolated territories and my clients thought they would feel safe if no other people were around. Many of the places were little more than campsites with a shed or two. The Jones were renting a 40-foot trailer. I pulled my pickup into their small clearing and got out.

Ed came out with his 45 pistol and said, "What the fuck do you want?"

Matter of factly I said, "I'm worried about your children."

In our sessions, he had told me how much he cared for his five-year-old boy and three-year-old girl.

"We don't need you."

I made sure not to make him try to scare me away. I said, "I just want to talk with you, would that be okay?"

"There's nothing you can do to help me, I am worthless," he said, as he lowered his pistol and staggered closer to me.

"Got any coffee brewed in the house?" I asked.

The months he had become used to being homey with me did the job. He seemed fairly casual as he went up the steps into the trailer ahead of me. Marjorie and the two kids were huddled on one end of the couch. As Ed moved into the kitchen to get me a cup of coffee, I signaled her to move to the other side of the room by the door so I could be between them and Ed. Keeping his attention on me, I maneuvered him toward the couch when I had my cup.

As he waved the gun up in the air he said, "Fuck all of this. Fuck my life. Fucking hell, you're all against me."

But he was moving toward the couch and not paying attention to his family.

Marjorie quietly went out the door that I had purposely left open, I said to Ed so that he would look at me and not them, "That's a nice pistol. I carried one just like it in the Nam."

Once the family had driven away, he seemed to forget about how angry he was. He grumbled, "Damn, I am out of beer." Great, I thought, if I can just distract him long enough he will probably fall asleep. And lo and behold there was a snoring drunk on the couch a few minutes later.

I drove back to my office and documented the whole event. Because of client privilege, I decided it was best to not involve the police at that stage of my career. A few years later, I heard the firing pin hit the bullet twice with one guy before he was willing to have me come to his house to talk to him. I ask if he would let the police come with me. Their first question was about his gun, where it was, and whether it was loaded. I could tell that the hundreds of times these officers had faced, had taught them how to protect citizens from themselves. In the following years, I let the police do the talking, rather than a counselor like me, but Ed survived my amateur heroics.

Chapter Eleven
Death

"War...is a human accomplishment and an inhuman horror"
James Hillman, 2004.

We get up early to move out with the wind whipping the fog around. The sky brightens and we make our way through dense brush. Most of the time, I keep Del in sight through the tall brush, about 10' ahead of me. Behind me, Greg is doing the same thing. It's scary when we all crowd together, but it's even scarier when I feel like a lone target that the enemy can pick off and sneak away with no one to back me up.

Two days later in the sweltering heat, I am eating a C-ration breakfast of ham and eggs which gets me going after a full 4 hours of sleep. The seemingly perpetual overcast remains as the clouds move on. Just as I get my water boiling with C-4, a sniper takes four carbine shots at us. The new Lieutenant (Lt) for the third platoon is grazed on his right upper arm. The corpsman patches him up. The second platoon leaves their gear and sweeps quickly toward the sniper. We are on high alert as we see the second move into the tree line across the sand. An hour later, small arms fire with a mixture of carbines, AK-47s, 3.5 Rockets, M79s, and M16s, erupts deep in that tree line.

"659922, 200 meters on an azimuth 13° east of North," says the second platoon on the radio. At 658923, our azimuth is 19° from North with three increments, and our elevation gauge is dialed to 55° to shoot 1023 meters. We launch a high-explosive round.

"200 meters to the left and 50 meters short with your spotter round," says the radioman out there. We make adjustments and fire another HE round. "25 meters to the right and fire-for-effect," we hear over the static. Our rounds are followed by the battalion's 81mm mortars that explode in the direction of the enemy. Then artillery rounds fly over our heads and strike the same spot.

It's difficult to sit still when I'm not sure if they have enough firepower out there. The first platoon departs at full speed. We reduce the perimeter's circumference and fill in all the gaps. The firing ceases, most likely before the 'first' arrives. Five minutes later, a Huey flies low over us, with the medevac chopper behind, safely out of rifle range. As the medevac lands, the Huey continues to patrol. We've only saved a few mortar rounds and we'll need more ammunition if attacked. The second platoon must be nearly out of all types of ammunition as well. At around noon, the two platoons return to our tight perimeter. Blood is on several guys' uniforms, including Harwell and Montgomery. When I return to my cocoa, it is sand-filled. I rip open the cookies and devour them.

Another bedraggled start to the day, after the third night of two blocks of 90 minutes of sleep, and today we have no food left to eat. Dawn is barely visible when we move out. The point people safely meet up with the recon guys we dropped off last week, who look dirtier and more exhausted than we do, which is difficult to imagine, but obvious. My mind supplies a picture of half as much sleep and twice as many miles, then sitting still in a hiding place for days. They travel with the CP group, depending on our security to protect them.

The amount of noise we make must be terrifying for them, but they are expressionless. Without the constant scanning that we all do, they are blank and alert. They appear to be more capable of reacting quickly and effectively than we are. Their expression and body language go beyond the angry, vicious energy we exude. To be alone in this scene, with only the gear on your back. No resupply of ammo, food, or water. So quiet the enemy doesn't know you are coming, or where you are staying.

We, on the other hand, need to exude being a hair trigger away from a wall of bullets flying toward the enemy. We make as little noise as we can but being around these recon guys makes us sound like clanging, brush-rubbing elephants. They silently pass between bushes. Their gear is taped down to keep it quiet. Even our ammo pouches make a noise as they brush against our legs. They carry survival knives, rather than K-bars, smaller and more utilitarian. The scabbard is taped down. Their canteens do not flop against their legs. All their straps are secured. As we walk back into the battalion area, the recon guys split off near headquarters and we go to our tents. There are a few hours before chow call. We get our gear in order with almost no conversation, except for people asking each other to do things for them. This routine is robotic.

Del heads to Australia for R&R. Jackson, who has been here the longest, takes over as our gunner. A reinforced platoon (the second) is dispatched in the late morning, with our gun. We are in our usual stretched-out, staggered line and barely out of sight of the Rear when the crazy sniper takes one shot at the Freedom Bird taking folks home. Or is this the plane with Del on it? If so, he is truly safe. No one is likely to shoot at him for five days. It is a stark contrast to watching where I take each step and scanning for danger.

It's a bright morning with a few clouds. The sunrise is breathtaking. The smoke from illumination rounds and airburst artillery fills the sky, which is a bright orange-pink stretching from the eastern horizon to the midheaven. After three hours of walking east, we move to a brushy hillside overlooking a broad valley, and set up in a long line, with fields of fire in front and behind us. We dig the mortar pit quickly and quietly. We have three grunt positions between us and the rocket squad to our right. For protection, the grunts dig fighting positions or hide behind natural hillocks. To our left is a machine gun team. We wait, as the clouds and overcast roll in. Unbeknownst to us, the rest of the company is sweeping toward us through the hilly area across the valley. A half-mile away, we hear a hand grenade detonate, followed by the rat-a-tat-tat of an AK-47. Marine firepower erupts for two seconds almost simultaneously. It is now clear that we are keeping an eye out for any enemy fleeing toward our dug-in positions.

Two hours later we are told the rest of the company will join us, "so do not shoot them." They have stirred up no further enemy. We see no one suspicious out in the valley. In the early afternoon, we set up a company perimeter. It is comforting to be back around Mo and his gun team. Mo's sense of humor and rolling efficiency are contagious. His inner-city smarts make us badder jungle fighters. Mo asks, "Hey Stick, what the fuck do you think Del is up to about now?"

I can see he is happy for his best bud and dreaming of his own R&R. I laugh, "He's fucking his brains out with some 'Round-Eyed woman." He smiles and chuckles as he sits down on the berm of his mortar pit. Like Del, he always looks comfortable, yet athletically ready to function, instantly. We talk about where we want to go on R&R. He is heading to Japan next week. I ask, "What are you going to be doing at this time next Monday?"

He laughs and says "I'll be with a beautiful Japanese woman, and I won't let out of my arms for the whole five days."

The next morning, we awake from too little sleep to a 75° slightly cloudy, windless day. The breeze, clouds, and temperature would rise over the next few hours. Once more, after breakfast, our gun moves out with the second platoon. We travel slowly because we are approaching the area where the rest of the company was hit by fire yesterday. Clint is 15 feet in front of me, carrying his M-79 at the ready. It shoots the same 40mm round as Puff, The Magic Dragon, but is a single-shot, rather belt-fed mini-cannon. For safety purposes, the round will not explode unless it has spun and traveled far enough away from the shooter. The rifling in the one-foot-long barrel starts the spinning. This spin also keeps the projectile moving in a straight line.

Clint is a tall blond guy who wears a bandana tied around his neck. As he comes upon a hooch 15 feet to his left, an old man appears in the doorway. Clint immediately fires a round at him. Not having spun enough to go off, the small projectile lodges deep in the center of the man's throat. We spread out and take cover. The old man is hardly bleeding. He twitches and struggles on the ground because he can't get a breath. After he is fully dead, the LT has the engineer remove the round from his neck and blow it up in a hole.

We move out again and let the villagers take care of the body. This old guy probably got recorded in "the body count" as an enemy soldier. I am trying to imagine what was, and is, going on in Clint's mind. Did he know this man was not a threat before he shot? Was he taking revenge for a recently lost friend or friends? Was he just an asshole? Maybe it's the thought, "what the fuck do I care?" Was this a better approach to warfare? Did he feel guilty? Then we meet up with the rest of the company at noon and it is in the 90s.

It is an almost clear morning with a slight breeze dying away as we eat our breakfast. We are cleaning weapons and keeping an eye out for enemy. The wind and cloud cover roll in with the increasing heat. Mo and I talk about our girlfriends in 'the world.' He says, "I dated six different girls as a Senior last year. Now I'm only writing to Mary Lou."

I'm feeling close to Mo than is probably safe, and I tell him about Mary Dyar being my serious girlfriend, but that I also write to Marjorie. I say that Marjorie I have an intellectual and sexual connection. Both girls are very passionate, but Marjorie enjoys mutual orgasms without intercourse whenever we make out. Mary would make my family happy and produce a middle-American lifestyle. Marjorie and I would be creating rebellious things together. The African American world of Mo's Los Angeles doesn't sound that much different from the world of a high school athlete in Anytown, USA.

"Well, Stick," he says, "you better keep both of them on the line, because who knows what the world is going to be like when we get back."

We mount up in the blistering heat of the noontime damp. The exact same wind that happens most days provides cooling every few seconds. We head out in an online sweep. The first platoon is in the vanguard. I am in the far rear with Igor protecting the back of the CP group. We are moving through hilly, brushy areas between rice paddies. An AK-47 opens fire from our rear. Those of us with clear fields of fire shoot back and the enemy breaks contact. We restart our movement. Five minutes later, the AK opens fire again. He is now almost out of range, so we pick up our pace and disappear over a rise.

Out of nowhere, there is an explosion off to my right, followed by screaming. I can see the cloud of dust the booby trap has created. We spread out to create a perimeter around the injured Marine. It had been a bigger explosion than a hand grenade. My mind is focused on my field of fire and at the same time trying to identify who in the second platoon is doing the screaming and how bad his injuries are. Five minutes later the medevac chopper arrives with a Huey escort. As the Huey patrols above, the CH-34 drops behind the trees inside our perimeter and pulls out again one minute later. There is a strange quiet when the last thumping sound of their rotors fades away. We are in the middle of nowhere. Someone I know is wounded or dead. No enemy is engaging us. Finally, an hour later we move out.

As we dig in for the night, an AK-47 and two carbines shoot at us. Massive firepower heads toward their muzzle flashes. They continue to fire. We zero in on their position with our mortars and fire-for-effect. Over in the area of the first platoon, someone yells, "Corpsman up!" A battalion 81mm mortar round lands near the muzzle flashes and produces an explosion twice as big as our 60mm rounds. A half minute later a barrage of five 81mm rounds tears up the VC's area. Then, another minute later, we hear the loud whistling of our big artillery overhead. The 155mm rounds, weighing 95 pounds each and twice as heavy as basecamp's usual artillery, create massive explosions in the enemy area and shuts them up. As the rain starts to fall, another medevac comes. We, again, have no idea who is wounded or killed.

In the morning I find out that Tater is one of the severely wounded guys. He is a machine gunner with the second platoon who took an AK-47 round in the gut and might not ever come back to the field. The other wounded are guys I barely know. Much like in high school, I know everybody in the company, at least by name or nickname. But I know and like Tater, whom I have played cards and talked with at chow hall. I know he is competent, and we'll miss his skills in tight spots. I feel a slight uptick in my anger and my desire to protect my friends.

We are out of food and have limited ammo. Mortars are reduced to a couple of illumination and white phosphorous rounds, so our squad has eight rifles and two 45 pistols for firepower. Not much for the space, we take up. Throughout last night, US artillery (105s) has been peppering the area we had been hit from. We head into that area just after the sky lightens. Our online sweep is covering about a quarter of a mile of territory, as we move slowly along. We clear five booby traps and discover fighting holes and several 6-foot-deep craters of 155s from yesterday. We find no tunnels, shell casings, or blood tracks; and are not shot at. Even some of the guys that have only been here for a month, look frustrated and angry. The couple of guys that joined us last week, look more terrified and confused than angry. It is obvious their nervous, unconfident movements make them stand out as more attractive and less threatening targets. They are likely to be a threat to us if they are responsible for an area being attacked. That weakness in our fields of fire feels like a magnet to the eyes of the enemy. I think of McCormick and I waddling away that first day and getting shot at. Then a few days later getting thrown to the ground by Mo. He may have been helping me, but he also did not want bullets drawn toward him. Thank goodness for Mo and Del, and their concern for me.

I do not want an invisible enemy to choose me in the line of men as a person unlikely to react instantly with overkill force. Do I shoot anything that moves? Do I carefully determine the identity of someone coming into my field of fire? I want to act angrily. I am beginning to form the idea to "shoot first and ask questions later." There is still a debate inside me about this. How would I feel if I killed an innocent? Do I think any of these people are innocent?

We finish our sweep and move in two columns to a location that the captain has designated for resupply about a mile from the enemy's territory. We set up our usual size perimeter, but we know we can only be effective for a few seconds with our limited remaining ammo. It's a relief to get resupply two hours later. It contains a mail call. While the Huey patrols above, we empty the CH-46 through the ramp door in the back. We load our magazine with 222 caliber Stoner ammo and position the mortar rounds near the guns before dividing our C-rations.

My mother and Mary Dyar have written me letters. Mom tells me all about Chris, Brad, and Barb. Mary is enjoying her time at the University of Puget Sound. Everything seems so unbelievable. 'The world' continues. How is that possible? I've landed in a self-centered existence that I need to maintain. The only priorities are my personal survival and the survival of my unit. We don't take over territories or control areas. We fight or die, and then we move on. The kinds of quick decisions I need to make have nothing to do with the life-changing decisions my friends and family are making. Each decision they make builds on the previous one, and I have not been present to witness their actions. I can't imagine their lives any longer. Would I be a freshman at Peninsula Junior College? Or would I have moved to Bremerton to attend school with Pesola and Dave Johnson? Could Mark and Dave murder someone? I am certain that I am prepared to act aggressively. As I shed the remnants of my old life, the snarl I feel influences more and more of my attitudes and behaviors.

This morning, having a cup of cocoa and cookies makes life seem bearable here in the Far East, roaming around the fields of Vietnam. Mo; 6' in height, solid neck, massive rounded shoulders on top of a heavily muscled torso, big biceps, and narrow waist, has a sour look on his face because he has the runs this morning. Every 15 minutes, he takes his E-tool out into the bushes to shit. An artillery barrage goes over our heads as he trudges the 20 feet to his shit spot on his fourth trip of the morning. We hear our incoming artillery's whistle, 30 seconds after he settles for his dump, but this time our 105mm rounds explode within our perimeter. We're safe in the mortar pits, but Mo is terrified by being completely exposed.

Our concern for him quickly turns into laughter. Mo, the bull, charges toward his mortar pit for cover, scuttling quickly because his pants are around his ankles. I believe he derives some satisfaction from providing us with some comic relief from the new kind of terror that misplaced American artillery has awakened in us. Even when mocked, he appears confident, despite the fact that he is clearly sick. To keep himself safe, his run across the dry rice paddy required athleticism and determination. His ability to do what was necessary without regard for our opinion of him, once again, aided me in learning what was socially acceptable behaviour in this setting. Something to do with growing up in the city? This man has taught me valuable lessons several times, including this morning. He is my best teacher.

We move out and start the next day of travel through a mostly sandy area. Every hour or two we move more cautiously through villages. By the evening, we have walked about 10 miles. A light rain cools us down to near shivering. There is no wind, but the temperature has dropped from 88° to 76° in just a few minutes. As darkness takes hold, a VC shoots two carbine rounds at us. One of the buzzing rounds misses my left ear by inches. In most parts of my body they could have hit, those 22-caliber bullets would have provided me with an exit from combat. A direct hit under my helmet or in the heart would get me dead, but even in the lungs, the corpsman might save me. But that slow-moving, small bullet would mean more pain than I am willing to face. All the grunts hustle into the fighting holes they have dug. We scramble into our mortar pits and fire an illumination round; the near darkness becomes daylight. We fire three high explosive rounds at the muzzle flashes.

The bugs, the filth, the hunger, and new terrors, like our misplaced artillery, are mounting up. It is bizarre how angry and fixated I become about the swarming flies, even compared to the bullets we just faced. I'm just on the edge of trying to shoot the bugs with an automatic burst.

I have last watch. The sky is clear when Bud wakes me. As the moon sets to full dark, the stars are incredibly brilliant. Every square inch of the sky is filled with layers of stars. It is pitch dark in my fields of fire. I had studied all the bushes before the moon set and can keep them from becoming the enemy by sheer force of will.

Shortly after another magnificent sunrise, the clear skies give way to high clouds. We pass the morning eating breakfast, cleaning our weapons, and talking in low voices, ever aware of our fields of fire. Even when we patrol, there is a constant awareness of my areas of responsibility, the same as there is sitting around out here. I trust the guys in front and behind me to overlap my area and to stretch further to overlap with the next guy's responsibilty.

Mid-morning resupply shows up, and Del returns from R & R. He is three inches taller than Mo and about the same weight of all muscle. We are all happy to see him again. He looks rested and well-fed. After we distribute all the supplies, I watch the big strapping New Prague, Minnesota farm boy laughing with Mo. Del is 6'4," long-armed, and only slightly less muscled than Mo. His constant closed-mouth smile is barely noticeable because his eyes are filled with ferocity and responsibility. Mo has the same expression but is more inviting to engage, as he leans slightly forward. Standing right next to each other Mo's head is held more upright, with Del's earnest look partially coming from the way his head is leaning toward Mo as he talks. They would be a formidable part of a defensive line in football. Even here in this sweatbox, they both weigh 225 pounds.

Speaking of heat baking the pounds off you, as the morning unfolds, the heat takes on a new level of intensity. By noon, there are heavy clouds and overcast. It is 97°. The breeze is a little slower than usual. There will be no shivering today. We mount up at 2:00 p.m. and sweep into the area the artillery hit yesterday. The first platoon, off to the right, is hit by mixed Ak-47 and carbine fire.

Del drops the gun with his usual skill, having not lost a beat by lying with a woman for five days. Watching Del, there is no wasted movement or struggling with straps. It is one aggressive fluid movement; from grabbing the tube and legs off his shoulder, flipping the canvas cup off the end, unbuckling and spreading the legs out at the guessed azimuth of fire, and the baseplate is planted. Bud determines the aiming spot and distance. Del adjusts the height and is now traversing as he looks through the aiming sight to the tree Bud told him to shoot over. Mo and Del's guns fire at the same moment. Those first two rounds are close to the target, but both are a little long. Butch yells, "Two HE and one Willy Pete!" We hear "Corpsman up!" from the first platoon's area.

Half an hour later, we go back to our sweep. The wound must have been minor. We turn the direction of our sweep, aiming toward the incoming fire from a minute ago. When we have gone a half-mile from where we had fired our mortars, I see the tail section of one of our white phosphorous rounds a foot from where I am walking. Did it cause any distress to the enemy? It is such nasty stuff, exploding in all directions in white fire. Once ignited by air contact, the WP keeps burning on anything it touches. There is no way to tell if the slightly greater skill and speed of Del, compared to Jackson, has made a difference.

Today begins like so many others, except there is almost no cloud cover and we didn't get any sleep last night due to the colonel's stupid decision to move during the night. There is no moonlight, as the first rays of dawn reveal more about my surroundings. I'm becoming more aware of two distinct ways I use visual data. The first is that my eyeballs appear to be directly connected to my trigger finger and the rest of my body for actions that must occur in a knee-jerk reaction to keep me alive.

The second type of reaction is a large, slow analytic reaction that requires me to recall similar situations and evaluate them in order to determine the appropriate behavior. Now that I understand the neuroscience of visual perception, this slower process takes at least a quarter of a second. If I don't have to evaluate, my body can react in milliseconds. If the shooting starts, can I dive to that low spot? My immediate past memory is constantly running through my mind, looking for danger or opportunity. At the same time, my trigger-ready body is alert to anything potentially life-threatening. If a bullet buzzes by my ear, my body will automatically accelerate toward the ground, while the immediate past in my memory will determine where I squeeze off my reaction after I hit the ground. As a clump of weeds appears in the dawn light, large sections of my upper brain try to figure out what it is.

If my brainstem recognizes a twitch of movement to be someone aiming a rifle, my body will fire four bullets into that clump before I realize what I'm doing. For the first milliseconds of new sensory input, the two processes occur simultaneously. If I still had to think for a quarter second, like when Mo yanked me to the ground a few months ago, I would have died several times by now.

There are several 3' high hillocks that could provide the enemy with cover, a dense pocket of trees behind those, and a sunken area where I can see no terrain features. Before I smash into the ground, I realize the hillocks are where I want to fire. From memory, I bounce up in the prone position and my Stoner sprays four rounds at each hillock. There is an exact, exquisite reaction coming from my memory as I see my bullets throwing dirt up on each hillock.

I stay low as I strip off my pack board to get at the mortar rounds. Del has the gun set up at the same time I have a round ready to drop. While we wait to see if it blows up in the enemy position, Greg has the next HE round ready. Del's first round hits the area of the hillocks, so we fire-for-effect; traversing among the hills. The enemy firing stops. Further to the front of our columns, I hear "Corpsman up." I become even more alert. A medevac will mean we will be an even more attractive target.

The VC's ambush position is hit with artillery and mortars all through the night. We split the company into two groups. We mortars stay with the first platoon, Captain Marks and the rest of the CP group. The second and third platoons circle several miles to the south. Our 30 Marines move two miles north in double columns, as clouds roll in and slow down the build-up of heat. There are only slight wisps of wind as we walk. At noon, we enter a dense, heavily brushed tree line and spread out into an online assault movement. We struggle out of the brush and come to sand. This is one of the few times I know what our movement is about. We are going to set up a blocking ambush just north of where the enemy had attacked us.

It is 102°, and the hottest day yet. The clouds have thinned out. It goes deathly hushed, as sweat pours from my body. After an hour of quietly sweeping through sandy hills and rice paddies with a few villages off in the distance, we dig in on a south-facing hillside with a lot of brush cover. Vietnam's typical wind finally provides some relief from the oppressive heat. Then comes the most difficult part of the battle: sitting and waiting. My lower body is safely in the mortar pit, as I lie on its edge. All five of us in Bud's gun team have our torsos just high enough over the berm of our pit to look over the sights of our rifles. Greg and Stan are to my left, with Del next, then Bud. We have open mortar rounds arranged to the side of the gun. Bud and I are responsible for also being sure no enemy are approaching from the rear. As always, in the near distance, we hear small arms fire and various explosions.

The tension level rises. Obviously, the second and third platoons have rousted some enemy. Are they going to come running straight at us? We overlook a rice paddy to the southeast of us. The paddy is city block-wide and that is where we expect to see the enemy come from. To the east, the paddy stretches for a mile between two outcroppings of brush-covered land that are a city block apart.

Four conical-hatted VCs in black pajamas dash out of the bushes. They are a mile away, our maximum mortar range. Butch, the mortar squad leader, orders Mo to aim in front of them after the VCs are deep in the paddy with nowhere to hide. When the round explodes in front of them, they turn around and run back to the western tree line. Then Del's round lands directly in front of them. As we fire for effect, both guns begin to traverse toward them. Bodies fly through the air. Instead of joy, there is a sense of competence and efficiency. I search within myself for the emotion I felt last year when Wiley Duckett kicked the game-winning field goal as time expired in the Homecoming Game. There is a void instead of exhilaration. I have great admiration for Mo and Del's gunmanship and coordination. They could blow up a moving vehicle a mile away on the highway.

20 minutes later, we can see Marines moving out into the paddy to retrieve the bodies. We have killed all four without a rifle being shot. We fill in our fighting holes and move east to meet up with the rest of the company for resupply. The Amtraks arrive at 4:00 p.m. We split up the food, water, and ammo. After loading our garbage and the water cans in the Trak, we put in the four mangled bodies of the VC on their stretchers.

The whole company moves in a double column an hour before sunset. This is another nighttime movement. Why? The Vietcong are just as likely to hear a big group of Marines in the dark as they are in the daylight, but we could step on anything like a pungy pit, land mine, or tripwires which are nearly impossible to see. Does the colonel think the point man can use a flashlight without getting killed? A mile to the north, I can see the summit of Marble Mountain. As night falls, we cross the massive rice paddy that abuts the mountain and runs alongside the road to our battalion area. It's terrifying to be exposed in the dark on the torturous zigzagging dikes. We are about a half-mile across the mile-wide paddy when we are halted for the third time. This time the front of the line comes walking back past us because they have reached an impassable area. We travel back the way we came for a quarter mile and start east again on a different set of zigzagging dikes. We are now closer to Marble Mountain. The paddy isn't as wide here.

The lead elements of the company go up a gentle sandy slope out of the rice paddy. Mo heads up the rise and I lose sight of him in the brush and darkness. Greg and Pops move up the sand hill I will be on in three steps. It is eerily quiet and feels a bit like walking around in our backyard because we are so close to the battalion area. The sounds in the nearby distance are "the rear"; aircraft and trucks around Da Nang, and mortars and artillery can be heard firing from 3/7 and we can't always hear the explosions when they land. At least we aren't as exposed as in that Godforsaken rice paddy with no cover. Seemingly out of nowhere, on the slope in front of me, there's a large explosion and column of fire.

In the dark, I can't tell who is injured or killed but it had to be someone in the mortar squad. At the same instant carbine and AK-47 fire pours from several levels of the sheer rock face of Marble Mountain. A small part of my awareness knows someone tripped a big boobytrap, but worrying about that could get me killed, so I keep concentrating my rifle rounds on the muzzle flashes on the cliff face. Minutes later, two Hueys arrive from our battalion area and pound into the mountain with machine gun fire. A Ch-34 medevac chopper arrives right after the Hueys and lands just on the south side of the rise that I am on. The bird is in and out in 30 seconds, as the Hueys keep the VC quiet.

It's Mo! Even a man as powerful as he is couldn't survive that massive eruption, could he? I hope there is some miracle and my big brother will come back to guide me through this insanity. I have an image of Boyd and Elliott being a few miles away. What would it be like if one of them was blown up in front of me? I feel closer to Mo than any of my high school friends and I have only known him for three months.
Years later, I found out that Marble Mountain had a labyrinth of tunnels and caverns inside its innocent exterior. There was a Vietcong hospital inside there, directly above the Marine AirWing Base, MAG-16. I had felt safe along this highway with people teaming along the road. There were restaurants in shacks, schivy houses, junk sellers, kids peddling, and beggars everywhere. I drank at the Airwing bar at the western base of the wall of marble, not far from that anti-tank mine explosion. The big Navy hospital was just across the highway and east of the village of Nui Kim San. Now as I write I have survived my travels through areas like this in Peru and Mexico. Were there guns pointing at me in those places, too?

Chapter Twelve
Shocked

"The ears...were hung by string around their necks...It's similar to the psychology that lies behind letter jackets"
                                        Karl Marlantes, 2011.

We move without Mo. Jackson has his gun. Tonight, we travel the furthest yet by foot and seem to be going in a 20-mile circle around 3/7. We make no contact with the enemy. As we set a perimeter at dawn, there is a low rumbling of thunder that sounds like a series of bombs or heavy artillery rounds. In the calm morning, a few high clouds add to the grandeur of the sunrise. We are just a mile from our battalion area. There is a bright orange and red cloud of smoke, shaped like a gigantic mastodon, that barely moves. It hangs in our territory and must have been caused by a large airburst explosion. This morning I get to have ham and eggs, with cocoa and cookies. I am in a daze. My head swirls around Mo being a mile away and maybe dead. Why we were moving in the pitch dark last night? I try to sleep to no avail.

Six hours later, we move out, as the Freedom Bird flies overhead. The engineers clear two booby traps. The blistering heat is dispelled slightly by some gusty breezes. The clouds build up, and the overcast thickens, while the heat builds. We arrive at the battalion area with barely enough time to get a hot meal before the chow hall closes. I try to watch the movie, Madame X, during which a VC shoots a tracer round over the screen, but my blood is boiling, so I head back to the tent. I can't stop thinking about Mo, the colonel, and the Vietnamese.

After a hot breakfast, we have another practice with the mortar. I am down to about 19 seconds from the shoulder to the ground. The leg strap is the usual hang-up. Except for Del, at around 12 seconds, I am the fastest. Most of the ammo humpers take 30 seconds, at best. The gun must be level, aimed at the target, and at the proper angle.

I pick up comic books and smokes at the PX on the way back to the tent, where we square away our gear. There is a bus with metal reinforced sides and rebar welded along the windows at the gate going to a USO show in Da Nang. The ride is not the uproarious joviality of typical teenage boys, but, I can feel the excitement. A divergence from boredom or terror, instead, round-eyed women, music, and round-eyed women may calm some of my anger and heavy sadness.

We file out of the bus and into a 5000-person outdoor theater. The band is on the stage and starts playing "These Boots Are Made for Walking." Then Ann Margaret and women in miniskirts strut on stage, and the audience erupts in cheers, hollers, foot stomping, and singing along. The 90-minute show is set in the middle of a sea of heat, dirt, bugs, bullets, death, anger, and injury. Would it lessen my rage if one of those women paid attention to me?

After the show, we mill around Hill 1 for an hour. Various American women work at the USO club and PX. There is such a difference in the feel of being around American women. They, having been raised like us, doing jobs related to combat and they have survived this difficult country. They feel like our sisters, our mothers, or our lovers. Because there never is any privacy, I never once masturbated during my whole 13 months in Nam. We often joke that they must be putting saltpeter in the water, so we don't get aroused.

The next day I wander around in a stupor for the morning hours worrying about Mo. Even though I didn't play cards with them, he and Del are my closest friends. We would have automatically gone to chow together, but I'm just with Del. After a silent breakfast Del says, "Stick, I've been okayed to go to the Navy hospital to see how Mo is doing." A flutter of hope wells up in me. "All I know is he is alive, don't get your hopes up."

Time goes the slowest it ever has the rest of the day. Finally, at 4:00 p.m., Del comes back. He smiles and gleefully says "Mo is his usual upbeat, humorous self" he chirps. "Who else could survive their legs being blown off and still crack jokes?" My feelings rush between elation and terror. I may still have a friend for life. But how can a rough-and-tumble inner-city East LA guy make it with no legs? Relief wars with sadness.

Two hours after Del's happy news, the company supply clerk, Puff Fitzgibbons, comes into our tent. Standing in the doorway he reports, "Mo died two hours ago. When Del was there Mo didn't know that he had also lost his dick and balls. He died in less than an hour after finding out." It made perfect sense to me. What did he have to live for? He was born five months before me. He died still a teenager, how many of us boys had depended on him as a role model to have dignity, grace, and humor in this Hell Hole.

For a few minutes, Del and I talk about God. It is nothing like the long philosophical discussions I had with friends in high school. I think he and I are trying to make sense of the horror we are feeling. How can it be Mo? He did everything to stay alive and then he steps in the wrong place in the dark and is gone.

The second platoon and Del's gun team get up early for the first chow call. We mount up and walk through the back wire as the sky brightens to its glorious colors. As the heat builds, we walk. The temperature is well over 90° before we finally get some relief at 9 a.m. from a breeze. My clothes, soaked with sweat, feel better in the wind. I am dry by the time the blistering heat of the day sets in. The heat almost feels friendly compared to the snarling darkness we have been traveling in the last week. The flies and the water buffalo can smell us. The chemicals from our soap are broadcast beacons. A buffalo screams in anger and terror, while the flies dive bomb in noisy anticipation of feasting on our skin. Nothing is better, or scarier than a clean Marine. Our patrol takes us into a new territory. We walk on sandy hills with vills every few miles north of Da Nang and cross a three-mile-long rice paddy. Although it is hard to believe the enemy is not aware of us, we receive no incoming fire.

The twenty-nine of us, the second platoon, and our gun team travel along in sweep formation on a search-and-destroy mission. I patrol with the memory of talking about God, and remembering my Methodist religious training, "Thou Shalt Not Kill," and continue the internal debate from the previous month about who to shoot and who not to shoot. Who exactly are the 'Good Guys' and who exactly are the 'Bad Guys?' The issue is that when someone appears in the dense forest, I need to resolve this 'Good/Bad' quandary quickly before they shoot me. As we sweep further away from the rest of the company, the impossibility of making a clear moral decision begins to sink in. If someone appears from the bush in front of me, ready to kill me, I will only survive if I fire first. I need to hit any VC before they shoot. Both the 'Good Vietnamese' and the 'Bad Vietnamese' wear black pajamas and conical hats, with nothing to tell them apart.

I continue to ponder God's directive, although the answers seem obvious, i.e.: Thou Shalt Not Kill, however, many of my friends have died. And my safety necessitates immediate action. The argument shifts to whether I am a stand-alone actor (as I have always been) or a component of the Big Green Killing Machine. What is my primary goal if I am guided by the Machine's thinking? I am responsible for all of the Machine's property. All of my friends and I are the property of the United States government. As a result, the government has ordered that I shoot first and ask questions later.

I begin an internal mantra that I will repeat throughout the rest of my tour. It's a long way from my high school morals. "Kill'em all and let Uncle Sam sort'm out." I've made my decision. If someone appears in the trees, I will do my duty with no thought, and then determine whether it is a little girl, an innocent villager, or someone attempting to kill me. Because I've always relied solely on my own moral compass, I need to practice this every step. I have to shoot first and think later, no matter what. The strong internal pressure to act in the way I believe is right must be pushed to the sidelines. Squeeze the trigger first, then consider it later, or simply let someone else consider it. Ironically, if I shot an innocent person, Uncle Sam will arrest me. After a trial, I'll be imprisoned, but at least I won't be in Vietnam or dead. As the day progresses, my resolve becomes clearer to me.

My utilities have remained dry through the night of walking. We get hit on the left edge of our line. Del's spotter round is long. We fire-for-effect after the adjustment and quiet the enemy fire. Heavy artillery blasts the enemy area for several minutes and then we start carefully moving in. Off to my right, a Marine yells bloody murder. As he walked through an opening between two trees, a branch that was stretched back with a tripwire swung back into him. The branch had pungy stakes attached. Four of the six-inch sharpened bamboo strips are embedded in his leg. The corpsman works on him to keep the poison on the stakes from getting in his bloodstream. 100 feet to my right, the engineer blows a booby-trapped grenade. An Antos joins us an hour later. The soldier with the leg wound is on a stretcher, strapped down on the Antos and taken away.

As we set up for the day, it is a clear morning with no clouds or wind. The calmness of the weather is short-lived. Large clouds slowly drift in. A breeze picks up, and the sky becomes overcast. Cruelly, the wind slowly dies away as the temperature climbs. By early afternoon, the heat is suffocating and there is no cooling air moving. The sky clears up and it heats up another five degrees to add insult to injury. Mercifully, two hours later a fresh wind blows in heavy clouds and cools us off with its brisk force.

At dusk, we are clearly preparing for a mission because we scurry around, eat in a hurry, and pack up to move out. We travel completely off a path tonight. Although we move quickly for Vietnam, we stop many times to assure there are no booby traps. We attract no enemy fire. Are we too small a unit to be worth an ambush? It seems like it should be just the other way around. We arrive at our destination just before dawn. We have walked at least 15 miles. We quietly dig in, chow down and get to our watches. Our perimeter is hidden in the rolling hills and bushes. Three times, our artillery hits an area a few miles north of us. I have first watch, as the heat builds.

Last night we slept, rather than our insane walking in the dark. There is a lot of cloud cover this morning. Gentle breezes pass through our position. We begin an online sweep toward the area where our artillery was concentrating, yesterday. The Lt, corpsman, radio operator, Aerial Observer, forward observer, and John, Stan, Bud, Del, and I are leading the way. "(T)hen a sound that makes you jump in your sleep years later, the cough of a mortar" (Yusef Komunyakaa) brings terror from up in the air. There is no way to plan ahead of time. A small mortar round, similar to the ones I'm carrying, is floating above us, zeroing in on one of us for an eternity of five seconds. It detonates near second squad, off to my right, striking no one. We continue to move toward the enemy. Our artillery screams overhead and explodes as the third platoon approaches the tree line in front of us.

Gunfire starts to the left of me, from first squad. We dive for cover and strip off backboards, as Del sets up the mortar. By the time we shoot the first mortar round at the enemy, we are engaged along our whole line of 29 Marines. The mortar is well protected behind eight-foot-high rocks. Persistent AK-47, carbine, and machine gun fire is coming at us. Two Hueys join the fight, roaring in over my right shoulder. The enemy must be well bunkered in because they keep returning fire between runs by the choppers. I spot two F-14s coming toward us from the south and each lets out two spiraling bombs. The air power produces a palpable increase in my feeling of strength.

Further off to our right, even heavier fighting begins. The jets change their course of attack. The rest of Lima Company is dug in and has been waiting for this large enemy force to run. The amount of firepower coming from their Stoners, mortars, rockets, an M-79, and pistols is impressive. Three of our the third platoon assault group have been hit. The enemy stops firing at us. The corpsman attends to the three wounded GIs. We now hold our positions, as the first and second platoons sweep into the enemy-held tree line. They receive small pockets of fire, which they suppress with quick, heavy Marine firepower. The jets and the Hueys continue to be a force right over our shoulders. They feel like an extension of my rifle, spitting massive firepower at the touch of my thoughts.

The jets leave. The Hueys keep patrolling as the two medevac choppers haul away our company's one dead and seven wounded, Marines. We have set up a strong perimeter with all of Lima. Two resupply choppers fly into the LZ we have created. An AK-47 opens up at the chopers and is abruptly silenced by the Hueys shooting a series of rockets at the enemy. I am holding a perimeter position, as the CH-34s are unloaded of supplies.

Butch jumps on the leaving choppers and heads to the rear to rotate back to the States. The feel of the mortar platoon has changed. So far, Butch's competent oversight has been a given my whole tour. He is clearly our leader. We are already weakened by the loss of Mo's fighting skills and good humor rolled in one package. There is an increase in the feelings that I need to be more effective. As evening sets in, the grunts diligently search within our perimeter for every possible enemy hiding place. I had fired all but two of my rifle magazines and we had used all the mortar explosives. Thank God for resupply. It feels equally secure to have full firepower again and to fill my stomach with some food for the first time today. We hear from the chopper crew say, "This fucking fuckhead of a battalion commander thinks the grunts should move during the nighttime." The column of fire in the pitch dark that caused Mo's death flashes through my mind and anger is rooted in my gut. We now have a more destructive enemy than the VC or the NVA, an idiot officer whose orders will get us killed.

There are spatterings of close-by enemy fire, as Lima Company is, again, moving throughout the night. The mild wind feels cool with the promise of rain. Two patrols of grunts are sent on sweeps around our perimeter. We're told not to shoot them because they'll be looking for enemy positions. Two large explosions occur about an hour later, indicating that they discovered some tunnels. Not far away, artillery continues to pepper the supposed enemy positions. Mid-morning, we head to the west. We are leery of every possible hiding place and move slowly. Yesterday the enemy ran from the jets and had placed booby traps in their retreat, which the grunts now clear. The VC knew we would chase them. They, of course, are invisible to us. We, on the other hand, as quiet as we can be, are a constant source of sound, audible from 50 to 200 feet away. Our itchy trigger fingers manage to protect us from harm. In the late morning, the breeze completely disappears.

Mid-afternoon the wind begins to slowly pick up. The heavy cloud cover that has been constant today thins out for an hour, followed by dark clouds. The temperature begins to rapidly drop, as the humidity rises. It is now colder than this morning. When we stop to clear a booby trap, I start to shiver, and the wind blows rain in on us. Shortly before the sun goes down, tiredness weighs me down. I know the dark is going to take over with a vengeance because the moon will not be up for several hours, and we again travel through the night.

The next day a bullet rips through my daytime sleep. Instinctively, I roll and bring the Stoner up to the prone shooting position. John, on watch, has already squeezed off a burst, and I follow suit. The enemy has again done its job of creating a feeling of unexpected dread to add to our fear. Not that is has become commonplace, but in any kind of weather or terrain, we are ready for an attack at dusk or dawn. Being hit in the middle of the day is unusual. If their objective is to get me furious, they are succeeding, moment by moment, day by day. Man, would I like someone to shoot at! I spend the late afternoon eating, preparing gear, and sharpening my K-bar and machete.

The engineers blow up two booby traps, while we move along in the dark. The two mortar tubes are closer to the front than the back of our 88-person columns. At each stop, we are alert to both sides, every other guy faces the opposite direction and checks behind himself periodically. A slight breeze makes the rain more uncomfortable than in the midafternoon. Although it is 75°, the rain trickles down my neck and feels cold, especially when we are not moving. This night has the feel of something bad happening, but it ends with no action except a sniper shooting three rounds at us just before full daylight.

In the morning, a few high clouds dot the sky, along with smoke from explosions. The air isn't moving. The whole scene of bright colors feels like a cartoon done by Impressionists. I eat my favorite breakfast of ham and eggs, cocoa, peaches, and pound cake. Harwell is always getting people to gamble their peaches and pound cake, so he has it most days. As the sky starts to lose its color, bigger clouds drive through our area. The heat begins to build. By 11:00 a.m. it is 95°. Short-lived breezes bring in a few clouds. A couple of hours later the Vietnamese 11mph wind arrives to tamp down the feel of the heat. Then the clouds cover the whole sky. We get a few hours of sleep.

On a spread-out poncho near the mortar pits, we have a poker game. The mortar men are the worst players in Lima Company. We are playing for payday stakes. I win $250. After dinner, we mount up, as dusk sets in. It is still strange and infuriating to be moving in the gathering dark. Now that it's pitch black, our double column stops frequently. How on earth will the point men see a tripwire? The damned new battalion commander! Six hours later, after the half moon, hidden behind the clouds, provides us with vision of more than two feet, there is an explosion at the front of the lines and a holler for "Corpsman up."

What a stupid idea to move in the night. It is obvious the thinking is to be less recognizable to the enemy. A Marine company being silent enough to not be heard is not going to happen. Yes, some of the guys who have been here for over six months are stealthy. The rest of us, with our heavy packs and a loose assortment of things attached to our exterior, click, clang and bump along. The point man must have been severely wounded, because we blow our cover of darkness, and call in a medevac chopper. 30 minutes later, after the medevac has left, we head out again. In the first hint of the lightening morning, we set up and dig in. Who do we think we are fooling? I do not have a sense of us being invisible to anyone who would like to see us hurt. The clouds clear to provide a full sky of colors, as the sun finally puts us in full light. Now we use the daylight to sit around and do nothing. The new, much more dangerous, enemy is stalking our lives…an obviously incompetent, bullheaded officer.

There is an hour of color as the sun comes up. I am doing first watch. It is a particularly warm morning. Then heavy clouds come in during my watch and keep the heat tamped down. Greg takes over for second watch, as I keep an eye out and I blow up my rubber lady. I try to sleep for a while with no luck, so I mill around, keep a low profile, a sharp lookout, and don't talk to anyone.

The day passes with no patrols or other war activities. Dinner is spiced up a bit by some wild onions we find near three hooches within our perimeter. Thunderstorms add to the background noise of distant combat operations as ominous black clouds roll in. The rain falls with a vengeance. After 30 minutes, the rain and thunder stop and the air becomes eerily quiet.

We mount up at dusk again. We move in full darkness and need to be only five feet apart to keep in visual contact. One grenade might get three of us at once. The terror of being alone overrides the terror of being an attractive target. We are stopped more than we walk. I try to calculate the best ways to survive with this new level of terror. No matter what I come up with, the clear risks of booby traps and ambushes, seem unavoidable. I slowly take each step with no idea where Bud stepped in front of me, and roll my rifle from side to side with special attention to the rear, as I am tail-end Charlie. The black behind us is complete until the waning crescent moon lightens the tops of the clouds a few hours before sunrise. We spread out to a much safer distance apart until we stop for the day and dig in. Exhausted and thankful I do not have first watch, I fall asleep without eating.

24 hours later, the sky brightens and we continue the in the direction of our nighttime movement. I am in a daze of tiredness and fury. In the heavy overcast morning, it is clearly so much safer to walk in the light. I imagine the point men feel this even more strongly than I do. Before dawn, the tiny, hidden sliver of a moon had produced enough light to allow us to see each other at eight feet apart. Now, with sunup, this tight grouping feels like a cluster-fuck. It seems that the whole company is one big attractive target until we get twice as far apart.

We have been out of food since yesterday morning. We drag into the battalion area through the front gate.

It is hard to believe, but everything here looks the same as it did before we started moving at night. I half expect to see a lot of dumb, dangerous activities. The feeling of being different from a Rear Echelon Mother Fuckers, REMFs, is stronger. Are they part of my new enemy, like the battalion commander? I can feel their eyes boring into my soul. They can tell how angry and dangerous I am. They know how to live in the rear. They can see that I have forgotten how to live anywhere but in intense danger. The temperature of the trapped air in the mortar tent is like an oven until we roll up the sides and let in the breezes. Even though we are still filthy after dropping our gear, Del and I head over to battalion supply to beg for a case of C-rations. The guy gives us one box. We split it up with the rest of the mortarmen and cook up a meal as if we are in the bush. Dinner is not for another five hours. I leave my gear piled up.

I drag over to chow call to eat. Even hot food can't break the feeling of being different. As I eat, I see Greg and Igor stagger in. Like me, they are covered with dirt from three weeks in the field. Heads down, not talking, an edge of anger on a vivid face of "I don't give a shit," or "Don't tread on me," which is the caption under the picture of a snake on many guys' helmets. You can almost see the REMFs pull away. In real life, Igor would be a guy to be picked on and made fun of. Today, he is left alone. Greg has such a sweet demeanor that people in the real world would tend to not notice him. Here, you can see an increased fear on the faces of the servers as Greg approaches them in the line. They slop Shit-on-a-Shingle on his tray. I hustle back to the tent to be the first back to the shower. The water is almost warm from the afternoon heat. I am still fucking angry! Damn colonel, damn VC, damn heat, damn bugs...

Chapter Thirteen
Before and After Vietnam
Hiking In the Dark

It was a Friday, three weeks before I was to leave for boot camp. At 7:30 a.m., I jumped out of bed and went straight to the shower. Then, I bounded up the stairs three at a time. When I rounded the corner into the family room, Victoria, British Columbia, shone brightly through the large picture window that overlooked Port Angeles and the Straits of Juan de Fuca. It was one of the few 80-degree days in Port Angeles. At the kitchen table, Mom, Chris, and Brad were eating breakfast. I took out the small blue mixing bowl I used for my Kellogg's Corn Flakes. I still missed the taste of Post Toasties, which were discontinued in grocery stores five years ago, I sprinkled sugar on top of the dry cereal, poured in milk to dissolve the sugar, and sprinkled another heaping teaspoon of sugar on top. I was ready for the day, after a glass of orange juice.

"I'm picking up Mary Dyar to go hiking at the Elwha River," I explained. I hadn't seen her for two weeks because I have been playing basketball, tennis, golf, and poker with my friends, even though I told her I would see her the next day when I dropped her off after we watched the movie, "Who's Afraid of Virginia Woolf."

Curly-haired little sister Chris, who seldom spoke up, said, "I think Mary is nice."

Mom mentioned that Mary's two sisters were role models for my big sister, Barb. Chris said, "I'm going over to Gail Thompson's house today."

"What are you two going to do?"

"Making a collage about migrant workers for the MYF meeting." The Junior High Methodist Youth Fellowship meets every Sunday at 7:00 p.m. Chris is the Vice President in charge of planning the programs like I had been in high school.

I told her, "There was a National Geographic about that in May of 1965 that had some great photos."

"How do you know that?" she asks.

I shrug. "I read every one of them in my Junior and Senior years."

Brad will be leaving in five minutes for two-a-day football practice to compete to be the quarterback of the varsity football team.

"Any chance you'll beat out Tom Fryer for quarterback?."

"No, his brother is the star receiver, and they practice together all the time."

"Is Steve Crumb giving you any competition for backup QB?"

Brad wiped the yoke off his plate with his last bite of toast. "We get the same number of snaps in practice, but I think I have him beat out.."

"Well, good luck out there today," I say.

I had lunch with Mom and then drove over to Mary's house in my Karmann Ghia. Despite the fact that I had not called as promised, she greeted me with a big smile and a picnic basket. We took a 6-mile drive out to the Elwha River. She told me she had decided to join a sorority at the University of Puget Sound. It came as no surprise to me. She was a beautiful, charming, intelligent, and civic-minded young lady. I was certain the sororities would compete to take her. I didn't tell her I'd won some money playing poker because I didn't want to hurt her feelings about the last few weeks since I'd seen her, I did, however, tell her about my golf outings with Ken, Greg Cushman, and Steve Colvin.

I carried the picnic basket and a bag of supplies for a campfire and such. Our two-mile hike was filled with laughter and serious talks about whether President Johnson will be able to end the Vietnam War that I might be fighting. Our politics were similar. We both abhorred the death penalty, thought our country should be finding a better way than wars to stop Communism and that women should have a lot more political and economic power.

We found a nice private fire pit on a small creek running down into the river, deposited our stuff, and went exploring our territory. When we returned and got the fire burning, we roasted our hotdogs and spread out her blanket to eat potato salad and the wonderful cookies she made for dessert. With all the talking and relaxing, neither of us noticed the approaching dark. Suddenly alarmed by how difficult it might be to see the trail, we hurriedly packed up and started walking. It was clear within ten minutes that it would be full dark by the time we got to the car. I said, "I'm not sure how long my flashlight will last, so we better wait to use it as long as we can."

The trail was well maintained but designed for single file travel. Despite that, I held Mary's left elbow and hand tightly and kept her on the uphill side of the trail. When it was completely dark, I was much more afraid than I let on. Each step seemed unknown. We carefully picked our way along, both focusing intently on the ground right in front of us, knowing without saying that a fall down the steep embankment to our left would be dangerous, if not deadly. I turned on the flashlight. This slowed us down, but it felt much safer to me.

Finally, I could see a lighter sky through the trees far ahead of us. Could that be the parking lot? I didn't say anything because I didn't want to get Mary's hopes up, but five minutes later, I was sure the opening in the trees was the parking lot and I told her. She seemed a little relieved but still hung on tight to my arm. The ride home was fun, as we were both more exuberant from surviving our adventure.

40 years later to the day, I was on a hike with the three other guys in the Men's Group I had been meeting with every other week for ten years. We were all experienced hikers, especially in the high country of the Olympic National Park. That day we were taking a day hike on a narrow plateau at 5000 feet elevation that is situated between the foothills and the 8000-foot Olympic mountains. The trail extends eight miles from Hurricane Ridge, where we started, east to Obstruction Point. Every six months, we men did an extended group experience in nature like this one. Half the time we stayed a night or two, but today we were only going to talk for six hours about childhood feelings of guilt and head back to Hurricane Ridge.

After three miles of hiking, we arrived at the best view spot. Sitting on our backpacking chairs, we took in the views of the inner snow-capped mountains of the Olympics to the south, and to the north we saw Victoria, Canada across the Straits of Juan de Fuca.

Martin heated up our nice meal of rice and vegetables. It was a gloriously warm evening and we continued talking well after dinner.

We started scurrying around, as dusk began to influence the sky. The trail at this elevation is often precarious, as the narrow footpath traverses through steeply pitched meadows with short-cropped vegetation. (Although I loved overnight backpacking with people, I did most of my hiking ahead of my friends. I often felt compelled to rush through every challenge and danger and didn't want to lose my concentration. So, nothing seems unusual to me as I took off walking alone back toward the car in the twilight.)

At the first big open area on a slope facing the mountains, I could still hear the men in my group as they discussed the safest way to travel in these conditions and picked their way slowly along the trail that was clear to my trained night vision. I didn't go back and tell them what I learned in Marine Corps training about peripheral vision being much better for seeing in the dark. When you stare at the trail there isn't enough data coming into the rods and cones to differentiate the vegetation from the line of dirt that is the path. By looking with the side of your eyes, the trail is obvious. Because of the stupid battalion commander who made us move every night, I got to practice this for three months. Finally, something useful from the colonel who was responsible for the deaths of so many of my friends.

The trail seemed obvious to me in the last vestiges of dusk. I could just barely see the guys in a tight group way behind me, as they picked their way along the other side of the next meadow. I kept my focus ahead of me and trusted my feet to know the course of the path. 20 minutes later, I could no longer hear the other men talking. When I got to the car, I put my knapsack inside and headed back down the trail to see if they could use my help, but they were in good spirits. Their eyes had become accustomed to the pale light of the last sliver of waning moon that was hidden behind the mountains and barely lighting the sky.

Chapter Fourteen
Infuriated Mortar Gunner

"War is cruel"

Karl Marlantes, 2011.

I wake up early and get over to the chow hall. The last three weeks have changed me in a way that the shower and clean clothes do not affect I don't notice anyone pulling away from me, but they probably are. I feel a deep bitterness in my gut, like a cobra ready to strike. Some guys from the second platoon join me at my table. We hardly talk, but we agree to meet for cards later. I stay in the chow line and get more food. On my third trip through the line, the first server shakes his head, "No."

The mortarmen are all awake when I get back, so I start to clean and straighten my gear. My laundry is stuffed in a White Phosphorus bag; a two-foot deep, rubberized, drawstring bag that is green like everything else. In goes my dirty set of utilities, five pairs of socks and my green hand towel to be picked up by a Donkey to go to the battalion laundry. We are issued

M-16s, another Matte Mattel stocked little rifle, to replace our Stoners. Although we are familiar with the Stoner and know nothing of the M-16, it looks better because the bolt is less open to the elements.

We go to the firing range in the late morning to practice with the mortar. Something completely unexpected happens on my first attempt. As I pull the strap through its buckle, the bitterness in my gut charges my fingers with aggression. I release the buckle in one fluid motion, and the mortar legs stretch and spread. As my right hand loosens the slide on the barrel and approximates the 53°, Del has called out, I can feel the aiming stake and drop the base plate and bipod directly at it. I set the dial to 53 degrees. The bubble is level. Return to the aiming stake. Re-level the bubble, ready for a mortar round. Nine-seconds! We take turns practicing for the rest of the morning. Del is the only other person who takes less than 30 seconds. My third attempt is seven seconds. Even when the buckle gets stuck on the fourth try, I viciously free it and am ready in nine seconds. The captain has been keeping an eye on us and conversing with Bud, our new mortar squad leader. Bud orders me to go to battalion supply and turn in my M-16, backboard, and ammo pouches in exchange for a .45 caliber pistol. I've been promoted to gunner. It reminds me of my sophomore year of football when I went from second team to starting defensive lineman.

Back at the tent, I break down the 45. I clean and lightly oil it. The magazines hold seven rounds, an inch and a half long, with a short projectile twice as thick as .225 caliber M-16 rounds. I check and clean all the bullets and the inside and outside of the mags. Before heading to the second platoon tent for the card game, I wander over to the PX. There is a new supply of comic books. I can't wait to find out whatced the Fantastic Four and the Avengers are up to. It is funny that a guy who loved Existentialist writers like Albert Camus is thrilled with comic books. I also get the Silver Surfer and Dr. Strange, and I decide to try Superman again, although I didn't find it very entertaining last time. After four hours of card playing and I never mention being the new mortar gunner. I eat dinner at the last call for chow. The outdoor movie will not start for an hour, so I read my comic books and find Superman too standard American rah-rah again this time, so I play some solitaire.

Another full night of sleep has me feeling rejuvenated. Igor and I have been assigned to burn the shitters. There are two cut-in-half 55-gallon barrels sitting under a plywood frame with two toilet seats mounted on the plywood, above each barrel. People shitting are in an enclosed plywood stall on a toilet seat. We slide the barrels out from under the hinged plywood on the back of the shack. The shit and pee sloosh around six inches from the lip of the half barrels. Igor and I can fairly easily lift them onto the Donkey. We put two fully burnt barrels with a couple of inches of diesel in them under the toilet seats and drive outside the berm on the south side. Then we set the full barrels on the sand, fill them up with more diesel fuel and light them. Black smoke billows up. The air is still, so the smoke goes straight up and is heavy enough to drift back down. We, thankfully, go back inside the berm and come back two hours later, when the diesel is all burnt off and the fires are out. We lift the cooled-off barrels onto the donkey and drop them off next to the shitter.

Mortars gear up with the rest of the company and head over to the Amtraks after early dinner. They drive us several miles east into the taller foothills with the grunts walking in double columns on either side. I'm carrying the mortar tube with the 15-pound baseplate as we dismount. My new weapon weighs 47 pounds and is held onto my back and left shoulder by the two-inch-wide canvas strap. We move out in a double column as soon as it is completely dark. A Chicom hand grenade explodes. I can't tell who was hurt or how badly because I'm toward the back of the line. The foolishness of moving at night is reinforced. Because it is a new moon, there will be no relief from the moonlight. The Chicom must not have been placed well or had very little shrapnel in it, because we keep moving without a medevac. A water buffalo starts bellowing about our arrival a mile away from the village we are headed towards. The rain falls gently at first, then the wind begins to blow it around. As we walk through the village a few old people are staring cautiously as we pass. The front of our movement has to stop every half hour, I assume to clear booby traps or to determine if tripwires are there.

The sand is almost dry as the sun rises. We settle in and set our watches for the day. Flies love my clean skin, making it difficult to sleep. The day goes by without incident until a sniper shoots at us as we mount up to leave at dusk. Another pitch-black night has us moving close together. The mortars are near the front of the two lines. With only a pistol in my hands, I feel naked. The mortar strap dig into my left shoulder. I feel like my junior high nickname, The Mule, as I lug 82 pounds of gear. With each step, I sink in the sand so far with the added weight, that it feels like I am getting nowhere, as we walk up a long gentle slope.

One hundred meters to our right, a bright crimson muzzle flash precedes an AK47 round whizzing by us. I have the gun down and a round ready to fire when the grunts stop returning fire into the darkness. Everything goes quiet. We re-pack the mortar round and head out. Each time we stop the mosquito air force bombards us.

Small breezes further chilled the air, in the cloudy morning. A few hours after sun-up, we set up camp. We are nearly out of ammo, so I'm thankful when resupply arrives by Ch-34s in the early morning mist. The night movements are bad enough, but to add insult to injury, it is my turn to pick last. I end up with ham and lima beans. I have yet to eat a can of these, except for one bite three months ago to taste them. I already feel hungry and now I only have three small meals for the next two days.

The choppers also bring the mail. I have a care package from my mother. Besides some cookies, she has sent the mosquito net I asked her for. I have to chuckle a little. I can't hold it against her for not understanding the danger a bright white piece of fabric might cause. The chuckle comes from my childhood sense that my mother might know my needs. The netting is pure, bright white, the size of a bedspread and will be like a beacon for enemy fire in the dark. Regardless, as I settle down for two hours of sleep, I fold it into a two-foot square and drape it over my head. I can still hear the flies buzzing, but it is like heaven that they can't land on me. I sleep on my side and leave a tunnel straight out from my air mattress to the open fresh air. When flies come in the tunnel, I blow them out. My left-hand cradles the muzzle of my pistol to hold the hole open.

When I get up for the mid-watch of two hours, it is clearly too dangerous to have this white flag calling out to my head as a target. It is one thing to have a white spot on the ground and quite another to have it moving around in the air. The camouflaged cover of my helmet is a lot safer, although its smooth arc is recognizable through bushes. The recon guys have twigs and leaves stuck into their camouflage covers. My second sleep of the day is much warmer, 89°, and the wind is really whipping around. I actually get some sleep in my new fly-protected environment. We eat dinner a few hours before dark. Mortars travel with the second platoon. As the first platoon is mounting up, a flurry of AK-47 and carbine fire hits us. It is coming from an area we have sighted in on this morning, so we fire for effect with both guns. I have the mortar down and fire in my fastest time yet. I know that the second of increased speed is about the unbarred disregard for moral principles. Del and I try to bracket the target area and traverse to the middle. The fight is over in 20 seconds. I hear two different yells of "Corpsman up." The first platoon, sans packs, starts an assault on the enemy position with the rest of us ready to support them. At dark, they return. They found no evidence of the enemy.

Now, in the full-pitched darkness. All three platoons move out in different directions. Throughout the night, we move slowly, stopping much more than advancing. If this had been an outing in my youth, I would have talked one of my buddies into sneaking off to explore the surrounding area. This wistful thinking barely cracks the harsh set of my jaw. Off in the direction the first platoon, we hear the explosion of an American hand grenade. Five minutes later, a Ch-34 and a Huey fly over us for the medical evacuation (medevac).

Before our night movement starts Bud says, "Stick, the captain said your R & R is approved and you'll be leaving with resupply the day after tomorrow." The darkness has extra terror, as I have something to look forward to. It is another night of stopping far more than moving. I try hard not to make rustling sounds, and can barely see Igor in front and Greg behind me.

Otherwise, I am all alone with a 45 pistol, prepared to end someone's life before they can end mine.

We walk on paddy dikes, as we zigzag across the broad expanse, with no treeline visible. An infinite rice paddy. The sky clears. A crescent sliver of the moon looks vivid and beautiful and allows me to see a few Marines further ahead. We naturally spread out our spacing. After an hour, a treeline begins to emerge in front of us. I get close enough to see that most of the second platoon is in the trees when gunfire breaks out. There is no place to get cover or set up the gun, so we move rapidly at a low crouch until we can spread out in the bushes just as the firing stops.

An hour later, we move deeper into the trees. The clouds obscure the tiny amount of light the moon permits us. Every time we come to a halt, the mosquitoes swarm. In the early morning light, we set up a perimeter around a small clearing surrounded by bamboo trees on three sides. A medevac helicopter manages to fit its spinning rotors inside the opening. The pilot appears to have his eyes attached to the tips of the rotors. On the three sides of the opening, he has only a few feet of clearance.

I can now see two grunts rush a man on a stretcher into the open side of medevac as the Huey patrols overhead. The bird slowly rises straight up. They veer to the right and fly away as soon as they are above the trees. We walk for another three hours and cover approximately two miles. We dig in and eat while keeping an eye on our area of the perimeter. The flies revel in the fact that we sit still and have food available for them.

I'm still having trouble sleeping during the day. I'm exhausted all the time. It's difficult to fall asleep in the morning. Today I get more sleep because three of us split the watch and I have the last watch. I sleep nearly three hours. The flies, only two inches away from my ears, will have to get through 12 layers of folded mosquito netting to wake me up. The heat and wind are at their usual levels during my watch from 4:30 to 7:00 p.m. It's familiarity reassures me. The high temperatures have ranged from 88° to 102° over the last few weeks. Instead of a daily high wind of 11mph, it has ranged from 8-15mph, though it has been 11mph for half of the last 25 days. Being able to depend on that same breeze makes me feel like I'm at home. The flies all day, mosquitoes all night, constant sounds of war in the distance or closer by, little else to think about, but fields of fire, stay quiet and watch where I step.

The clouds thicken and we heat our dinners in the last bits of light. By the time we move out, it is full dark and has started to rain. This kind of crazy, nighttime movement is what got Mo killed. Nearby, I hear the explosion of a Chicom hand grenade. Although I do not know where the first platoon is, I am guessing they tripped it. How did no one get injured? We keep moving but stop for long stretches. The rain has ended and my clothes are completely dry. Jarringly, there is the metallic sound of the spoon plinging free from a grenade. I have at least three seconds to determine the best place to eat dirt. There is a slight depression in the sand eight feet to my right in the direction of my fields of fire. I pick that position, instead of lying next to the bush right in front of me. Three long seconds after I am prone with my pistol looking for the enemy, the grenade explodes 30 feet away, followed by "Corpsman up." The colonel got us again, that fucking asshole. My itchy trigger finger can imagine taking out my rage on him. I never saw his face in his three months of commanding us, but I built a picture of an overweight guy, who didn't like to get his hands dirty. I always see him leaning over a map, pushing the pieces that represent us into territories he knows nothing about.

Well, tomorrow will have me out of the field to get ready for Bangkok. From what I can gather from the guys that have been there, the Thai government oversees prostitution. All I know is, that I will be away from constant gunfire for five days. With clean sheets, a girl, dancing, drinking and eating good food. Having had only one attempt at intercourse in the backseat of Marjorie's Hillman Minx, I really have no experience, except masturbating to women in magazines back in high school and junior high. A medevac lands and a minute later takes off from the first platoon's area. The Huey is patrolling the mile in between us. No enemy soldiers make themselves known.

Chapter Fifteen
"R & R"

"How can you return home if you've never left?"
Karl Marlantes, 2011.

R & R stands for Rest and Recuperation. Everybody in the combat zone gets one five-day break at a port of call in the Western Pacific. I can think of little else as the clouds clear up to a massive array of stars. It's June 25th and the large crescent moon makes this our easiest night movement, yet. Still, there is little hope of seeing a punji pit, (a hole, camouflaged with a ground cover over thin bamboo slats to match the area around it. Poisoned, sharpened bamboo stakes line the bottom and sides of the hole). I might see that camouflage in daylight. Maybe tonight, a careful pointman will be able to see a thin wire and keep from tripping a booby trap.

The moon sets after midnight and the claustrophobic dark surrounds me. I am alone with the dark shadows of the only two guys I can see. Gunfire erupts as we move through bushes. My mortar quickly down and on the azimuth the company radioman got from the invisible grunt radioman. We fire a round, the grunts adjust us and we fire for effect. The enemy fire abruptly stops. I later found out that one of my HE rounds exploded right on a muzzle flash. My first confirmed kill. It feels satisfying to know I reduced the length of time of the firefight. The second platoon and the company CP group escaped with no injuries. The rest of the night of walking has a more intimate sense of danger because we know the enemy are near and they know we are here.

We dig in at first light. I begin the long minutes of waiting the two hours for resupply to show up to take me away from this shit. I hear the birds in the distance and hope wells up, overtaking disbelief. Am I going to be out of the only environment I have known for over 100 days? It feels like I have been here for two lifetimes. As the bird flies out with me sitting on my flak jacket, we receive fire and the chopper's M60 machine gun provides a comforting, powerful response, which shuts up the carbine that has poked a hole in the rear part of the bird's body. There are eight other holes that pre-existed this new one. None of this seems to faze the crew. The pilots, behind their black face plates, are impossible to read. The gunner is hanging mostly outside the bird, next to me. I have Greg's rifle and return fire with the gunner, who has a blood-thirsty look tattooed on his face.

At the battalion area, I get my orders to be at the motor pool at 8:00 a.m. tomorrow. I spend the day washing as much dirt off my body as possible. I pack a draw-stringed rubberized white phosphorous bag with a couple of pairs of socks and my ditty bag with toothbrush and stuff, grab early chow and head over to the jeep that is waiting to take three of us to the airport. One is a Rear Echelon Mother Fucker, (REMF), and the other two brother grunts. The REMF is all clean, shiny-faced, with polished boots. The grunts, like me, have boots with no black leather left, that are the same color as the sand, scuffed light tan. They are going to Japan and Australia. We share stories of what we have heard is available in Japan, Bangkok, and Australia. Most of our sharing is about how you pick up a prostitute. I picked Bangkok because it sounds like the easiest process for getting together with a girl.

I hear gunfire in the distance as I walk across the tarmac of the Da Nang airbase and board a commercial flight with 40 other guys. When we get up in the air, I imagine the little sniper taking his daily fight against the imperial force of America by shooting a round at us. There is no sound of combat. For a plane loaded with 19-year-old males, there is very little chatter happening. Life is serious business with objectives and boredom. Most of us are grunts.

When we get outside the airport in Bangkok, a row of taxis awaits us. A small smiling guy, (who I have always thought of as much younger than me, but now I realize he was in college and therefore, my age), introduces himself as, Hoy, the translator for the taxi he is next to. We agree they will be my exclusive cab for the five days for $55. I hop in the back and Hoy turns around from the front passenger seat and introduces me to the driver, Al.

Hoy suggests getting some clothes first, so he takes me to a Men's store. I get shoes, socks, two pairs of pants and three shirts. He then tells me about the hotel options. I pick a mid-range hotel and we head over there. Hoy helps me navigate the front desk, while Al waits outside. $55 for the five nights. I tell Hoy to pick me up in two hours to go out on the town. I take a long, hot, soapy shower and watch the dirt and grime flow down the white tile even on my last rinsing. There is a nice restaurant and I eat an early dinner.

At 5:00 p.m. we head out. Hoy explains that there are all kinds of bars that are regulated by the government. There are small, quiet bars with 10-20 women available to interact with. There are big, fancy, loud bars with hundreds of women all wearing number badges to help GIs identify them. I chose a medium size place, Marvin Gardens (probably because it reminded me of Monopoly).

Hoy and I walk into the small dance hall room. We pick a table near the dance floor. Hoy says I should take my time. The girls are out dancing on the dance floor. There are 50 working women here. Five other

GIs are spread out around the room. They are each with a girl. I pick Number 35. You would think she was Marilyn Monroe with how nervous I feel. She and I dance together and I feel calmer and turned on. She has a nice rhythm and seems quiet and confident. She joins us at the table so Hoy can translate for us. Her name is, Susie, she says. She speaks English, but not as well as he does.

Hoy takes me up to the cashier, who is behind a caged window. I pay him $55 for Susie for the five days. Al drives us back to the hotel. I have had a couple of drinks and we make out in the backseat. She is an expert at just the right amount of passion and erotism to wait for our joining in the hotel room. I tell Hoy to take the night off and I'll call him in the morning.

When we get up to my room, I am feeling like the virgin I am. The only other time I tried to have sex was with Marjorie, the woman I eventually married, about a year ago in the back seat of her Hillman Minx. It was so awkward that I never got my penis inside her, and we had to get each other off by hand, which we had done many times before that. Marjorie had been experienced, but not enough to make up for my lack of knowledge. Susie, like the beautiful professional she is, knows just what to do. She suggests we take a shower together first. I have a hard-on the whole time and appreciate the smell and feel of her naked little body rubbing on me. This being my first experience between the sheets, she guides me into her, as she moves in seductive ways. She draws out the intercourse by having us both stop moving until I cannot take it anymore and have an orgasm. We rest in each other's arms, as I smoke a cigarette. I didn't realize at the time that I was going to have to relearn all this sexual stuff when I wasn't with a professional. I had to figure out the give and take of pleasure. She then starts working me up again. This time we go much slower. I crash into sleep when we are done.

Susie and I wake up and go to breakfast. Today is Thursday. She goes to the doctor to get a checkup for Sexually Transmitted Diseases twice a week, Tuesdays and Thursdays. She asks if I want to go along. I call Hoy and we drive to her parent's house, where she lives when she is not with a GI. It is a polite friendly experience with Susie translating, as her parents speak no English. Then we are off to the doctor who gives her a clean bill of health, much to my relief.

Driving in Bangkok is quite an experience. The downtown one-way roads are at least six lanes wide. All the fast-moving cars are small, lots of scooters and motorcycles. Every few blocks there is a roundabout, where no one slows down at all. Cars are weaving through the lanes and flying off at their desired streets. We decide to find a back-alley place to eat on our way to the harbor and the Hanging Gardens. This little restaurant, with only outdoor seating, has really good food. Then the trip to the Hanging Gardens takes us past a bronze statue of Buddha 40 feet high. The street goes straight at it until it curves around. The Gardens are unbelievable, flowers are suspended above all the floating shops, houseboats, and restaurants. Hoy and Al wait in the car as Susie and I head down onto the docks. It smells wonderful to be surrounded by flowers.

Friday, we decide to go to the Zoo. It is big and well-kept, somewhat like the zoos in Seattle and San Diego, but with more hot-weather animals. We spend a couple of hours in the snake area. The vendors drape a 20-foot boa constrictor over Susie and my shoulders and take our picture. Then they allow the snake to make a wrap around my chest. Its four-inch-thick body feels like it could crush me in an instant.

At Hoy and Susie's advice, we book a seven-course traditional Thia dinner at one of the nicest places in town. Susie decides to go home to pick up her nicer clothes. We drop Hoy off at school. I tell Hoy Al can take care of us this evening, so we won't need him until the afternoon tomorrow. Susie comes out from the back of her parent's house and is dressed in a beautiful kimono. Al drives us to our restaurant. We sit on the floor and enjoy the attention of five different attendants, while we savor each course.

The next day we spend a lazy morning walking around near the hotel until we find a nice-looking restaurant serving American food. The following day is my last one away from combat. I wake up next to a beautiful young woman, on a comfortable bed with clean sheets, in air-conditioned comfort. I haven't had hardly a thought of the boys back in the field. It is so unknown what they might be up to. Even though almost every day was the same; same temperature, same wind, same sand, and rice paddies, same gunfire and explosions; all the meaningful moments were the highest energy in my life and dramatically different from one another. My brothers are doing something at this moment beyond my ability to imagine.

Writing now, as I reflect on these five days, I realize that I kept my combat troop out of my head while I was with Susie, and I seldom thought of my friends from ancient times in Port Angeles, either. Even when I have written to Marjorie, the high-energy states of combat are left out. Therefore, all that has meaning is left out. My mind has learned to create a narrative as if I was only relaying information to myself.

We grunts don't rehash the combat we survived; we haven't even talked about Mo's death. Instead, we robotically move on to the next startling event. This self-contained process developed over the 100 days by never having an outlet for the need to tell someone about my peak experiences. You may know the feeling after you caught a big fish, and you are just dying to tell your friends and family about it. The urge gets less imperative after many tellings. I can remember the feeling as I wrote my first letter three months ago to my mother. Everything I needed to say would terrify her. Even Marjorie: the stuff that is important to me, is unfair to have her thinking about. Besides the fact that I would sound like an exaggerating fisherman because every minute of every day was so far out of what they can imagine.

It is a similar feeling thinking about what to tell the guys. They have been filthy, starved, and dodging bullets, while I have had five days of fantasy. Nothing I have ever done is like this R & R. It would be unfair and impossible to try to recreate and share what just happened to me. Whose story is bigger? They won't need to tell me about all the peak moments while I was gone. But when I get back, I will be able to see those moments on the changes in Greg's face. Things will further harden him. His already reserved manner is more able to not relay things that desperately need to be talked about. The last five days have been big events for me to not tell, but I can't share with my brothers. And, I have been too removed (between my clean sheets) to be able to really hear him, or anyone else, about what they had been through.

Susie and I make love before and after breakfast. I pack up and send her home with Hoy and Al. I drink two Bloody Marys at breakfast. My flight is at 2:30, so I go down to the bar and start drinking in earnest. As Hoy and Al take me to the airport I am feeling no pain. If I am terrified to return to combat, I can't feel it.

Our 707 lands at Da Nang. As I step out of the plane I can hear gunfire in the distance, but there is a feeling of competence and little need to be wary. The jeep waits with the other three guys I rode with on the way here. We head to the battalion area and go our separate ways. I report to the company office, drop off my gear at the empty mortar tent, and walk over to the club to see if they have any beer. I am still drunk from Thailand and want to be even drunker. The club closes at about dinner time. I am in the chow hall when several Lima Company men come in. They shuffle from exhaustion and are covered in dirt and dust. I can imagine they were up all night and then spent the day coming back here.

I tell the guys back at the tent about my $55 for Susie, the cab and the hotel. I am in alcohol-inspired high spirits. They are interested, but quickly get themselves ready to crash. We have been told that we are moving out tomorrow to a Rocket Watch site on Hill 41, whatever that is.

CHAPTER SIXTEEN
GOD

"We don't want to think that something as ugly and brutal as combat could be involved in any way with the spiritual"
                               Karl Marlantes, 2011.

All of us in Lima Company head over to the motor pool area after morning chow and mount on Amtraks and tanks. We travel mostly on dirt roads to Hill 41, 10 kilometers west of the battalion area. This job is called Rocket Watch. We are in a heavily fortified position on a 41-meter (a 12-story building) high hill. We are now 110 men, up from the usual 88, thanks to the addition of two tanks and two Antos. Our job is to watch over an area from which the VC had often shot rockets targeting Da Nang Airbase during the two years of the war. The hill overlooks rolling densely forested hills with the mountains further west.

The bunker I am assigned to faces west and is the next position from a tank to our right. The bunker has one step down outside the doorway into a flat spot carved out of the hillside. Even Igor ducks down to get under the roof made of sturdy lumber with dirt piled three feet high on top of it. The west-facing side is a double row of sandbags seven feet high, so we can all stand up inside. There is a six-inch rifle slit, chest high all the way around the out-facing walls from which to fire out into the valley. My cot is against that west wall. Del is along the shorter north wall. Igor is just inside the door on the east wall of sandbags. Greg's and Stan's cots are against the south wall. The bunker is almost as big as our tent back at 3/7, with room to walk around. It has several more cots that we don't use.

Before we arrived here, this TAOR (Tactical Area of Operational Responsibility) had been manned by the command post of the Third Battalion of the First Marines, 500 men. We are to carry out all the same responsibilities they did. Our job is to patrol the area around here that has a strong VC presence, is heavily booby-trapped and mined, and to defend this hill. It is a different feeling throwing all my gear down in a protected area like this bunker. I don't feel safe, like at battalion area, but I don't feel exposed, either. We sit around and look at each other for a while. Eventually, we break out our C-rations in the 101° heat and have dinner.

After dinner, Del and I have another conversation about God. I talked about God at least once a week in high school. I would sneak out of the house and meet with one of my friends to discuss what we thought God was like. I had a long story of my opinions that I had perfected by lying in my bed after these discussions and replaying and critiquing everything I had said. Now I am feeling some of the eagerness I had last year to get back to my spiritual/philosophical journey. Del had studied no philosophy and had unquestioning spiritual beliefs. When we start the night watches, our conversation ends. This is the last time in Vietnam that I will talk about God, but my inquiring mind keeps wandering what I believe about killing for the rest of my tour.

During first watch, I listen to the tanks freak out about the bushes that they are sure are VC. They will get better and a little less afraid as the nights in this place wear on. Tonight is the first night many of them have been outside of the protection of concertina wire and the berm surrounding the rear.

The sunrise is multi-hued, but because I am on the west side of the hill, I only see that half of the sky. There must be a brilliant sunrise on the other side of the hill. It is clear skies, except for the many bright-colored remains of explosions. Each cloud of smoke is transitioning from reddish orange-yellow straight above me to an almost purple in the dark of dawn to the west. The type of smoke makes a difference in the color, as does the steep angle of the rising sun blocked by the rest of Hill 41 behind me.

After breakfast, my gun is sent out with the third platoon on a search-and-destroy mission. During the patrol, I replay my talk with Del about God and reinforce my mantra that I need to shoot first and ask questions later. At every step, I must remember the logic of blindly doing my duty of protecting myself as government property.

Chapter Seventeen
After Vietnam
Fumbly Fingers

I hadn't bothered calling Ken, and instead, went straight to his room at the 101 Motel. I could relate to him more than anyone else because he had also experienced close-quarters combat. Across his small kitchen table, we were facing each other. He pointed his two index fingers at me, while I had three fingers pointed at him; the index finger on my left fist and my right fist index and middle finger. He'd tried to match me ten times in a row with no success. We'd been playing this game, Fumbly Fingers, for four hours, nonstop since midnight.

It's similar to Rock-Paper-Scissors, except you have four options rather than three on your two hands. With closed fists, the two players face each other, tap their hands three times, and then simultaneously extend one of the four configurations of their index and middle fingers. Ken's right-hand fingers were attempting to match my left. Each hand must extend one or two fingers. I'll try to match him after he matches me. The player with the most successful evasions after three rounds advances to the next challenger.

That night, I noticed Ken was agitated, which often leads to repetitive plays, so copying his most recent configuration wouldn't be a good idea. He might also try to follow me by matching my last play, in the hopes that I will play it twice in a row. Then he did mimic my last move, but I had switched to two fingers on my left hand and one on my right. Eleven in a row, while we spent the entire time talking.

Our philosophical conversation had been growing for the two weeks we had been back home from Vietnam. We continued with yesterday's logic and went on from there. When we arrived at an irrevocable conclusion that didn't make sense we went back through our conversation in reverse for as far back as a few hours to find any point that had debatable logic. We were sort of like mad scientists trying to explain the world.

Periodically through the night, we traced back hours in our conversation, and we said things like, "I said 'People act from self-interest' when you said 'We all act toward our survival.'"

Then Ken said, "I said that after you said, 'People stick together for the survival of the pack.'"

Concept #5 came from concept #4, which came from concept #3 and on and on for however long it took. This was like the memory ability we both had to remember every blade of grass our ball was near in 18 holes of golf or every detail of the scene in front of us with our faces in the dirt in combat.

"People are motivated by a need to feel superior to others," Ken said.

"They seem to be acting from insecurity to prove they aren't inferior," I said.

"Exactly, then they surround themselves with people who will buy into their bullshit and give them a sense of understanding of the world they are terrified of."

"They're compulsively predicting what will impress the people around them as if reality is predictable," I said.

We have gone over this before and made the mistake of thinking reality is predictable.

While we talked, he threw out two fingers on each hand two times in a row, while I dodged with two fingers on one hand and one on the other two times. Then, I successfully copied his last play with two fingers on each hand just as he switched to the index finger on his left and two fingers on his right. I started thinking I could read his mind and I might set a new record of 28 tries without getting caught. Bam!

We both extend only two index fingers and Ken rolled off his chair in relief and exhaustion. Well, 14 passes are the most either of us had ever gotten against each other. Ken got Dave Musielak for the record, and I got Mark Pesola for 18, once. Elliott totally refuses to play and also never talked philosophy with us.

Ten years later, I was still in Port Angeles, but in the house, I bought when I was a fireman in 1971 and Ken came knocking on my door. We hadn't talked for five years. He looked like the successful grade school teacher that he had become. I had completed a 28-day inpatient alcohol treatment program three weeks before and hadn't had a drop of alcohol for seven weeks. I knew he and his wife, Marjorie's sister, Shirley, have a boy about eight years old that I knew when he was three and they now live in Gold Hill, Oregon. Ken brought a six-pack of Lowenbrau into the house, and said, "My Dad just died. I promised him I would get drunk for his wake."

I didn't say anything about my weeks of sobriety and cracked open a beer. That started eight more years of drinking that led to four more DWI/Driving While Intoxicated arrests, which could have ended my career as a combat veteran counselor before it really got started. I was lucky it didn't and so were hundreds of combat veterans who felt understood by me.

That night back together, Ken and I headed downtown to Loren's Tavern. Ten years before, Loren let us drink at his tavern, even though we were only 20 years old after our time in combat because Loren thought it was ridiculous that combat veterans were too young to drink. We each gave Steve Harris $5 and he gave us a baggie of marijuana. Then we played pool and drank beer until Ken wanted to crash at my place and be ready for the funeral the next day.

When we got home, Ken flopped on the couch and said, "My unit got wiped out twice in Nam." I was surprised he mentioned combat. All those marathon conversations in 1968 and he and I never talked about combat. Nor did Ben Elliott ever tell me about his experiences, although I knew he got wounded once. I later found out that Ben roomed with Wiley Duckett in Seattle that first year and the two of them never talked about Vietnam, even though Duckett's experiences were as intense as mine. Ben went to his grave with his stories on December 29, 2011. I knew Ken got wounded twice in situations where his Company was almost wiped out. Could I face the stories he might tell?

He went on, "Dickson hauled me to the helicopter after the VC cleared out because of the Hueys blasting them. Our other 86 guys were dead. Two months later I was holding Dickson in my lap as he died and no one else survived."

I said, "I thought that was going to happen to me on December 27th. The whole second platoon got cut down in front of me. The NVA fire was so thick I was sure the rest of us would all die too." The fear we were going to be wiped out happened several times for me, while Ken was the last man or two standing those two times.

At Ken's dad's funeral, both of us were in our suits from high school and never mentioned the Nam. He had a confident smirk, as he talked to whoever came his way. I ventured from his side to talk to other school chums, then wandered back over to pick his brain. Every summer he made extra money by fighting forest fires. He and Shirley had three kids. As the crowd of 50 people started thinning out, he said, "I'm driving back home today, so I'm leaving now to make the eight-hour drive."

It is the last time I saw Ken around his old friends. He never attended any of the class reunions like I always did. Our talks of life and God have disappeared into the ether.

Chapter Eighteen
Rocket Watch-Hill 41

"But before society sends high school kids to do our killing in battle, those kids have to transform the way they think of themselves, or they are not going to be very effective killers"
Karl Marlantes, 2011.

At the first hints of light, it almost feels like home to be back on the Hill, as we lie around on our cots talking. In our stooped doorway, a rat pauses. 51 years later this is still the most giant rat I have ever seen. Its tail barely clears the right side of the two-foot opening as it turns its head back from the left edge to see if it wants to come in and steal any of our stuff. It looks defiant and calm. Clearly, it knows how to handle Marines. It meanders away. From the foot of my cot, a centipede about a foot long scurries along the sandbags. It vanishes into the structure of the roof above my head. Later that day, we capture three of these insect pests with a metal illumination canister and burn them with C-4. The flies are worse here than in the field. As the day wears on the urge to open fire on the flies grows. They are aggressively focusing on my face and ears.

The Company, including us mortars, gets busy cleaning up the area and building new structures. For four months I have not done anything like upkeep. In the field, it was one day at a time, and move on. In the base camp area, we leave any upkeep to the REMFs. Here, we clean and store our gear, clean and sharpen our weapons, clean our bodies, eat, sleep, and goof off. We are all working as a unit to make this hill more livable and safe.

For the third day in a row, there is no air movement in the morning. Clouds cover the sky. We mill around, as the temperature rises around 10:00 a.m. By noon, everyone has their shirt off, except Igor. It reaches 94° at 1:00 p.m., as the usual wind blows around. We spend the day playing cards and standing guard duty. This almost feels like spending time last summer after high school with one of my groups of friends. Perhaps it was a day when we went to the beach but didn't swim. There were poker games every evening, so I won't have contacted my girlfriend, Mary Dyar. I'd be with a group of boys acting like eight-year-olds because I didn't drink alcohol yet. Throwing rocks in the water, constructing driftwood structures, grab-assing, and conversing about life.

Here in Nam, we do nothing but pass the time. There will be no grab-assing, throwing rocks, or discussing our lives. We've built our structures like men, and we're not going back to school this fall. Our sole purpose in life is to survive. We won't be boxing up groceries for elderly ladies on the evening shift like I did at McGlenn's Thirtyway.

After we eat our C-ration suppers, Del and his gun are attached to 20 guys from the second platoon, and my gun and I are attached to the third platoon. Both groups do perimeter patrols for five hours. We are moving slowly through the trees in pitch dark until midnight when everything slowly changes in the light of the large gibbous moon. It is a surreal scene. Grunts, in bright moonlight that is filtered by the trees, judging the danger in the area around us, watching our every step in the sand between the trees. The world is immediate, almost as if a rifle round has already ripped through the air near us. As the vicious mosquitoes attempt to distract us from our job of staying alive, each turn of the head is planned for maximum awareness of possible death-defying actions.

I have seen dozens of ways my buddies have been killed or wounded. All those ways constantly play through my mind, and my awareness scans for dangers I have not thought about. What could happen as I round the tree in front of me that Greg passed ahead of me? Where could an enemy hide? Could a knife come flying out of the bushes? So far, I have not seen anyone wounded by a knife attack. What about the branches above my head?

When we get back to Hill 41, we do not have to stand watches. We go right to our cots and sleep for the rest of the night and early morning. There are no thoughts left of my friends in the Real World.

Mortars stay on the hill for the whole day. We redo the sandbags around the mortar pit. To fill the plastic-fibered sandbags, I use my entrenching tool, E-tool. When the E-tool is filled with sand it fits perfectly into the mouth of the sandbags to fill them. This will make a Cadillac of mortar pits, dug two feet down in firm dirt with a wall three high of sandbags on the ground around it. The sandbags are a foot from the edge of the pit. This means we can sit on the ledge with our legs in the pit and lean against the circle of bags. Only our heads and upper chests are in harm's way. Since the enemy has to shoot up the hill at us, we are safer than we ever are out in the field. Over the months, the bags had become worn and torn in places. We dump out and refill half of the bags.

The Antos guys want to know what we found on our patrol last night. They seem less afraid. They acclimatized faster than FNGs, probably because they have been in-country for months before they had to learn to sleep in the bush. While we are talking, we hear three thumps of a 61mm mortar being shot in the distance. Everyone scrambles for cover. With a faint swish, one round blows up on the other side of the Antos. The grunts radio in the coordinates of the incoming mortar. The Antos and our mortars fire at the same time.

Six 106mm recoilless rocket rounds streak at the tree line. Our annoying little mortar rounds start exploding out there before the dust clears from the rockets. Much like shooting at flies with a rifle, this has a futile feeling. It's likely that all the firepower hardly bothers the enemy. They were probably well protected underground before their mortar rounds exploded in our encampment. I hear no yells for "Corpsman up" and our boring day continues.

During first watch, it becomes deeply dark. Puff, The Magic Dragon can be heard flying high overhead. Suddenly there is a metallic pop in the sky and it is daytime. Puff's illumination round floats down on its parachute for 20 minutes sputtering out when it's 100 feet up. Five minutes later, Puff brightens our whole perimeter again.

We mortars mount up with the second and third platoons and snake our way down into the tree line to the south during another colorful Vietnam sunrise. We have all our gear with us, so I know we will be sleeping in the field tonight. On our third stop in the first mile of travel, the engineers blow up a land mine near the front of the column. I am only 100 meters away. The explosion is a 30' column of fire two feet around, going straight up in the air. The pang of the image of the column of fire that blew off Mo's dick and legs reminds me not to get any closer to the people around me. We can play cards and fight together, swear and crack jokes, but except for Del, I want to keep them at a distance. I don't want to get a close to anyone as I was with Mo.

Del seems only slightly different now, a month and a half after his best friend's death. He is a little more alone, more sullen, less jocular and more businesslike. He and I have not gotten any closer, as I have probably made the same changes. The businesslike nature of every breath I breathe is the focus. If I miss a twitch of movement on the horizon, I may die. If I miss the spot Pops has already stepped on, I may go up in pieces in a column of fire and at worst not die until I find out my dick and legs are gone.

Early evening Lima Company sets a perimeter and we mortars dig our two mortar pits. An AK-47 sends three rounds toward us from long range. We pop five rounds on top of the muzzle flashes. Like many nights, that is the end of active engagement for that day. We fire two rounds into other areas from which the enemy may fire. With the mortars sighted in and dinner eaten, we start watches in the full dark. The crescent moon will not help us until it rises at 1:32 am. I, of course, have my right aiming eye functioning with full night vision. I am on second watch, as the moon from behind the clouds slowly changes the nearby ghosts into bushes. The wind barely stirs the air. We are all alive and uninjured, with an intense fear that tomorrow may not go that way.

We have walked and fought for five more days and are now back on Hill 41. The Fourth of July came and went with no fanfare. I am standing last watch. The guys in the tank next to us have been quiet the whole night. As the moonlight fades in the west, the clear skies light up from the east. For 15 minutes I can hear no gunfire or artillery, simply looking out over the sandbags to the lightening terrain. The varying hues of the hills and valleys are beautiful and peaceful. I can almost feel the rhythm of the land and its farmers.

Out of nowhere, bullets are flying in all directions. On the left edge of my field of fire, several enemy are firing from the tree line. The mortar is dug in next to our bunker. In the near distance, I hear the "thump" of a 61mm mortar heading up in the air. I yell, "Incoming," and it explodes in an open spot on our hill. Greg drops a round down our tube and we see it explode 50 feet short of the treeline with the muzzle flashes. I traverse left, crank the angle lower, and fire another one. It blows up harmlessly 25' short. Cranking down more we fire-for-effect, sending six rounds at them in quick succession.

The tank turret slowly turns in the direction of the incoming fire. About the time we shoot our second spotter round, the powerful 90mm projectile erupts out of the tank. They are shooting line-of-sight and the explosion is right on target. The enemy keeps firing. The tank rips five more rounds into them, as we drop five HE and three WP on them. Two Huey gunships roar in low over our hill, and fire rockets into the enemy just over our heads. The enemy goes quiet.

The captain orders the first platoon to sweep straight at the enemy position. Part of the third platoon moves out in a rapid column to the right of the enemy. Part of the second platoon does the same thing to the left. We remain alert with the mortar, ready and waiting for the grunts to make contact. Five minutes later, there is a muffled explosion in the tree line and the shouting scream of a Marine, followed by "Corpsman up."

The grunts remain out beating the bushes. Periodically, they intentionally blow up a boobytrap. There is one big explosion muffled by being underground, as they are collapsing a tunnel or bunker. The medevac chopper hauls out the wounded in the distance, as the Vietnam breeze picks up in the 100° heat at 2:00 p.m. We can only watch and wonder, who? The perimeter defense of our hill is very thin. We cover wide fields of fire. Luckily for us, the enemy does not attack our position. When the grunts return, a long boring day ensues.

We send out patrols for three days into the varied terrain. The smallest one I went on was 16 guys: my mortar team of Greg, Igor and Larry, plus a machine gunner and a rocket man with their ammo humpers, a corpsman, a radio operator and six riflemen from second squad of the first platoon. Today, all of Lima company is set up out in the bush. It is solid high overcast this morning. There is a listening post (LP) of four Marines 500 meters in front of Greg's and my position. I am on the sunrise watch. At 5:30 gunfire breaks out, but not toward us. The almost constant gunfire and explosions in the distance go on while the closeby fire splits through our scene, then suddenly, it's abruptly replaced by the dead calm of the morning. Over the next hour the yellows, oranges, pinks and purples slowly turn toward gray as the tiniest of breezes keep the building heat from being too intense. When the breeze dies down, the heat rises. The LP radios that they are coming in and three grunts walk past us with no bandages or signs of being hit.

My gun is sent out with a two-platoon search-and-destroy mission to sweep the area the LP was hit from. It is ominously quiet by the time the heat reaches 99° at noon. Two hours later, we hear a roll of thunder and we can see the build-up of dark clouds to the west. The thunderheads keep getting closer and vibrate the ground. After walking through the bushes and trees for three hours, we come out onto a gigantic dry rice paddy. It is a somewhat rectangular-shaped paddy, with a bulb of land protruding into it from our right. As we halt, our patrol is stretched across the open 2000 meters.

A wall of rain is visible coming down on the east edge of the paddy. As it starts moving toward us, I quickly strip off my clothes. I get all soaped up just as the downpour arrives. I am rinsed and clean in seconds. This is my first shower since arriving on Hill 41, 19 days ago. It feels incredibly luxurious and refreshing. By nightfall, I am dry as a bone and we set up a perimeter.

My day begins with the last watch. We've set up shop in a wooded area. My breakfast is a B-3 Unit of C-rations, consisting of beef steak, fruit cocktail, crackers, and peanut butter, with a two-inch disc of half-inch chocolate candy. The morning drags into the afternoon, and the suffocating boredom seems to last forever. I almost feel relieved when we mount up. We mortars are the sweep action's tail-end Charlie. An American hand grenade goes off somewhere to my left, followed by heavy gunfire from carbines and M-16s. Before the last bullet is fired, I hear the yell for a corpsman. We are directed to set up a medevac perimeter. 30 minutes later, a Huey comes streaking over our position and makes several passes, as they look for signs of enemy. The Huey then returns to escort the CH-34 in for the medevac. After this intense hour, we move slowly through the brush again. The feelings of boredom are in my memory along with the hyper-alertness of each second for the last hour. Now we know there are enemy around. Well before dark, we set up for the night. Heavy clouds roll in for an hour on a stiff breeze.

I settle into first watch and the western edge of the night sky begins to darken. The terror of the day hangs around like an animal you cannot get to leave you alone. The clouds clear for the first time in five days and I am again startled by the number and intensity of the stars. There are no blank spaces. The sky is so bright, I feel like I ought to be able to see clearly in the pitch dark by their light. When I look out into my fields of fire, I can only make out the shapes of the darting and imaginarily-moving bushes a tiny bit better than on a regular overcast night.

Before the first light of morning, we have eaten our C-rations and mounted up with our four meals and all our gear. That means we are going on an extended patrol. It is pitch dark for the first half hour. There are no stars visible through the heavy cloud cover. The air is not moving. The sand between the trees is firm, making patrolling easy. One 15-minute slight breeze cools the air. A hint of dawn light allows us to get further apart, as we move through trees and brush with all the usual ground-pounders of Lima company. We are 90 heavily armed guys. Three M60 machine guns, six guys carrying five of the new LAWs to replace the heavy cumbersome Bazooka 3.5mm rocket tube, both mortars, an FO, an AO, most of the CP group with the captain, along with the three infantry platoons. As the heat hits blazing, we move into rolling sand hills and out of the trees. The front of the column must be entering a new area, as we stop for long periods which must be to clear booby traps.

In a pause of traveling, I am lying on my left side, pistol out and ready, and I scrape out a cone-shaped hole eight inches deep. This is the type of tan sand that is the worst to walk in. I'm on a slight incline that raises 100 feet in 500 meters. A biting red ant goes tumbling into my trap. It aggressively attacks the side of the hole, only to fall back to the bottom. After five minutes of this entertainment, I see a larger black ant nearby and scoop it into the hole. For ten minutes, I watch their efforts to get out and to stay away from each other. The black ant keeps struggling sluggishly at the steep sides of the hole. The red ant scurries around, attempting to pester the black ant and scrambles at the sides to no avail. I, embarrassingly, drop a lit cigarette into the hole and take sadistic pleasure in the increased activity, particularly from the black ant. The red ant eventually falls to the burning cigarette end and is fried crisp. I cover up the entire scene because it is time to leave.

We hike 12 miles before late afternoon and are in an area of brush and trees again. As we dig in and set up the perimeter, I hear a single 45-round fired, but there is no following sound of a bullet flying through the air. A Marine is yelling and someone yells, "Corpsman up." The second platoon machine gunner shot himself in the foot as he attempted to pull his pistol out of the holster. They patch him up and secure him for the night because they do not want to give away our position by bringing in a medevac at nightfall.

Chapter Nineteen
NVA Rocket Attack

(Official report by my company commander, Captain Greg Marks)

A special event occurred just before midnight on the night of 14-15 July that no one who was there can forget. On this night during the darkness of the moon, an NVA Rocket Battalion had slipped out of the mountains to the west and into nearby lands, and launched a salvo of 122mm rockets on the Da Nang metropolis. Starting at 12:15 a.m., 15 July eighty rockets fell on the US Air Force Base, supply depots, and various military facilities in Da Nang causing extensive damage to jet airplanes and the airstrips. They were launched from a site close to our area of responsibility, but not within it. The loud, outgoing "swoosh" noises made by the rockets were imprinted on us forever.

Lima Company strongly suspected that an attack might occur on this night, and made plans to react if it did. As soon as the rocketing began, the company executed its plan. The first part was to report azimuths and suspected coordinates of the outgoing rockets and to deliver heavy fires from previously selected weapons upon those sites and possible assembly areas. Five separate compass azimuths and coordinates from five separate locations were reported to Third Battalion/Seventh Marines's operations section. Concurrently, the company fired from Hill 41 two hundred 81mm mortar rounds, seventy-five 60mm mortar rounds, and all twenty 90mm high explosive rounds from the tank which stayed nightly on Hill 41. The US Army had a searchlight crew that also used Hill 41 as home. This crew had been integrated into our reaction plan and they used their bright lights to sweep the area around Hill 41 to expose any ground attack that might be employed to keep us held in place. At this time Hill 41 was defended by just one platoon reinforced by everyone not otherwise employed--about forty Marines and five Army soldiers.

A district (county) government headquarters, Hieu Duc, was located 2500 meters north northwest of Hill 41, and a US Army major advisor was attached to it. He gained access to Lima Company's radio frequency and screamed his protest about our firing into areas where he had patrols. He demanded a cease fire. The company commander denied his request and told him to get his head down and get off the company's radio net. He managed, however, to put a stop to Lima Company's artillery fire missions designed to interdict NVA withdraw routes and suspected launch sites. Lima Company continued firing its weapons from Hill 41 nonetheless.

The second step was to have the two platoons that were patrolling a short distance from Hill 41 meet the company command group at a predetermined place. From there the company was to make a hurried night movement to a suspected NVA assembly area and engage him in an unexpected night attack. About the time the company rendezvoused, the plan was thwarted by the First Marine Division, also monitoring Lima's radio transmissions, who ordered the company to hold its position.

For three frustrating hours, we waited. At about 4:00 a.m. Lima Company was ordered to secure a helicopter landing zone for the insertion of Kilo Company, 3/1 who would subsequently search the area. When they did, they found the firing sites. The greatest concentration of these sites was found to be within 400 meters of the Hieu Duc District Headquarters exactly where we delivered much of our fires the night before and where the Army advisor wanted us not to fire. (His patrols were not decimated, there were no casualties. I suspect they were not in the area at all.)

Lima Company won the admiration of our 3/1 hosts. We demonstrated that we were a fighting Marine rifle company. The first Marine Division also recognized the company's fighting proficiency by directing Lima Company to reinforce other battalions.

At 11:15a.m. on 31 July, Lima Company was relieved of duties with the Third Battalion, First Marines and returned to 3/7's TAOR. Upon arrival, the Company was immediately ordered to reinforce a battalion for Operation Pike.

***

The two days Capt. Marks explained above seemed like all the others to me. We had met up with the rest of Lima Company in the middle of the night and sat around until sunup. Lots of the big enemy rockets were flying from nearby and US artillery fire was heavy, but no one told us line troops what was going on.

We start the morning with an early patrol four days later. My gun moves out with the third platoon and a canine team, (a Marine and his German Shepherd, who stay separate from the rest of us). We head in the direction of the foothills. The canine Marine has his M-16 slung over his right shoulder. His left-hand holds an eight-foot canvas leash haltered to the dog's chest. The dog is sniffing everything as we move along in a search-and-destroy sweep. We cross open grassland, as we come out of the heavily forested area surrounding Hill 41. The grass is a foot high and brown, inter-spruced with clumps of bushes every few hundred meters. A half mile away to the west, a mottled range of hills rises 50 meters above our current elevation. The hills are the same colors as the flatland around us, except containing more green bushy areas.

We have cleared three hand grenade booby traps before we arrive at the low range of hills. There are boulders and natural ditches running through the hillside that we could not see from the distance. We are halfway up the long, gentle slope of the hill when an American hand grenade goes off on the right flank of our line of attack. I hear two Marines yelling and screaming. The corpsman patches them up as we set a perimeter for the medevac. I wonder if the dog would have found this trap if it had been on that side of our line.

As we crest each hill, the mountains on the western edge of Vietnam are visible again in the distance. Every time we have operated near the western mountain range, we have had lots of enemy contact. We are now halfway across the narrow country, 16 miles from the Pacific and 16 miles from Laos. Clumpy bushes have taken over most of the grassland. Single trees border the shallow slow-moving rivers. The slope of the land undulates. Rolling between gullies eight feet deep and rises at the same height. We move into a double column to travel along a deep draw with a 20' wide creek which we walk in.

Luckily our jungle boots will allow the water to drain out once we start walking on dry ground again. Heavy bushes and trees cover the rises on both sides of the creek. We are invisible to anyone in the distance but completely exposed to the 15-foot sides of the creek. The trees have trunks from six to 30 inches in diameter, with bushes six feet tall clogging our journey.

Just before dark, we travel through smaller trees with no other vegetation. Everything is brown instead of green. The trees and the stems of the bushes look dead as they have no leaves or color. (I discovered that I was walking through areas sprayed with the defoliant Agent Orange from the air. In 1984, the Washington State Department of Veteran Affairs provided us combat veterans with an 8 ½ by 11-inch map of Vietnam with marks to show all the areas I walked through, on which days, and when they had been sprayed). An eerie light develops as the overcast thins and the full moon takes over from the occluded sun as night falls. For two more days, we walk around in this bizarre terrain.

The day starts on Hill 41 with high clouds filling the dawn sky. Different from the usual overcast, the sunrise sky peeks above the clouds on the eastern horizon in a rainbow of colors. The sun is obscured and the puffs of explosion smoke are in varying degrees of gray to black. The night on my cot with the air mattress on top on Hill 41, has restored some of the vigor the constant walking had drained out of me the last three days.

For the last two years of my high school life, I had always made sure I was alone at breakfast time. My Dad left for work at 6:30 and that's when I went up to the kitchen to eat. The rest of the family got up after 7, when I was down showering and getting dressed. Being on the Hill milling around is starting to feel like a home and a family, except there is no place to be alone. By carrying a sense of irritability and avoiding contact, I have learned not to be my bubbly, interactive self.

The sun heats up, and I wash my utilities and hang them on a line, knowing they will be dry in an hour. I walk around in the pair of green boxer underpants I keep tucked in my pack. I strip down my pistol and the mortar and meticulously clean and lightly oil them, carefully avoiding eye contact with my comrades. By midday, I am ready for a card game to lighten up my surly attitude. On several guys' helmets the phrase "Don't Tread on Me" is written, and I have the same feeling to keep my fellows at a distance, especially the newcomers.

In the distance, B-52 bombers can be heard flying toward us. A line of bright fire with smoky eruptions blossoms along the foothills. A second later the shockwave of that train of 50, 500# bombs makes five seconds of earthquakes. The fire plumes had risen 30 feet in the air. Now the stillness feels complete. Would this make the enemy closer to us more afraid or more angry and aggressive?

The day wears on with no action, so the bombing did not make them angry enough to attack. As late afternoon arrives, heavy, dark clouds roll in. The heat stays oppressive for several hours until we hear the deep rumble of thunder, making the roar of the earlier bombs sound like children's toys. Rain starts, as choppy wind whips around us. A half-hour later, at 6:30, the soaking downpour stops. The air cools from 95° to 79° and stays that way for the rest of the night. The next morning starts with a sniper trying to kill us. I am on last watch. Firing back, I protect my comrades as they rouse from sleep. The moonlight is augmented by the palest beginnings of a cloudy dawn. After a few seconds of return fire, everybody eats their breakfast. The day's march begins early. Most of Lima Company heads toward the south in a double-column movement. Sporadic breezes temper the rising heat. We mortarmen return to our most common position at the end of the two lines. It feels strange to trust my back to Joe and his M-16, but I wouldn't feel any safer if my 45 pistol was covering our back.

When the full blast of the heat through the heavy clouds reaches its zenith, the wind picks up and provides some relief. The second platoon is left behind in a well-concealed area of bushes and trees. They are digging defensive positions as the rest of Lima Company, 65 guys, head west for two miles, then south again for two miles. We spread out and move north in a search-and-destroy sweep back toward the well-hidden second platoon. Three AK-47s open fire at us. We return fire and start to run to find them and they abruptly stop firing. There is no place for them to go besides heading north.

I hear a brief firefight 500 meters ahead. As our sweep returns to the second platoon's ambush site, I see three black pajamaed guys sitting with their hands tied behind their backs. Hard looks set their jaws. They have white towels on as blindfolds. One of them has an unlit Vietnamese cigarette hanging out of his mouth. Several Marines have M-16s trained on them, but we all keep our distance. Two of the VC are 19-year-olds. The other guy is about 25 years old and has a sadistic smile on his hard-set face. There is a four-inch scar running from below his Adam's Apple to just behind his ear on the left side of his neck. We secure a wide enough perimeter for a chopper to come to pick them up. It is a relief to have the temptation removed of venting some of my distress on these vicious-looking guys. More and more revenge is part of me. The prisoners will be taken back to the POW camp at the base of Marble Mountain to be interrogated.

We have not received enemy fire for two days. Daybreak settles in with a breeze and soft rainfall. The sounds of combat are way off in the distance. Pops, with his handlebar mustache, is acting imperiously. He must believe being 21 makes him superior to us. He seems like perfect career-military material. He is not very efficient, is hard to get along with, has no sense of humor and often acts in a belittling manner. He'll fit right in with the lifers.

The rain stops and my gun team heads out toward the east with the first platoon. The hills in this area are not like the range of foothills in front of the mountains. Rather than stretching in a continuous line across the horizon, they roll between large areas of flat land. Each hill is about 100 feet tall. As we crest one of the gentle slopes covered with bushy grass and sparse bushes, I can see all the land to the ocean 15 miles away. In the lowlands, the greenery is thicker and taller, dotted with scrubby trees ten feet tall. There are no rice paddies visible near us.

We traverse down the side of the third hill and gunfire breaks out on the far right of our 30-man sweep. The base plate of my gun hits the ground as I pull the bipod legs open. The grunts 200 meters away have not called in any coordinates, so Greg drops in an HE with one increment to shoot 500 meters in the direction we think the fire is coming from. First squad of the second platoon is on that flank and radios that we shot 100 meters to the north of the target. I move the legs of the mortar. We fire another round. We are 25 meters long. The base plate settling in the firm earth will increase the angle of flight and shorten the distance of travel, so we fire for effect with me traversing the area of the enemy It has been 30 seconds from the first gunshot to quiet intensity. The rest of the night I feel keyed up.

In the calm morning, the almost constant clouds break apart. The sunrise illuminates the entire sky brilliantly. How can such a beautiful place hold so much horror? We form our perimeter near a slight rise. The mortars have visibility in every direction.

The slowly drifting colorful puffs of smoke in the west illuminate the reflected light. The eastern half of the sky is a vibrant array of oranges, reds, and purples.

I cook my last C-ration meal alone with Al. He is calm and quiet as usual. The scared look that is always on his thin black face has hardened just slightly in his two months here. We watch as the heavy clouds obscure the colors and a breeze picks up. Cracking the calm, three AK-47 rounds rip through our area. We have almost instantly dropped a round down the tube. The grunts on the west side of the perimeter open fire. They adjust our fire and we drop two more rounds into the again, quiet morning. The raw edge of alertness matches the disappearance of color in the sky. Would I be seeing any colors now, even if they were there?

For the next half an hour, every detail of the perimeter is clear to me, but everything appears black and white with shades of gray to brown. It is as if I have no time for colors. The world is not about colors, it is about bare-bones survival. By noon, my level of awareness has gone back to its steady state with an uptick of hostility and alertness. The wind matches my disposition as it blows the clouds more violently than usual. Nothing has changed and everything feels different. No rain, no sun, no enemy, no safety, no color in the glum. No one to kill and an increased desire to blame my distress on someone.

The day marches slowly on with resupply arriving by CH-46 in the early afternoon. The dual rotors whip up the wind. Dust bellows 20 feet up, filling the whole perimeter. The Huey gunship patrols above, obviously aware we were shot at this morning. As soon as the birds fly away, we gear up to move out. We move fast in a double column for the last four hours of daylight. Is it a blessing or curse to have no enemy or booby-traps to vent our rage and terror?

The first hints of dawn lighten the last watch and overcast rolls in. I stare out into the rolling hills as an AK-47 opens fire on us. One of the rounds buzzes and snaps by my ear and slams into a tree behind me. The wood shatters. That heavy rifle round tears a chunk three inches wide out of the bark. It has missed my prone head by just inches. This is now the third time I have heard a bullet this close. My memory is beginning to be able to determine the distance and direction the bullet is traveling as it moves past me.

The skills I learned as a high schooler to fit in are being replaced by cataloging different types of danger. Rather than picking up cues from peoples' tone of voice or facial muscle movements, now it is the subtle differences in the sound of a bullet after it has traveled 500 meters or more. Here there are no bullies to avoid or pretty girls or friends I want to hang out with. There are mortars, boobytraps, punji-pits, bullets, hand grenades, knives and rockets. Learning the vagaries of these sounds is my life, or not learning could be my death. The brazen enemy this morning has probably escaped without being harmed and we suffered no casualties. The day then begins like the alarm clock has gone off to send us to school, but it is a Sunday, so in The World, we would not have to be at Sunday School until 9:30. Here, there is no going back to sleep with this much adrenaline flowing through our systems. We are going to head out and find someone to kill.

With the heavy clouds and overcast skies, the wind and the heat abruptly pick up in the late morning. We plow through thickly bushed terrain and look for the enemy or traces of the morning attack. It is slow going as everyone is clearing their own trail through the brush. My machete, as always, is razor-sharp. The three-foot high hard-stemmed brush snaps back unharmed unless the stem is struck with a downward blow at 45°, and we have to force our way through the bigger trees unless they are small enough for a perfect strike to remove it from our path.

By late afternoon, in the gusty breezes, we catch glimpses of Hill 41 in the distance. We drag in two hours later and start the boring process of being in a somewhat safe place for a while. There is a mail call waiting for us. Dinner and a funny letter from Marjorie slightly take the edge off of my hostile, withdrawn alertness.

We board CH-46s first thing in the morning and fly back to 3/7's TAOR (Tactical Area Of Responsibility) near Da Nang. A break in the ever-present heavy clouds allows for an aerial view of the sunrise. Everything at the Lima Company tents is exactly as we left it, but there is no sense of coming home. There was no sense of leaving a familiar place when we left Hill 41. My "home" has become the "bush."

We arrive just in time for a hot breakfast of oatmeal, toast, and sausage. We get orders from the new company clerk, whom I don't know, to return to the company area to resupply before we embark on Operation Pike. The PX is open on the way back, so I buy a carton of Parliaments and five comic books. We sit on our gear for a couple of hours. I'm too preoccupied with The Hulk and Spiderman to notice anything else. "The Silver Surfer" is a new hero in my entertainment world. His all-powerful face is always filled with a harsh, troubled expression, while nothing changes his stony features. Despite the fact that they are all fighting evil, he has no connection with any of the other super heroes.

We walk out of the south end of the barbed wire. The fantasy of fighting evil is replaced by the reality of not knowing if we or the enemy are evil. I only know I want to kill them before they can kill me. Every step contains a vivid sense of wanting the opportunity to hurt them and anyone who protects them. "Kill 'em all and let God sort out the good from the bad."

A brisk wind starts whipping around in the afternoon. There is more gunfire and explosions here, around

Da Nang. We do not know it, but we are heading toward the most intense sounds in the area. We are simply a hundred guys walking in a double column staying 20' apart scanning for someone to vent our rage upon. We travel about 15 miles. It is now clear that we have moved into an area with lots of action. I have mixed feelings of terror and anticipation. Will I get to satisfy the urge to kill that fuels my careful and aggressive movements?

Chapter Twenty
Salty

"Killing someone will affect you"

Karl Marlantes, 2011.

It's luxurious to wake up on a cot in the rear after six days in the bush. We are not going to "the bush" today, so after breakfast, I head to the front gate to go to China Beach. There is a Marine Airwing base at the foot of Marble Mountain that opens at 11:00 a.m., so I stop for a drink at their club. It is a plushy brick building, with comfortable chairs and nice big windows. It costs a dime for a beer. I order a screwdriver for a quarter and keep to myself. After two more, I head out for the front gate to try a Scivy House at Newi Kim Sahn. It is a family hooch about 20' from the dirt road. The Mom and Pop have me sit at a Formica table and present their daughter to me. She and I head into the back room that has a mattress on a platform. She puts a condom on my penis and we go straight to intercourse. Within a minute, I pull out and take the rubber off and go back to work to have an orgasm inside her. Many years later, I began to wonder if I have a child in Vietnam.

I put on my clothes and walk out to the busy road and get a ride to the beach. The waves are ideal, 12-footers. Del, Stan, Bud, and Greg arrive around noon and join me. I spend the next three hours bodysurfing or lying in the sun drinking beer while my pistol sits on my towel. I fall asleep despite the fact that I am not a napper. We all head back to get supper at the chow hall. After watching It's a Mad, Mad World for the third time in six months, I find a Bid Whist game that Harwell invites me to join. I do not even notice that I am the only white guy at the table. It is so much fun to be playing a card game that requires thinking with a group of talented, dramatic, fun people. Even with all my experience with Bridge and Pinochle most of these guys are better players than I am. The game breaks up at about midnight and I wander back to my cot and fall asleep.

Early in the morning, the whole company of 89 guys moves out through the wire on the south side. I am feeling "salty." The vicious look is a permanent feature of my face and body language. I have got a portable radio about the size of a deck of cards with an earplug. I am walking alone, even though Stan is ahead of me, and Joe is 30' behind me. They don't know I am listening to the Armed Forces radio station. Before this trip, we got an order to get rubber canteens. The battalion commander's order explained that the metal made too much noise. The rubber canteens taste like drinking out of a water hose. I kept my two stainless steel ones. Again, the colonel clearly demonstrated no knowledge of the kind of noise and smell a Marine unit made.

We cover at least ten miles by noon. This terrain is flat as far as the eye can see, with the hills 20 miles west, vaguely visible in the overcast. The heavy tall brush makes the going tough. A row of scraggly 20' high trees run along what must be a river. As the afternoon wears on the bushes give way to wild grass that is three feet high. For the last four hours, we see no cultivated land. At the edge of our rifle range, trees are surrounding the area, creating perfect cover for any enemy. Even though it's easier to walk through the grass than bushes, it feels futile to put out the effort to not be picked as a target. I walk with as much aggression as I can portray. I stay alone and low, as I slowly and thoroughly scan my fields of fire.

We take care to avoid bogs by walking around several of them. The wind picks up and brings some relief in the 98-degree heat. As the pointman approaches a tree line with dense brush, a Chi-com hand grenade detonates, followed by the expected Marine scream. Captain Marks rushes the rest of us into the eight-foot-tall, thick-stemmed bushes for cover. My swagger has been replaced by wariness and anger at the near impossibility to get through this area. I force my way through each clump, while I keep an eye out for tripwires and listen for the rustling of an enemy attempting to flee or charge us.

The corpsman has quieted the wounded Marine. The pointman was wounded, and he must be mobile because we move again. All hell breaks loose from off to the right of our line. There is no place to set up my mortar in this five-foot-tall brush, so I return fire with my pistol. Our massive wall of bullets rips through leaves and slams into tree trunks, but we will never know if it contacted human flesh. Brass (spent shell casings) is flying everywhere in this, recon-by-fire. Within seconds the enemy has gone silent, and I am confident there will be no trace of them. It's the middle of the night, when heavy clouds roll in.

While I am on last watch, it gets overcast. By the time we eat breakfast, the temperature is rapidly climbing. Bud says, "Your gun team and I will get on helicopters with the third platoon to provide guard duty for a week on a bridge on Highway 1." What a relief to stop moving at night. The birds drop us off and we set up a perimeter at the southern foot of a bridge.

In two 12-hour shifts, five grunts guard each end and watch who comes on the bridge. The rest of us do two-hour shifts, once a day, with the 22 caliber M-1 carbine, that we were issued for the purpose of detonating floating explosives before they get under the bridge. I'm in the middle of the span in the 100-degree heat at 2:30 p.m., when a clump of bushes floats toward me on the surface of the water. The water moves steadily and the carbine is easy to aim, so I plunk a round into its center, creating a small splash and no explosion.

On our last day here, I notice my bullet will skip off the water if I shoot far enough out. I shift my aim to the north where the bend in the river is wider. After I skip a beauty, I notice there are people out in a rice paddy along the path of my deflected little round, so I quit my game and go back to watching for slow-moving bushes.

A half-hour later, a crowd of old Vietnamese women comes up onto the roadway at the north end of the bridge and heads toward me. At the same time, Jackson comes to take my place from the other direction. The oldest of the women talks fast and shows Jackson and me a nine-year-old girl with a crude, bloody wrap on her shoulder. I go get Ken, the platoon corpsman. While no one is paying attention to me, I slink away to disappear into perimeter duty.

The next day, the 28 of us board the same CH-46s we flew in on and fly inland and south to meet the rest of the company. The day starts with a light breeze and soft rain. A quick breakfast and we take off toward the foothills. By mid-morning, we have stopped to clear five booby traps. We are in an area with a heavy enemy presence. Gunfire is almost constant, coming from within five miles of us. We switch to an online sweep. I crest a sandy hill with my ammo humpers and Bud around me when the heaviest gunfire I have ever experienced rips through every air molecule. Our return fire is instantaneous. Two seconds later there are several yells to "ceasefire." From the bullet end of all the noise, we just felt the power of a Marine company.

It seems impossible that no one got hit. I'm relieved because I was unable to get a mortar round-off before the ceasefire. As I walk down the hill toward a draw, I hear we were in a firefight with Foxtrot Company of Second Battalion/First Marine Regiment. That's Ken Boyd's company! Could I possibly come out of this nightmare into something that seems real?

As our two lines pass through each other, I ask the first guy I come close to if he knows Ken. He does not. He looks like an FNG and says most of the old unit was wiped out before he got here. One of the Foxtrot guys seems salty enough to have been around a while. He and I talk for five minutes. Foxtrot had lost most of the company two times this spring. He says Ken was wounded in both of those battles and has been sent to Japan to finish out his tour because of his two long hospital stays. He does not know for sure this is Ken Boyd, but the guy was the best poker player in the unit, and his personality features of being cocky and nervous, match Ken.

In my six months, this is my first conversation with someone from a different unit while in the field. What a mixed bag of feelings. Wow, the power of two Marine companies, even if one of them is a bunch of new guys. I think of Ken, and what it would be like to fight alongside him. I realize these were a bunch of kids, and we are too. I can almost imagine the next few Marines I pass hanging around in high school. They don't seem nearly tough enough to have produced all those bullets.

CHAPTER TWENTY-ONE
PRISONERS

"You can't force consciousness or spiritual maturity"
Karl Marlantes, 2011.

Choppy breezes break up the cool morning. Clouds cover the colorful sunrise, as the heat suddenly climbs. This terrain is much hillier. Again, there are no cultivated areas. Scrub trees and thick-stemmed bushes fill the hillsides. We are sweeping down the side of a hill when we get hit from the left flank. There is no place to set up the mortar.

The second platoon captures two Vietcong. Several Marines are lightly wounded. The Vietcong sit on their haunches. Their arms are over their heads with their hands tied together behind their necks. Rags are tied around their eyes. Our ChuHoy is crouched down by them doing his interrogation. We move out with three Marines guarding the prisoners.

In mid-afternoon the wind is stiff, and the moisture seems sucked out of the air. After a week of high humidity, the dryness feels foreign. We hack our way through the heavy brush, then we approach an area that has no trees. To make way for the medevac to land, the grunts chop out the 3" thick, rock-hard stems. The opening in the trees is only twice as big as the diameter of the blades of the CH-34. The pilot descends slowly, battling the wind. The bird hoovers two feet from the ground, and the wounded are helped onboard. The ChuHoy prods the prisoners on. The helicopter lifts straight up and away to the right above the treeline. Resupply is flown in the same way an hour later. Two Huey gunships patrol above us for an hour.

The morning sky just begins to turn red and orange in the east, when heavy clouds turn it back to all grays. Gunfire can be heard in the hills around us. We prepare and eat our hasty breakfast, with careful attention to the perimeter. The heat and the wind pick up quickly by 10:00 a.m. Today, for one of the few times that happens during my tour, we know what we are doing. Lima Company is to drop into the area of heavy fighting further into the central highlands. We cram as tight as we can get into CH-46s. The bird can barely lift off with our weight. 13 Marines plus gear weighs about 2500#. We zoom low over the heavily brushed rolling hills. I have the mortar tube on my lap, my legs out the door and my feet on the skids. I can see ten bullet holes letting the light from the outside stream in the chopper. The helicopter's machine gunner, to my left, is strapped in a swivel seat halfway out of the bird to allow him to pivot 180°. I have my flac jacket folded in half and sit on it to give me the only cover available. As we approach dangerous-looking territories, the gunner fires long bursts into the brush.

The hills get higher and more rugged and we start being shot at. Two new shafts of light appear near the front of the bird. The light skin of the helicopter could be poked through with a knife. There are artillery explosions and Huey gunships peppering the area we are heading into. Our chopper descends rapidly to get rid of us. It is hard to tell what we are jumping into. The ground is invisible under heavy bushes. The three helicopter crew members are yelling at us to jump.

With the skids still five feet from the top of the bushes, I jump and plummet like a rock with the added weight of the mortar. Now, I can tell these bushes are 10 feet high with arched three-inch-thick stems. My right foot strikes a trunk and luckily it travels up the outside, rather than the inside, of my leg. As I zoom past that stem, I drop another five feet to slam hard against the ground and roll with my mortar to quickly get up and clear out of this dangerous, blind setting. The vivid thought of that horizontal trunk going up the inside of my leg heighten the feelings of danger. Those damn, chickenshit helicopter guys are not worried about us at all. If my nuts had been destroyed, would I let myself die like I think Mo did? He was alive and joking until he found out he had no genitalia. We scramble toward the rest of the company through the heavy brush.

The beautiful sunrise is quickly dulled out by cloud cover. We eat our C's, fill in the mortar pit and fighting holes, and mount up. The side of my leg has no ill effects from scraping along the lethal hardwood stalk in that 12-foot plummet yesterday. After we walk for an hour, we are hit by small arms. The gun is useless in this terrain, so my body takes straight to the ground. As the bullets fly at us, leaves are dancing and stems shatter. Simultaneously, from behind and in front of me, Marines holler in agony.

As I shoot my 45, I am aware to not get down to my last magazine. If, and when, I get to that magazine, I will count the times I squeeze the trigger until I have one round left to use on myself rather than be captured. When the firefight is over, we have one dead Marine and several wounded. We dig in around them and set up for the night.

We ran out of water yesterday. This morning thirst and hunger build. When the Ch-34s of resupply try to land, they receive heavy fire and pull back out. We feel like we are holding the enemy off enough for them to drop in, but they pull away repeatedly. Huey gunships strafe the area. We have several ambulatory-wounded and a dead Marine. We are told we will have to move to an area where the flyboys feel safe.

Twelve of us are dispatched to carry the body. He looks like you or me lying on a poncho. We work in two teams. One man on each corner and two guys holding the middle of a poncho. The body slides around like the bag of water it is. We have no handholds. After half an hour, we let the second six relieve our tired muscles. The terrain is treacherous, ducking under the hardwood stalks, climbing in and out of gullies, and worming our way through trees.

Mid-afternoon we come to a rice paddy in one of the valleys between the rugged hills. There is a board trail on the south side that runs for a half-mile along the edge of the paddy and has no cover from the steep treed hillside 300 meters away on the north side of the paddy. After planning the movement and resting for an hour, the company strikes out double-time to the east. It is my turn to carry the mortar, and not the dead guy.

As the first grunts get a quarter mile along the fully exposed trail, they begin to be shot at from halfway up the hillside on the opposite bank. They start moving faster and firing back. There is no place to get cover. When I move out into the valley, the path feels too dangerous for me, so I climb up the slope and work my way through the brush on uneven terrain. It is exhausting. I debate dropping down to the trail and trying to run in the open. Although I am exposed most of the time anyway, the enemy are shooting at the trail, not 20 feet above it, where I keep fighting my way along.

All the other 85 guys cross this opening on the trail. Four more guys are wounded before we reach a knoll rising from the east end of the rice paddy that is 50 feet high and 75 feet wide. We are bunched together to be out of range of the well-dug-in enemy. Two Marine Air Wing F-14s head straight at us from the further east. As they get near us, we see two finned bombs spiral out below each bird's wings. We watch as the four bombs look like they might not clear the hill we are behind. The bombs whoosh by us and the big explosions on the enemy-held hillside give me hope we can make a break for it.

A couple of grunts are sent across the open area to the north of our hill, only to be immediately hit with weathering small-arms fire and are forced back to our trap's safety to wait for more bombing runs. For 13 runs, the F14s release 4 high explosive bombs right over our heads. Every third or fourth run the grunts try to get across the opening to no avail. I climb down into the rice paddy with its foot-deep green stinky water and fill my metal canteen. I have never used the iodine tablet we are issued for water purification, but today I drop in four of them and quench my desperate thirst.

On the fighter jets' 14th run, they release their loads at the same spot as usual. Instead of spiraling, the bombs tumble right at us. For sure something is wrong, and no way will the bombs get over us. I have already kissed my ass goodbye, as the barrels of napalm sail over our heads. Much of the enemy-held hillside erupts in red and orange fireballs with thick black smoke around it and the enemy no long issues death from their bunkers. Got to love those flyboys.

At an awkward run, I take my turn and carry the body across the opening past our knoll. Blessedly, the napalm stopped the enemy fire. The thick stalked hardwood bushes are taller here. We are stooped with our load under their arching growth. After an hour in this clogged valley bottom, we head up a grassy hill about 500 feet high. We set up a perimeter and the chickenshit choppers bring in resupply and get the wounded to medical care. The flyboys are hidden behind the black face shields of their helmets, so I cannot tell if they feel guilt or anger. I know I am furious with the danger they have put us in so they could have this safe place to land.

The air slowly warms up throughout the morning. The sand is soaking wet from last night's rain when we start preparing for another day of humping this hilly, densely vegetated, enemy-held territory. The overcast is thick. We are well aware that we are in the backyard of a disciplined, well-organized, and trained enemy force. Their uniforms were green or khaki with helmets. Lima Company typically engages VC soldiers who wear black pajamas and are not as well equipped, nor coordinated in their random acts of violence.

Two days later, we wake from sleeping in a relatively flat lowland area of scattered trees and scrubby grass and head east in a double column towards a grassy hill with no trees. After all the bright greens of the heavy brush we have been fighting our way through, this feels drab. The hill is a big, flattened cone 200 feet high, a half mile away. We trudge through the undulating flat land, cross two small creeks, until we traverse the side of the hill about halfway up its side, then head down.

By mid-morning, we come into an area of low, steep hills with more bushes. The second platoon of 22 guys is sent on patrol to scout for any enemy who might be following us. An Aerial Observer radios Jack Brown, the new company radio operator, that they see an enemy force of fifty, which is preparing to ambush our whole reinforced battalion at a water hole. The second platoon spreads out in a blocking position, while the other 66 of us maneuver toward the enemy. We move rapidly in online assault formation for 1000 meters. While the company races to the enemy's location, a coordinated airstrike is called in on the enemy's position. When the close air support expends its bombs and other ordinance, Lima 6 requests they continue to make dummy runs and strafe with their machine guns.

The enemy, not knowing the approaching jets are without ammunition, continues to hug the ground, waiting. This allows us to get closer. The enemy is on a slight rise above a stream. While they have their heads down and are confused by the dummy runs, Lima Company forms a two-platoon assault line, and as the last jet roars overhead, the company jumps into the attack. We rise with whoops and yells and charge across the stream into the enemy's position. The fighting becomes hand-to-hand and is over quickly. The assault lasts only five to ten minutes. It took us another two hours to search the area.

Blood darkens the muddy stream.

The enemy dead are big men, in light gray uniforms with distinctive, non-Vietnamese features, maybe Chinese. The results of this attack are 40 NVA killed, and we suffered just one walking wounded. Many of my fellows are exuberant about our success. Although I stay out of the celebrations, it feels satisfying to have repaid the enemy for some of our recent losses. This is no game to me. We had not just kicked the winning field goal. We had not died, and nothing more. My mood is as dark as the overcast dusk. By my turn to stand watch at 3:00 a.m., it is pitch dark. Alone, filthy, exhausted, and fuming, I wait for another day of the misery of warfare.

CHAPTER TWENTY-TWO
BEFORE VIETNAM
FIRST INEBRIATION

With our suitcases in hand, Ken and I hopped out of his brother Bob's car at the Seattle ferry terminal in Winslow, Washington. Bob was attending Gonzaga University on a Fulbright Scholarship, having picked it over the Vanderbilt Scholarship he was also offered. Bob had been my campaign manager when I unsuccessfully ran for Student Body Vice-President last year. Ken and I would be sworn into the Marine Corps the next morning at 9:00 a.m. in the lobby of the downtown Seattle YMCA, where new recruits could stay overnight for free. The weather was perfect for our half-hour ferry ride across Puget Sound. The Cascade Mountains framed Seattle and the surrounding area from the top deck of the ferry's bow, and as we left the Bainbridge Island harbor, we walked back to the fantail to watch the Olympic Mountains appear to the west behind the foothills of Bainbridge Island.

When we got to our room at the "Y," Ken showed me a purple velvet bag in his suitcase that his father had given him to commemorate his going into the service. It held a bottle of Crown Royal, a smooth Canadian Whiskey. I had seen Ken drunk twice before, once at the homecoming dance and again when we went backpacking with his brother, Bob, and Ben Elliott in August. On that backpacking trip, I had tried to drink one of the 24 beers we brought but I couldn't stomach the stuff. I carried eight of them on the two and a half hour hike up to Boulder Lake, thinking I could get some beer to stay down that evening. No such luck. My stomach started rolling in protest after the first gulp, so I gave up, and there was more beer for the three of them.

At the YMCA that evening, Ken opened his treasure and poured himself half a water glass of whiskey. I poured enough in a glass to cover the bottom and threw it down like medicine. My stomach rolled for five minutes. When I felt better, I downed another dose of the same size and had the same reaction. This ritual went on while Ken and I talked, and he calmly drank about half of the bottle. I managed to hold down five swigs and felt some warmth in my cheeks. Ken was slurring his words and weaving when we walked down the hall to Bobby Lovell's room. Lovell was a friend of ours from Port Angeles who was there for his induction physical for the Army. Ken finished another full glass of the expensive whiskey as the three of us talked for an hour.

Ken struggled to stay upright on the way back to our room. I draped his arm over my shoulder and maneuvered him down the hall, as he bumped into the wall several times. He flopped in his chair and asked me to refill his glass, which I did. I poured twice as much as before into my own water glass this time. I had no worse reaction than I had with my previous smaller doses and the glow I was feeling increased. Four larger doses later, I was calmly sipping the whisky and feeling great. The few ounces I drank to finish the bottle created a feeling of euphoria I would chase for the next 21 years. Ken finished his glass and promptly fell asleep on the easy chair.

When I woke in the morning, I felt no worse for wear. My mouth was dry, but I felt ready to tackle anything the Marine Corps would throw at me. The bunch of guys who had been around the YMCA the night before was waiting out on Fourth Avenue for a bus that arrived at 10:15. There was a lot of grab-assing, joking, and jostling typical of 18-year-old boys. Ken groaned periodically and looked miserable. A big strong looking guy for Wrangle, Alaska, Bob Smalley, said, "You better get your goofing around done now because that won't be allowed where we are going." Although what he said had a ring of truth, I couldn't imagine any setting that could keep Elliott and me from goofing around.

Four hours later, inside the San Diego Airport, a crisp Marine met us as we followed the civilian passengers into the terminal. With a hard-set face, he yelled, "All you Marine recruits get in four lines right over here." We shuffled to the area he'd identified. "Cram yourselves together asshole to belly button. Stand at attention, eyes straight forward, and don't move." Three other plane loads of recruits arrived and were packed into our tight formation. 80 of us guys packed in a space the size from the basket to the free throw line on a basketball court. It felt bizarre to not look at the facial expressions of all the travelers passing by us. Finally, the Marine marched us out to the sidewalk of the busy six-lane street. He spread us out facing the road in a stance he called "parade rest" - feet spread, hands held behind your back, a rigid spine, eyes straight forward, and no movement. For the half-hour, we stood there, Navy guys drove by, yelling taunts about "Jarheads." We stood still. Then I was getting an idea of what Smalley was talking about. Standing at shocked attention, my mind darted every which way, but somehow, I managed to keep still. When we filed on the bus the Marine driver was yelling at us the whole time. Calling us "maggots and pukes."

"Get in a seat at attention and don't look around, or say anything, you maggots." He drove like a maniac on the freeway, often turning full around to yell at us. At one point he spun around and stared at a guy a few rows back and bellowed, "Are you eye fucking me, faggot?"

At the Marine Corps Recruit Depot, the bus driver instructed us to run out on the asphalt and stand on the painted yellow footprints. The footprints were in four rows facing a stucco building. I ended up next to

Elliott about halfway back in the second and third lines. On command, the first four guys ran in the door to the building. Two minutes later, the next four ran in. My four, with Ben, ran in the door to find four barbers' chairs holding four bald Marines. Their skulls were bright white. As the barbers whipped the capes off them, the shorn recruits hustled out the door to my right and the four of us were unceremoniously draped with capes and the fastest haircut you have ever imagined took place. My barber made eight passes, baring his electric clippers hard into my skull.

The door to our right was a supply room where the four guys in front of us were standing at attention, each with a pair of pants, a bright yellow sweatshirt, flip flops, and boxer shorts in their outstretched arms. They turned in unison and went out a door to the right where I could see naked recruits in a locker room. We four got our gear and moved into the locker room. We were given white cloth bags and a magic marker.

A harsh Marine, fully clothed, said, "Write our names on your bags, you maggots, put all your clothes and belongings in it and kiss the world you knew goodbye." Then he left us sitting there naked.

A half-hour later when all 80 of us who had come in from the airport had been in the room for several minutes, he burst back in and told the guy closest to the shower room to file through the running showers. When I got in there, steam was clouding the bank of shower heads. There was no place to walk except through the scorching water. As I turned the corner to the bank of showers facing the other direction there was no steam. The freezing cold water knocked off most of the hair that still clinged to me.

When we finished showering, it was the middle of the night. No one had given us any instructions for hours and we sat naked on the wooden benches until the first hint of dawn. Then, our drill instructor, the harsh Marine from last night, told us to get dressed. In our canary outfits, we were marched over to the chow hall, ate breakfast at attention, and filed out five minutes after we'd arrived. We spent the day at "attention," ramrod straight, feet together, hands straight down at your sides, no movement, and eyes straight ahead. We marched from one check-in location to another, with the same rigid posture and no bobbing up and down. The sky was darkening, as we lined up outside four Quonset huts. Elliott and Mike Clark were with me in second squad. We rushed in, made our beds as instructed, and stood at attention next to our bunk beds. I had gotten a top bunk near the back. Mike and Ben were just to the left of the door. The DI yelled, "Go to bed."

Two hours later, I was still wide awake, when I heard Elliott whisper to Clark, "What have we gotten ourselves into?" The door burst open, the DI flipped the bright lights on and in a frantic voice said, "Who said that? Get at attention, you maggots."

Elliott admitted to the horrible offense and was forced to do push-ups until he could do no more. The rest of the night was completely silent. Two days later, we were finally taken to the crappers. No one had had any need for a bowel movement in those first three days of constant tension. Tiny round turds that looked like a cross between deer and elk poop were all that came out of anyone.

Chapter Twenty-Three
Visiting Ben Elliott

"When I was fighting...either I felt nothing at all (about killing) or I felt exhilaration akin to scoring the winning touchdown"
Karl Marlantes, 2011.

The rear feels secure, and I roll to a sitting position on my canvas cot. I know I want to find a time when the line to the shower is not too long. There is a heavy overcast and clouds. I put on my spare utilities over the grime of my body and walk over to the mess hall. After eating, the PX is open and I grab a supply of comic books. At the tent, I can see the shower through the rolled-up sides, while I lie on my cot and savor the ongoing superhero stories. Despite the cool 80°, there is a constant line at the shower. There are only slight wisps of wind here and there. The other companies that use the one shower, Kilo, Mike & India (K, M & I) are mostly out in the "bush." When there are only two guys waiting, I go over to the shower. We haul five-gallon water cans up the ladder/steps and pour them into the 55-gallon barrel. As I wait, a stiff breeze picks up and the five-gallon cans have warmed up in the now 97° heat. Filth begrudgingly flows off my body, the mosquitoes will love me now.

We all throw our laundry on a mule, clean weapons, sharpen knives and machetes, and so on. Harwell is playing Bid Whist in a Mike Company's tent, and I join him. After a few hours, the game ends, and he and I look for a poker game. Within an hour, he has won his usual $100 and bids us farewell. Before it's time for dinner, I win some money. The rain falls as the movie begins to play. I give up on the movie and find Harwell for a six-hour Tonk game, where he gets all my dough again.

It is a wet rainy morning out in the bush. The trench around Greg's and my tent has kept the water out, except for a small trickle along the side of my air mattress. He is last watch when the listening post creeps back in. It was another night spent somewhere outside of Da Nang. Our maps show us where, but we are far enough away from the battalion area to have no familiarity, as we have never traveled here. I have never been in the same place twice, although I've walked for more than 150 days.

We eat breakfast in the early morning light. The mortar pit is large, and we fill it completely. We're on our way when I notice an explosive flash in the bushes half a mile away, followed by the thrump of a 61mm going off. When I yell "mortar," everyone dives for cover. The enemy is well aware of this distance. The soil is soft, so the round sinks in before blowing up, and we're close to the ground, so the shrapnel's cone-shaped path goes up between two Marines and hits no one.

The second platoon fires while they charge the enemy. To make sure I don't hit them, I drop a round a little beyond them. They radio Jack, who instructs me to back up 100 meters. The running grunts conduct reconnaissance-by-firing. When the second is a quarter-mile away, the enemy fires back with a few AK-47s and then goes silent. Then the rest of us chase after them, to no avail.

Back in the rear a week later, the world of no wind continues as it has for the last week. I finish with breakfast early, so I can catch a ride into Da Nang and get a bus out to the TOAR of First Battalion/Seventh Marines, Elliott's unit. This is the first time in my tour that I know we are not leaving tomorrow. Just 14 months ago, Ben and I had been considering going into the Coast Guard for four years instead of this insanity. Neither of us was any good at following orders, therefore, we decided the shorter time in the service would have us less likely to get in trouble. Six of us from Port Angeles went through boot camp together, but Ben's infantry training was with a different unit than Boyd and I, then he flew to Vietnam the day after Ken and I did. His unit, 1/7, is the next TAOR (Tactical Area Of Responsibility) to the east of my TAOR. Ken had been assigned to the much more dangerous area near the mountains on the Laotian border. I know from letters from home that Ben is with 81mm mortars, so he is probably at their base. I am really excited to see my friend, who is more of a goof-off than I am.

I am the first guy to finish breakfast and get to the front gate at 7:00 a.m. I catch a ride into Da Nang with a dump truck. The driver knows Da Nang well and tells me where to get a local bus that heads west. In town, I find the intersection of the dirt road heading west off Hwy 1. A rickety city bus rolls up with people hanging all over it. An old woman with betel nut teeth (black gooey stuff that all the adult Vietnamese out in the bush chew) moves up one step so I can get a foothold on the bottom step. I am hanging outside the bus, fully exposed in my Caucasian skin and dirty green utilities. My only protection is my holstered 45 pistol with three rounds in the magazine. Until two weeks later, I had no idea how many enemy combatants roamed around this stretch of highway.

The bus bounces around for five miles. A family and three toothless old men, all carrying bundles and supplies, get off at the first group of huts and I can stand inside and be much less exposed. All of the people, mostly women or very old people, have on black pajamas. They are sullen and don't make eye contact, which is good for me. The sand berm of 1/1 appears ahead on the left. The driver stops without me giving any kind of notice. I walk in on the dirt road between two piles of garbage with kids and old people searching for valuables, just like at 3/7.

One of the gate guards says, "What do you want, Marine?"

"I'm looking for Ben Elliott. He's with 81mm mortars."

The same guard says, "You're fuckin' outa' luck. Elliott's gun is at a remote site on a rocket watch for a month."

"What about Don Reardon"?

"Reardon is KIA. He got shot in the head two weeks ago." Don was my sister, Barb's age, two years older than I am. Although we went through boot camp together, I didn't know him well. The friendly guard tells me I can find a place to crash at the mortar area. The mortarmen are happy enough to meet a friend of Elliott's. They get me over to chow, then set me up with a cot and directions on how to get to Ben in the morning.

The same routine as yesterday at 3/7, I am first in line for chow and at the front gate 15 minutes later. The first vehicle going out is a road grader, which is headed right past Elliott. The operator is happy to have another pair of eyes and hands me his M-16 to keep watch for VC. The driver and I do not talk on the noisy, bumpy ride. I hop down at an area of bunkers and sandbags. Marines are milling around not looking scared. They know their territory well. On the other side of two bunkers, I hear, "Mule!"

Big, handsome Elliott acts like it is an everyday occurrence for a high school friend to stop by. He has not heard that Reardon got killed. With a mature look that I never saw in training or high school, Ben is concerned that I am out in this area with only a 45 pistol.

He says, "There's been a lot of action around here, lately. A jeep will stop by in an hour with their mail call and it's heading into Da Nang."

He goes on, "You better get a ride with him and not risk going back to the base and then riding the bus again."

We fill each other in on our families and an hour later I head back to my battalion area. I feel strange that it is all so matter-of-fact.

My return to the 3/7 battalion area at dusk has a more global feel to it than it did yesterday. I have a broader sense of the area around our TAOR. The gate guards greet me in the same inviting manner that 1/7's guard hosted me. Our territory has a little less of a dangerous feeling. I head to the movie because I have missed chow.

In the morning, we are rousted out of our cots early to get over to eat. I hustle over because I want to get as much food as I can, especially after I missed dinner last night. Then we put on our gear and head out the front gate. We have used this westward route three times before. Lima Company spreads out into a sweep across a flat area, two miles west of our battalion area.

After moving across a mile-wide dry rice paddy, As we assault, Ak-47s and carbines hit us from three spots at once along the brush line. We return devastating fire, while the close-by artillery pounds them into submission, and we move on, scan carefully, and get even lower to the ground. We crest a long, low sandy hill with bushes every few steps, only to be hit again. This is not simply harassment fire. Charlie is trying to keep us out of their territory.

When we start our movement again the terrain looks familiar. Oh my gosh! We are crossing the road I had been on two days ago in a city bus with only three rounds for protection. As I cross the road heading north, we get hit for the third time. Now I am grateful for Elliott getting me safely out of this area. His unit's behavior makes more sense now with brazen enemy interspersed throughout this territory. They were safe in their fortified position. Maybe we are pushing the VC along with our assault, or maybe we are fighting different troops every half mile, and the people from the last firefight are hiding behind us.

The third platoon corpsman patches up the three grunts who were wounded in our five skirmishes today. Then we set up for the night.

I bask in the stunningly beautiful morning, somewhere in Elliott's territory. The few high clouds mix with the explosives' smoke reflecting the sun. I watched the sky unfold on last watch. Now the rest of the company stirs around. Everyone is preparing their breakfast, so we must be heading out early. I have a cup of cocoa in the cool, breezy 75°. Beefsteak, potatoes, and gravy with crackers and cheese with pecan roll make up the hardiest meal I get out here in the bush.

After we fill in the mortar pit and fighting holes, we start a movement through the scrub brush. The area is dotted with clumps of dense, impassable bushes and small, 20-foot-high trees between the sand and hard-packed dirt. It is scary walking because the passable ground, although not trails, is ripe to be filled with booby traps. In fact, we clear three of them before the air heats up. The wind also makes its presence known for the first time in more than a week and heavy clouds have rolled in.

In the heat of the afternoon, we spread out into a sweep into a village of 15 huts. The left side of our assault fires a few rifle rounds over the structures. Although, on high alert in the center of the sweep, we receive no incoming bullets. Half an hour later, the first platoon escorts a VC to the command post. He is a little taller than the usual Vietnamese, maybe 5'7," with almost a smile on his face. His black hair is in a Beattles' cut without hanging over his ears. His skin is clear and smooth, his lips are full, and his mouth is open slightly, revealing straight white teeth. He looks athletic and confident. As I study his face, I notice the angry intensity of his eyes below his full eyebrows. His neck is held up straight, with his small, rounded chin slightly recessed from his mouth. His ears are sticking out and nicely shaped. He may be a Vietnamese-Chinese mixed-race person. The barely recognizable fear in his high cheekbones is hidden behind his purposeful manner. This is certainly a worthy opponent.

He seems to exude the same sense I have, that if only three or four enemy corner me, I will figure a way to kill all of them. His eyes don't scan us, but I can almost see his mind as it looks for any opportunity to take some of us out.

Stationary heavy clouds hang in the morning sky. We move shortly after first light. Our detainee remains with us. He's near the front of our double columns, and our mortars are near the back. This territory is novel and distinct. The dense brush is difficult to cut through with bamboo interspersed. Between the bushes are flat, uncultivated areas. To see the closest Marines in the brush, we must be only 5-10 feet apart. Then, as we approach an open area, we spread out to our standard, hand grenade-safe distance of 20-30 feet. Because of this fluctuation, we move slowly through the open areas at first.

In the bushes surrounding a small clearing, we set up a perimeter. The two mortar tubes are on opposite sides of the opening, so each gun is only free to fire over the heads of the other without hitting the tall trees right behind it. When the two choppers land, a ChuHoy hops out and immediately starts viciously interrogating the cocky prisoner. I have watched the cruelty of these ex-VC ChoHoy interrogators several times, now. This looks like more of the same. The two of them are 40 feet away from my gun. When the pistol-whipping and cutting stop, the VC is forced onto the chopper. When the bird is well-away, I see a body tumble out of the side door.

We stay in the relative safety of our position for long enough to eat our first meal of the day and then move out again. Different than the recent flat exposed areas, these brushy areas are filled with rises and depressions, allowing for instant cover. Incoming rifle fire hits us within an hour of our patrol. I get the gun down and a round away in 10 seconds. The grunts yell "ceasefire," as the enemy disappears. We walk another hour until a hand grenade blows up at the front of the line. We head out again 20 minutes later, so the corpsman must have been able to patch him up to become a "walking wounded."

The enemy strikes us hard in the moonlight. During a lengthy firefight, we use all of our mortar rounds on three different enemy positions. Several grunts are seriously injured, and two Marines have been killed (Killed-In-Action). Due to the dense brush and the threat of the enemy, the medevac hovers 30 feet above the ground, drops a stretcher cable laden with mortar and rifle ammunition, and quickly lifts the dead and wounded. The chopper and the Huey gunship are constantly firing to lessen the incoming fire. We're halfway through the night before we try to sleep.

Then, as the moonless dawn brightens, the grunts return fire to the west, as we receive incoming rifle fire from three areas. I shoot a mortar round at the center muzzle flashes, just to the right of where we sighted in last night. I traverse to the other two enemy areas, and Cowboy drops in two HE and one WP on each spot. I adjust and traverse back to the middle target, which still sends forth death at us. As I fire the tenth round of the 50 seconds, it blows up on top of a muzzle flash, the well-equipped soldier's attack is abruptly stopped. I count that as a confirmed kill.

Our grunts have remained hunkered down in their fighting holes. The enemy continues with scattered harassment fire. I can imagine them dragging the body away under that covering fire. Ten minutes later, all goes back to quiet and damp. Three Marines have been hit. From the mortar pit, I can see one of them being placed on a stretcher. I feel more vulnerable until I see the stretcher-bearers move back to fighting positions and we wait for the medevac.

Ten minutes later a Huey suddenly zooms low overhead and strafes the silent area the enemy had been in. He circles up and does a perpendicular run, and fires rockets and machine guns, as we hear the thump, thump of the CH-34 medevac coming in. It lands near the stretcher, and lifts off seconds later, as the grunts get their brother to care as quickly as possible. A deathly hush returns, as the sound of the two helicopters fades away. Do I feel safer or more terrorized without all that intense noise? Hyper-alert with no clear threat, or viciously suppressing enemy fire? Resigned to knowing we will sweep the enemy area and find no trace of them. Another day in paradise with the growing dichotomy between wanting to be safe and wanting to hurt someone.

I feel all alone as I eat my dinner, still not knowing who got medevacked or how badly they were hurt. Was it one of my old friends, or just some Fucking-New-Guy? The four of us in the mortar team are assigned to a fighting position and the mortar pit for night watches. By midnight, I settle down on my air mattress while Joe does first watch in the pit. At 2:30, Joe carefully nudges my boot to wake me without me killing him.

Chapter Twenty-Four
The Grind of Existence

"I am afraid I know how the winning chimpanzees felt. There is a very primal side of me"
                                            Karl Marlantes, 2011.

The ground undulates in rhythmic waves to wake me up. Sound follows seconds later, made by tremendous explosions of bombs from B-52s, off in the distance. It feels like a force of nature. Man is powerful enough to shake the ground miles away and I want to take a human life for the wounded and Mo dying.

Writing now, I wonder what my life might be like now had Mo lived. He was such a healthy, fun-loving guy. Would he have been the only guy I kept in touch with back in the States? Would I have gotten to know his family? Would I have learned about the inner-city and Black culture? How powerful am I today in Vietnam with his influence over me? It serves me well to feel as powerful as a god, as I seek puny mortals upon whom to exact my revenge.

Lima beans is the final meal in my pack. It alleviates my gnawing constant hunger. I clean and lubricate both my pistol and mortar. The filth on my body aids me in combating the powerful Vietnam insect air force, and I refuse to waste even a tablespoon of my precious water cleaning the grime off. I make my way into the bushes to poop. Because the constant tension isn't going to loosen my bowels for another ten years, a nice clean turd drops into the ant-torturing size hole I dug. I grab a handful of nearby sand to clean my hands before I continue on with the business of living in the bush. When we come to a halt on a sandy hillside, I dig an ant trap hole and torture and kill two of them. I rush to find another to satisfy my growing craving for killing and death.

The clouds break up as I finish last watch and the guys begin to move around. My hunger slackens with my second meal in the last ten hours. I try to remember when I was the hungriest before Vietnam. It had felt unbearable the few times I missed a meal. Hunger grew and grew. This morning feels worse, even with two meals in my gut, but I am used to it and I do not even fantasize about chow back at the battalion.

The clouds have fully occluded the sun and the temperature rises. We cover up our perimeter holes, imitating the VC's ability to leave a place looking like we had not fought from there. The 47-pound mortar feels natural strapped over my left shoulder. Both Del and I carry the big baseplate because we have been in many different types of soil. In the sand, the six-inch

(5lb) base plate never stops sinking deeper, which means, after every shot, I have to adjust the level. The 12-inch (10lb) plate takes two shots to pack the sand and the angle stays the same as I fire-for-effect.

The area of this patrol seems familiar. About noon, we come upon the same village where I forgot my fancy watch in the mortar pit when we filled it in. Could I just move out of the line and dig down 18" and retrieve it? The problem is, that I do not know exactly where it is in the covered-over pit. Oh well, because I have not got to play cards with Harwell much, I have won enough money in poker winnings to buy a few more.

At the peak of the heat in the early evening, we hear a rumble nearby. This has become a ritual for the last few days. Rain will fall at sunset. The rumble gets closer and is clearly thunder, not bombs, artillery or some other American explosives. I strip off my pack, put on my poncho and get protected from the half-hour downpour. We move through the rain for another hour until it is fully dark. As we dig in, a carbine rifle shoots its pesky 22-caliber rounds through our perimeter. Little buzzing bees dangerously zip by. Seeing the muzzle flashes allows me to sight in and drop three rounds on the spot in seconds. Odds are, I only disturbed the dirt, and that VC has gone on about his business.

The morning starts like the last few days. The heavy clouds drift apart as the hidden sun lightens the sky.

In the windless daylight, the clouds build and the heat intensifies. By mid-morning, I hear an ascending 707 fly low overhead and know the battalion is near.

Thunder rumbles in the distance, at 3:30 p.m. We trudge the last hour home in the rain and exhaustedly dump our gear on the floor of our troop tent. We drag ourselves over to chow. I am disappointed to see the PX is closed, so, no new shipment of comic books until tomorrow. Back at the tents, we are introduced to the new Navy company corpsman, Brian. He is what is called a "Shake-N-Bake," an NCO, Non-Commissioned Officer, at pay grade E-6, Petty Officer First Class, who went to an NCO school to be promoted from E-3, Seaman, to fill a critical shortage in junior noncommissioned officers. Like a fast-food restaurant turning uncooked food into an edible product in minutes, he jumped several pay grades to more responsibility. I'll wait and see if he is as incompetent as most of the Staff Sargeants I had met in the Marine Corps.

Clouds fill the sky this calm morning. The temperature is the usual 80°. After we eat breakfast and clean all our gear, the order comes to be ready to move out in the afternoon. I get right over and wait in line for the shower. I will fight the bugs attracted by the soap and clean skin, this filth is more than I want to stand. Wet down, soap up, pull the chain again and watch the dark brown water go down the drain. It feels very different to have clean hair, face and body. Our laundry is brought back at 2:00.

The usual breezes never materialize. The heat does its daily climb to a humid 93° a little later than the last two weeks. It reaches this peak at 3:00, the rain starts and we climb into helicopters. We land in driving rain. An intense wind accompanies the chilling drop in temperature to 73°. Bullets come at us from a treeline. We scurry about, to get into an attack formation. As we sweep down a sandy hillside, two Huey gunships make passes perpendicular to our approach. Their rockets and machine guns fire into the dense tree line we head toward.

The wind fades away, the temperature increases and the rainfall continues. The enemy fire at us, despite the constant passes from the Hueys. About 500 meters from the enemy-held tree line, we are told to take cover and watch for enemy movement. The Hueys move off. I hear what sounds like a Buick passing overhead. It is a 16-inch-in-diameter artillery round from the USS Missouri's guns, miles out at sea. The artillery observer, AO, adjusts their fire over the radio and a whole herd of Buicks passes overhead, exploding all throughout the enemy-held territory.

The Hueys come roaring back, and fire rockets 100 feet in front of us. Then, we sweep into the base of the hill that the enemy are dug into. No one is firing back. The bombs must have caused them to use their escape routes. As we search the brush-covered sandy hill, we find heavy bunkers, tunnels, trenches and fighting holes. As the rain finally stops, we set up a combat perimeter to allow us to explore the tunnels.

A guy with a K-bar in his teeth, his 45 in his right hand, and no shirt on, drops into a tunnel. This scene is probably being replayed across the face of the hill. Each platoon has a "tunnel rat," an athletic smaller guy trying to fit where the tiny Vietnamese can go.

After blowing up all the tunnels, we move out to the next hill. As dusk sets in, we can see taller hills to the west. We, the CP group and mortars, array around the nearly bare top of the hill. The grunt platoons surround us. We dig the pit and fire aiming rounds at three possible areas the enemy could attack from. Four of our ammo humpers man two positions on the perimeter. With our aiming-stakes set, most of our ammo opened ready to drop in the tube, we cook up our dinner. What a first day for our new company corpsman, Brian!

The morning is shattered by incoming gunfire and a mortar round blowing up inside our perimeter. I roll off my rubber lady and slide into the gun pit. We fire three quick rounds over our aiming stake and adjust 50 feet to the left and fire three more. The sun has not fully lit the dawn. "Charlie," as usual, is invisible. Two minutes after the firing stops, the captain sends the second platoon on a search-and-destroy sweep. The rest of us remain on high alert and wait for the enemy to be flushed out. My mind races through different scenarios of where and how Charlie might run at us.

I thought our rapid response would yield some enemy, but the grunts find nothing. Two Marines are wounded and patched up. Breakfast is a dreary affair. No one talks. We are spread around the mortar pit as if Al, Greg or I have the flu and we don't want to catch it from each other. Earnest, down-turned looks reflect our shattered lives. What Hell we live in. The aggressive mosquitoes give way to the flies that are hungry for my washed skin. The thousand-yard-stare is evident on all of us who have been here a while. It is a way to hold focus on nothing and be alert to any danger. Look at nothing and see everything.

At noon we mount up and head out. The heat comes late through the dark clouds. As light rain wets us, we clear our third booby trap of the morning. Just as I dry out in the heat of the afternoon, it starts to rain in earnest. Thunder heralds even heavier rain. We walk through an open area of knee-high grass and enter a heavily brushed tree line. I have my 45 held at my side ready to use its ineffective bullet or two to add to our attack or defense. As dark sets in, we slop out a mortar pit, throwing wet mud away from the edge so the water will not drain back in. Still, the bottom of the pit has an inch of mud. As we cook dinner, the rain stops. I am thankful I have my Rubber Whore and my half a wool blanket, or tonight would be cold.

I can't believe that my buddies back home are ready for yet another year of college, while I am ready for another day of killing and warfare. The overcast morning is a continuation of the last few days. Are my old friends thinking about girls, sports or school? Are any of my old chums thinking of coming to this hell hole? The rain from yesterday has soaked in and now the ground is dry. I break out the peaches and pound cake and a cup of cocoa and partake in "Bush Luxury" followed by ham and eggs. I just get a poker game started when the word goes out to mount up. Although the mud of last night covers parts of my skin, I am still quite attractive to the flies. One big one dive-bombs into the corner of my mouth. When I try to knock it away, I smear more dirt on my face. I look around at my fellows and I see that most of them did not take the time to shower the day before yesterday. The dried mud of last night mottles the deeply ground-in dirt of the last two weeks, and no flies buzz around their heads.

We head toward the foothills with the mountains behind them. Up one hill, down to a broad flat land, up a little higher hill, down into a heavily treed valley with no resistance, yet.

As we climb a fairly steep, sandy hill in the mid-afternoon, at the peak of the heat, the usual wind starts. Then, we are shot at from the trees behind us, A knoll with a clump of trees provides me some protection as I dive toward the dirt. I can tell we will never get the mortar set up in this steep terrain, so I return fire with my 45. Back down the hillside, I hear a Marine yell in pain. On the hill below me comes a shout for "Corpsman up." Brian, with a determined demeanor, heads down the hill in a crouch. The gunfire has stopped. The screaming Marine slowly quiets down, as the morphine takes effect.

We trudge on and the rain falls in a steady drizzle, and the wind whips around. By the time we are soaked to the bone, thunder proceeds a drop in temperature. After the rumble of thunder quiets, it continues to rain. The CP group has found a broad, flat area the size of two football fields to set up our perimeter, where the wounded Marine is brought for more protection. The wind dies down, then goes away, as we prepare our dinner. Tomorrow will be a lighter pack with no food in it. Resupply will probably come with a medevac in the morning. This is a strange thing to be grateful for. I have concern for my fellow Marine, yet I'm thankful that food will arrive.

While I am on watch in the middle of the night, we receive fire from three AK-47s. I set the gun for the angle to reach 800 meters and look through the tiny sight at a muzzle flash. My first round blows up on top of the flashes, that end abruptly. I traverse over to the flashes to the right and fire-for-effect. Before those rounds even hit, the enemy has gone quiet. None of us are hit. I have my fourth kill. It had been too dark for enemy soldiers to truly aim their very efficient weapons. The dark is usually our enemy, but tonight it saves us.

Days have passed, and we are awoken in the battalion area by the ground rolling violently and the sounds of a nearby bombing. That is probably where we will head today. So much for the luxury of a five-foot-long cot and hot food. Today, I will again bring my little portable radio with an earplug. After chow, we hustle over to the motor pool to get on seven, Six-By's. Two jeeps with quad-50 caliber machine guns are our intimidating armament, as the convoy leaves the gate.

We head north on Hwy 1, rapidly, to begin with, then when we leave the densely populated areas, we slow down to check for mines. In an area of immense rice paddies, we disembark and zigzag across a paddy on the dikes. Although it is rice paddies full of stinky, green water, the dikes are solid enough that by the time I get to them, I am still on solid ground, even though we mortars bring up the rear.

We enter a tree line as the perpetual cloud cover rises. The armed forces radio station plays in my ear. No one, except my buddies, knows anything about it because only I can hear it. In October 1963, in Mr. Kennedy's Sophomore Biology class, Mark Pesola, "Fazz" was secretly listening to the World Series on this same type of portable radio. He had the little radio in a book with the center of the middle pages cut out and an earphone wire running up his back under his shirt to his right ear. The class buzzed along nicely when Kennedy noticed the wire in Mark's ear. Kristie Eyre and I shared the lab table in front of Mark and watched as he had to give up his ability to follow the World Series. His beloved Dodgers would have to get along without him. If I get caught here, I would have to give up my entertainment, but I knew I was just as valuable to the company with only one ear listening. I only have a pistol to respond to incoming fire, and besides, we make a lot of noise to enemy ears with years of experience in ambushes.

By noon, the thick clouds are back and the wind picks up. We walk past three 500-pound bomb craters, which have pools of water eight feet across, 30 feet below us in their steep cone shapes. I'm hot enough, that it looks tempting to climb down and dive in. The enemy had to know of our arrival, given the early morning bombing, so they made themselves scarce. In the late afternoon, heavy rain falls and lets up a little later. As we dig in for the night, the same sound as this morning comes from a near distance, but the ground does not shake. The thunder brings black clouds and more rain. An hour after dark the bright moon must have come up because, even through the clouds, the pitch dark has turned to an eerie phosphorescence.

Chapter Twenty-Five
The Glory of Killing

"I turned murderously angry"

Karl Marlantes, 2011.

Three weeks later, we finally straggle into the rear in the pitch dark. Six more guys were wounded, with Miller from the third platoon sent back to the States with his foot blown off. This morning we woke up in the bush to no heavy clouds and only a slight overcast. By 6 a.m., the usual clouds had rolled in. This weather pattern has had wind every afternoon and none in the mornings. Generally, it is becoming less hot. We have not had a day in the 100s for a few weeks. The nighttimes have been cool, in the '70s instead of the '80s. Exhausted, I crash on my cot.

I walk over to breakfast by myself. Today, I am going to use the ocean for cleaning my body, so I don't worry about getting a shower. After eating, I get all my gear cleaned and hung up by the time the PX opens. I get my comics and smokes, stash them and head for the gate with Del. We catch a 6-By (a troop transport truck that carries six guys per side). The beach is not too crowded. I swim out past the breakers and float on my back for half an hour. The dirt slowly comes off my skin while I swim underwater. Now that I am clean, I lie out in the sun and fall asleep.

An hour later the beach is too rowdy to sleep, so I get a beer, ride some waves, get another beer, and listen to the music coming from the shed used as a bar. I carry a hopeless, vicious edge throughout the day, but I barely remember how to have fun, as I go through the motions, I even fake a smile and laughter.

Del and I head back to the battalion area. I find an afternoon poker game. After winning $40, I search for a Bid Whist game. The game is like Bridge, except Spades are always trump. I am getting better and seem to be more of an accepted part of my Black brothers-in-arms style of banter. As an example, when you "trump" someone's trick, you whip the spade down with a flourish. The game breaks up in time for chow. After dinner, I sit on my cot and write letters to Mom and Mary that talk about my day at the beach without mentioning the beer. Then I write to Marjorie about being in the field for three weeks, leaving out the blood and guts. I explain how good it felt to let the dirt soak off in the ocean.

I see now, 51 years later, that I tried to make all three women think highly of me. The character they knew has become fictional but needs to be preserved to come alive again when I'm in the States. The movie is Madame X. The Club has beer again, so I skip out on the movie and slowly drink the two they allow each of us. When I get back to the tent, everybody is crapped-out, so I go to sleep.

The morning is announced by two mortar rounds blowing up inside the berm. The rounds land on the far side of the battalion area and are of no threat to us, except the next ones could land anywhere. Fully awake, I head over to chow. Clouds roll in. After breakfast, the clouds have moved on and we have a rare morning of only high overcast skies. I have not seen a dynamic sunrise for weeks. Back at the tent, I read my comic books until it has warmed up enough and no one is in line for the shower. Everybody back in the tent slowly gears up. A Mule pulls up to our tent with mortar rounds, ammo and food. We fill our canteens from a "Water Buffalo" (a 500-gallon tank with a spigot towed on a trailer).

At noon another round of clouds pass overhead and we pile into choppers. My portable radio is in my shirt pocket. I am ready for the make-believe world of being a pin on someone's map moving us to a new location. The ideas of that pin mover have almost nothing to do with the actuality we will find on the ground. It is usually easy to imagine the strategy they had, but the reality is that the terrain is going to dictate how we move and keep ourselves safe. Once we land and spread out, the radio goes on in my ear. I walk in stark reality.

In these seven months, I have killed five people, been shot at a hundred times, and seen muzzle flashes and enemy running, but I have never once, shot directly at another human. The music in my right ear doesn't make me any less alert and aware. The troublemaker part of me is awakened in a new way. The boyish joy turns on part of me that "lights up" at being able to use that rebellious part of my brain that is unconcern with the consequences that might come from authority figures. In my youth, I always got one of my friends to follow my rebellious adventures. Here I am alone. The powers-that-be have reached a new level of estrangement from my need to control my own surroundings. Firepower protects a Marine. It depends on rapid response. "Shoot first, ask questions later."

The moral and strategic process to determine where each of us sets our next footfall will have more to do with how this war turns out than what the Rear Echelon Motherfucker does with his pin. Only a few times in my walks around Vietnam did the REMFs actually know where the enemy was.

After we eat breakfast, the company splits into three patrols. My gun, three ammo humpers and Bud, go with the first platoon. The other two platoons mount up for separate movements. After walking through low rolling hills for two hours, we approach a narrow rice paddy with a dense tree line on the other side. We pass the first trees and spread out into a search-and-destroy online assault formation. This is not a time for listening to the radio. Every sound is important. I need both ears, so the wire to my ear is buttoned up in my breast pocket. We hack our way through the brush, which forces us to travel slowly. Mortars are with first squad, on the far left of the assault line. The rocket and machine gun teams are with second and third squads to our right. The whole platoon is only covering an area 100 meters wide. As we fight our way through the bushes, I periodically lose sight of Joe or Cowboy on each side of me, even with this close spacing. Word is passed down the line to halt. The engineer, who was walking with second squad, comes right behind us toward first squad.

An hour later, I assume they have quietly disarmed a booby trap because we move again. The engineer stays attached to first squad. As the wind gets unusually stout, we hear gunfire nearby. This must be the second or third platoon. We may have scared up some enemy and run them into our comrades who are hidden in ambush. The gunfire seems to be a half mile away and there is no place to set up the mortar to assist them. The combination of a few enemy weapons and a lot of M-16 firing is quickly over.

We move through the afternoon, and clear booby traps three more times. As we approach the first rice paddy we have seen since this morning, we dig in in the sandy terrain that borders it. Our gun pit is part of the perimeter, which allows us to fire because we are free of the 10' tall bushes we have been fighting our way through. Carefully cooking dinner in the bottom of the mortar pit, I feel very exposed as dark covers any enemy movement in the distance. For the first time in weeks, no evening rain falls.

Growling thunder and pouring rain dominated last watch. An hour before dawn, the wind blows away the rain clouds. The thunder quiets in the heavy overcast. The ubiquitous sounds of far-off combat are more evident now without the last hours of thunder. Everyone stirs around to get hot food. I wonder where the rest of the company is set up. Are they hidden in wait for us to push the enemy to them? Or will we move to a hidden place and attempt to ambush the enemy that they flush out? It is a different feeling when I know there are enemy present and there will likely be a confrontation. I would rather nothing happens than get a chance to hurt them. Not because I am feeling high morals, but because of the terror of the random chaotic violence. I make sure I get a cigarette lit before the last heat tab goes out. We throw the dirt from the sides of the pit into its muddy bottom, pack up our wet gear, and walk.

After we have covered a lot of distance in our double, staggered lines, we skirt around the edge of a rice paddy in the afternoon. It feels safer to be spread out compared to yesterday being bunched up hacking through the brush. As I throw my poncho over me and my gear, I am almost dry, as a brisk wind picks up and heralds the fall of rain. As we pass through the sixth heavily brushed area that sits above the level of the rice paddies, a ChiCom hand grenade blows up in front of me, just beyond Cowboy and Joe. Johnson, from first squad, screams. AK-47 fire explodes at us through the pouring rain. My choices are few. There is no place to find any cover, so I dive violently into the mud, slamming down hard in the same instant as bullets whiz around me. A long two seconds later, everything is quiet, except for the Marine yelling. The first platoon corpsman, Tony, hustles by me in a rapid crouch.

For the next hour, I have no idea what is going on. When we move out again, I assume Johnson is patched up because we have not called a medevac. We now know the enemy knows exactly where we are. I wonder if the people who move pins on the map know we are so exposed. We set up for the night inside a tree line, five miles away from where we were ambushed, and start watches before full dark because we are told we will move out at 4:00 a.m. This means to me that we will move to a place the pin pushers think the enemy will not know we have set up.

Like the 27 "bulls-in-the-china-closets" that we are, we break camp as quietly as possible in the pitch dark. We travel a mile to a draw with a small stream running through the middle of it. We are placed perpendicular to the flow of the stream and cover a line about 300 feet (100 meters) wide. Before the first hints of dawn, we are in our slightly protected, hidden places. (This reminds me of playing hide-and-seek with my four-year-old grandson, who is almost always visible as I look up from counting to 20. We, Americans, seem about as effective at hiding from the VC as he is from me.) Hours later, we move out, hike for a few hours, and set up for the night.

When we wake to another wet morning, we break camp slowly. It is damp and the sky is filled with heavy clouds and overcast. The wind whips around. It is the perfect morning for cocoa and cookies. We walk for an hour and stop to eat. I am nice and dirty again huddled in my poncho over my heat tab. The flies hardly notice me. At the crack of gunfire, I eat dirt. Instantly, I get hold of the mortar, turn the legs in the direction of the bullets, and send out a round. The muzzle flashes are further away and a little to the left of the mortar's flight. I correct and we fire-for-effect. As usual, the enemy stops firing before the volley hits them.

The rest of the company meets us at 6:00 p.m., and the rain starts again. The wind dies down and the rain lets up for the first time today. As dusk fades into darkness, everything is quiet. No moonlight brightens the backs of the clouds. It is going to be a dangerous night. The noise of the breeze in the bushes could hide the sounds of the approach of a VC. The rest of the night is terrifying, but uneventful.

The sunrise fills the sky, with a mix of colors. There are a few high clouds and no wind at all. The purples brighten to oranges and the panorama gets more dynamic. It means we survived another night of sleeping in terror. The enemy in this territory has done a good job of keeping us on high alert. They have hit us at all different times of day, snipers in the morning, dusk, daytime and night, and full attacks three times this week at various hours.

We are spread out in our perimeter. The soil is covered by short grass interspersed with bunches of taller clumps. I wonder what kind of snakes hang out around here? There might be tripwires hidden below the thick shorter grass and tied between these clumps. Areas of trees and brush surround us. Many spots could provide cover for the enemy, but we are 88 guys with a lot of firepower. Probably a little intimidating to take potshots at. Everything is dry, after yesterday's blistering heat with no afternoon rain. I cook breakfast, and the morning drags on. No bullets go out or in. Many of us clean our weapons and sharpen machetes and K-bars.

A CH-46 stirs up a dust storm to bring in resupply. We mount up an hour later and walk down a grassy slope from last night's perimeter. We force our way through the heavier and heavier brush, especially in the numerous gullies. We stay away from trails or roads, but the pointmen find booby traps five times, anyway. The brush is thick and over my head. My radio is playing "Red Rubber Ball," as we get hit while I am below the line of fire in one of the gullies. We stay down, as the exposed grunts return a wall of fire. I scramble 100 meters up out of the gully to a grassy area out of the tall bushes. Although we cannot see any muzzle flashes, the grunts have given us coordinates and we fire a few rounds to help keep the enemy fire suppressed.

Next morning, an incoming burst of AK-47 fire wakes us, followed a fraction of a second later by the haunting quiet of steady rain. The company's response in the first fraction of a second is a cacophony of explosive sounds. The enemy has done its job well. They have disappeared and we are shockingly awake. We send four mortar rounds to join the destruction of dirt and bushes where the enemy had been. More wind than usual for the next hour, makes us tense and on high-alert.

It is dark and I try to sleep to no avail. Dawn makes sleep less likely, so I crawl into the mortar pit with Cowboy. I get my heat tab started in my makeshift stove and cook ham and eggs. While I smoke a cigarette, I see the rest of the company start to move around in low profiles. Is the enemy watching for an opportunity to hit us while we become visible? Morning progresses. The wind dies to a dreary breeze with hardly any sounds from us big clumsy Marines. These exposed, high-alert time periods extenuate the difference in our strategy to pack and produce massive firepower, to the VC's quick strike and disappearing abilities.

We have so little control over how we deal with the enemy, that there is no reason to debate which style is better. The pin pushers move us to the next location and tell us what to carry. We choose the way we take each step and search-and-destroy any sign of enemy. We start a sweep through the area the enemy has fired from. Often, like this morning, we "search" by "recon (reconnaissance) by fire." The treeline they were in is filled with our face-moving lead, which we believe will protect us. We fire a heavy barrage, scamper forward, fire another barrage and get closer. No enemy fire comes at us. This technique provides a feeling of safety. If the enemy is protected in those bushes, they need to keep their heads down.

Even though we search the area for two hours, we find zero evidence that the enemy was ever there. The fog rolls in as we move out in a double column. Fog, rain and wind surround us as we travel for the next six hours through rolling hills, and gullies with streams, while the engineers clear five booby traps in the stiffening wind. We finally stop on the crest of a hill overlooking lowlands with mountains to the west. Thank goodness I have had a lot of practice using my Zippo. The recessed filter of my Parliaments keeps my cigarette from getting totally soaked. Against the edge of the bottom of the mortar pit, I can make enough of a windscreen to get my heat tab lit and I have a hot supper. The temperature has not really changed all day.

Heavy rain, fog and wind blow through my poncho tent and get into all my gear. The wind dies down at about 4:00 a.m. and the rain stops for two hours. The fog lifts by the time we start cooking breakfast, but the rain comes back, chilling the air. The rain is gone quickly and the temperature climbs rapidly to the warmest day we have had for weeks.

The rain in the night has given way to high scattered clouds. We seem to be in no rush this morning, so I guess we will wait here for resupply. After nine months, some of the patterns have become predictable. A whole school year in this hell hole. It feels like an eternity or as if I arrived yesterday. Time makes less and less sense. It goes in slow motion in action and doesn't seem to move any other time. I eat the last meal in my backpack and dry my gear by shaking the water off it. We have had contact with the enemy almost every day on this operation and have moved around on high combat alert, but there is usually nothing to do. Vietnam is all about nothing to do, unless we're walking or fighting. The overcast thickens and the morning heats up. Resupply comes in by CH-34s at about 11. We have them in and out within ten minutes, then pack up and move out. Not a bullet has flown in either direction yet today. Off we go into the "I do not know where."

The next day, we slog around, eat breakfast, and break camp. All of us hear the "thrump" of a 61mm mortar and scramble for cover. This unique sound is caused by the shotgun shell and small explosive when it blows up at the bottom of the heavy steel mortar tube. Other types of explosions aren't muffled like this horror. From one edge of the bottom of the mortar pit, I wait a century for the sudden swish of the deadly round. Because it is coming in almost straight down above, there is no place to hide. If it hits in the mortar pit we would all four be seriously injured. If it lands one foot outside the pit, we won't get a scratch. We would have about the same likelihood of injury or death lying flat on the ground, due to the conical shape of the blast zone. It will kill or seriously injure a person eight feet behind where it lands, three feet in front and five feet to the sides. But while hugging the ground two feet from where the round hits, you might not get a single piece of shrapnel. No matter what, you won't have time to even twitch between the swish sound and the explosion.

The quick swish proceeds an eruption 20 feet to my right where no one is cowering. Although we heard the "thrump" there is no way to identify the direction it came from, except vaguely east. Back to my cold turkey loaf 15 minutes later, we are ordered to mount up in. We finish our food, fill in the pit, and strap our gear on.

We're in a sweep movement toward the east as the rainy, foggy morning gives way to cooling temperatures. We move carefully through three different bushy treelines, with the second platoon in front of our two mortar teams. We clear seven booby traps by 2:00 p.m. and see no other evidence of the enemy. We have walked eight miles when AK-47s and carbines fire at us from three areas in front of our line. Three mortar rounds slam into us. Our wall of bullets instantaneously acts as if we can push their bullets back at them, but several Marines get hit, as I hear

"Corpsman up" to our left and right. Our fire tones down the enemy, however, they continue to attack for five minutes. Two Hueys come racing in, strafing them. Between the first three Huey passes, the enemy maintains the same rate of fire. We stop shooting the mortar for fear we'll hit the choppers. The enemy goes quiet. We scurry forward and, of course, find no blood trails, shell casing or any evidence they were ever there. The two dead Marines prove these phantoms were not figments of our imagination.

The Hueys patrol overhead, as the medevac comes in for three wounded guys and the two bodies. The bird is 100 meters from my part of the defensive perimeter, so I can make out that one of the guys assisted onto the bird is a card-playing buddy of mine. I do not recognize any of the rest of the guys.

We mount up an hour later and head further into the highlands to the east in a double column. The clouds part enough for us to briefly see the almost full moon. After walking 12 miles, we finally stop for dinner. My ammo humpers only have five rounds left. Each rifleman, machine gunner, grenade launcher and rocket man saved a small amount of ammunition. Luckily, the enemy does not attack during the night.

Everything is subdued in the wet, cool morning filled with fog, rain and wind. The fog is thin. The wind is mild. The rain is misty. We trudge away from our nighttime defensive position. A carbine round whizzes between Bud and me. The company returns fire for a couple of seconds and the world goes back to hush. The captain puts us into an online assault formation and we move toward the source of the bullets. We get hit hard. At least twenty enemy, dug into the hills on either side of us, have us penned down in a brushy valley between the two ridges. An enemy mortar round explodes, throwing a Marine body in the air off to my right. He is too far away for me to recognize him, but he is from the second platoon's part of our assault line. The enemy's fire is disciplined. Besides their short bursts of AK-47 and carbine fire, their attack is accented by mortars, two rocket rounds and machine-gun fire. They get more aggressive as the seconds go by.

Del and I, both, have run out of mortar rounds. My trusty 45 pistol may come in handy as a last line of defense. The terror is building in me as I realize this could easily be the end. We probably have another two minutes before the helicopters get here with their firepower. Battalion artillery slams into the enemy area, but Charlie's fire gets even more intense. I must remember to save one round for myself if I start shooting with my last magazine. I hunker down as tight to the ground as I can get and pray earnestly. "God, if you will get me through this one, I will pray to you every day, read the Bible, attend church services and follow your path for me." The grunts continue to hold the enemy off with M-16s, machine guns and grenade launchers. Our artillery rounds come rapidly. Through all the noise of the fire-fight, the distant sound of Hueys can be heard. The enemy pumps more firepower at us. They must know they only have a few more seconds to wipe us out.

The ememy continue to shoot at us, even though the two Hueys strafe them with machine guns on their first air assault. By the third pass, a little less fire is directed at us. It does not feel like the answer to my prayers. It feels like my viciousness has expanded to include my whole company, the battalion artillery and the Huey gunships. A man-made response to the devil. Is there a way to get through all their bullets to exact our revenge on them? Not yet. They haven't completely ignored the Hueys, but they have more firepower than we do, unless the jets get here soon.

After the Hueys have made 13 passes of machine-gun and rocket fire, two Navy F-14s roll in low on each hillside spiraling bombs at the enemy, who shuts up. The jets make three more high explosive passes, followed by Napalm's oily-looking fireballs that burn 30 feet high. It is now 20 minutes since our first casualty. I only feel a mixture of desire for revenge and wanting to get a hole dug to hide and no feeling of gratitude for surviving. I have forgotten about God and don't feel any relief. Only, "What is next"? The pin movers in Da Nang now know that there had been a dug-in enemy on the route they had us walk.

I know we will find a few tunnels later, but there is no evidence of their firepower. As we lick our wounds, the feeling of who the enemy is has expanded to include the Americans who push us around from their safe comfortable settings in Da Nang, Saigon and Washington, DC. I have a sense of fury at the incompetence and arrogance of my government and military, and an acute desire to get at that enemy. Resupply is brought in by a CH-34.

Much like my internal rage about the position I am in, the wind whips the rain in all directions. It has rained off and on all night. I wake up to an 11mph wind at an unusual time in the morning. It feels surreal for the wind to be at its afternoon intensity now. The whole company set up in a dry rice paddy and putters around for breakfast. An active village with purposeful inhabitants is to the north of us.

An old Vietnamese man leaves one of the hooches with a bowsaw, that is two feet from the bowed handle to the blade and is three feet long. As I eat my turkey loaf and watch him head to a spot in the paddy where four dikes come together at 90° angles. The paddy next to the one we are in is filled with water. The other three, including ours, are dry. He saws into the dirt of the dike between the soaked paddy and a dry one. He works hard on the first slice and makes a series of cuts two inches apart in a three-foot section. Each cut is skillfully straight up and down, the same way I, 51 years later, cut my homemade bread each morning. He cuts loose the bottom of a slice of solid dirt, allowing the paddy water to flow through the two-inch opening he creates. He carries this slice on his bow saw, with his free hand to keep it together, to a three-foot-wide gap in the dike between us and the dry paddy to the west of where he cut. He firmly places the slice against the edge of this opening. He goes back over, pries another slab loose, and adheres it to his first slice to build the new dike in the opening. Back and forth he goes for 30 minutes. He has built a solid dike and the water has filled a third of the dry paddy. It is amazing how perfectly level each paddy is. Women and kids move into the drained, damp field of rice. They harvest. A 10-year-old boy dances around his massive water buffalo and attaches the bundles of grain to his animal. When he has a pile six feet high, he guides his animal back to the village. He and the unburdened beast return. The process goes on all morning. By the time we move on at noon, the new wet paddy has filled evenly with a few inches of water. The old man can be seen changing paddy openings in the distance.

It is a chilly, damp mid-October morning. The sky is overcast. Not even sniper fire last night. The full moon is somewhere up there above the thick clouds. We are told to mount up for extraction, as the transition from moonlight to sunlight is complete. This is easy because I have no food left. By the time it is full light, we are packed up and hunkered down in our protective perimeter. It is ominously quiet. These three weeks were a more intense way of life, with combat 19 out of 22 days, in territory unfamiliar to us. We moved every day. I feel detached from the guys in the company who have not been through one of these three-week stretches before. This is my fourth time away from the battalion area for longer than two weeks. My routine is down pat. Get your limited sleep between watches. Pack up after I sleep, and always keep a sharp watch for the enemy. The sun and stars have been invisible almost the whole time. Rain, clouds, overcast and cool nights, every day.

The silence allows me to hear the far-off, faint sound of "thump, thump" from the dual rotors of Ch-46s. The terror of being announced as a target mounts and wars inside me with the anticipation that I will be out of danger soon. Let me stay safe in the cocoon of my vicious, alone persona, as my comrades, with our firepower, provide the meager protection between me and the enemy. The birds land. The enemy takes potshots at us from three different directions as we hustle into the exposed aircraft. There are several shafts of light in the bird where bullet holes have pierced the thin metal of its skin. Two new holes appear between me and the cockpit.

As two Hueys fire at the muzzle flashes, our chopper takes off with the troop entry ramp still down, forcing the last Marines to run and jump on. We bank quickly to the right, then arc up into the air and away from the gunfire. When we're high enough to be a nearly impossible target for small arms, I get a sense of security. Nobody speaks in the bird. When we disembark at battalion, the silence continues.

Chapter Twenty-Six
After Vietnam
Washington State University
Cougar Union Building

As I walked out of the dorm and up to campus, I was greeted by dry heat. Four days ago, Ken Lindsey and I drove across the state to Pullman, WA to begin the fall quarter of 1968. Ken was one of the brightest students in my graduating class and is now pursuing a career as a veterinarian. We were in the same Methodist Youth Fellowship group and got along great. I had only gotten him in trouble once when we were late returning to the group camp on Lake Adwell in a canoe. He had introduced me to several other Juniors like himself on the tenth floor of Goldsworthy Hall Men's Dormitory. Josh Hampton, one of his friends, and I shared a small room, 1025. The rooms around 1025 were mostly occupied by 18-year-old freshmen. On my floor, I was the only 20-year-old freshman. Five guys were juniors. I was self-conscious and unsure whether I was respected, liked, disliked, or feared.

I crossed the street and climbed the first flight of stairs, looking for attractive females rather than land mines. I had two hours before Composition 101 class, so I decided to do some socializing.

The cacophony of coed voices welled up in front of me as I swung open the outside door of the CUB, Cougar Union Building. The long hallway with the cafeteria at the end was full of students scurrying about in groups of twos and threes, while some leaned up against the walls to chat. I thought to myself, "Will some girl think I'm interesting enough to talk to?" I wondered. How could I stand out in this crowd of people I don't know? I've always been a member of the student council to meet new people, but here I knew no one I walk past. Ken's junior friend, Harry, lived down the hall on my floor of the dormitory, told me that the Associated Students of Washington State University would meet next Thursday. Maybe I could get to know some people there.

The din of conversations in the CUB was incomprehensible. I stood for a moment at the arched enteryway to the hundreds of full tables. It was a sea of happy college kids. I wondered, "What are all these people talking about?" I found an empty spot between two tables of jabbering young women. I still didn't recognize anyone. I was dressed like everyone else was, in jeans and a short sleeve shirt. No one seemed to give me a dirty look, in fact, they didn't seem to notice me at all. I got out my three-ring binder and opened it to a blank page of notebook paper. I decided to figure out if there was a pattern to the conversations that people talked about so urgently. My theory was that I would find out they were talking about school, football, politics or philosophy. I put those categories down the left-hand margin and I left the bottom half of the page open for categories of discussion I hadn't thought of.

A girl with straight long brown hair behind me was talking about what she had for breakfast this morning. Next category: Talking about Themselves. I put one mark in that category. When she finished her explanation, the redhead with glasses to her right talked about her dinner last night. Another mark. I listened to the next table and heard a curly-haired girl talking about a Calculus assignment. A point was awarded in the top category, School.

A very nicely dressed tall girl in front of me was telling her friends how she chose the shade of pink lipstick she was wearing. There were now three points for talking about themselves. Her neighbor told a story about being at the hairdresser and the guy at their table said his haircut wasn't as good as his barber back in Spokane gives him. One more vertical mark and a diagonal through the four existing marks and five of the first six conversations seemed to be people who like to listen to themselves talk.

For the next 90 minutes, I zeroed in on conversations as far away as I could hear. I made 152 marks on my paper in the following categories: 130 were in Talking

About Themselves, 10 in School, eight in Football, two in Politics, and two in the new category of Talking About Their Families. No one mentioned Vietnam or the riots in Chicago this past summer. All my fantasies of college students passionately exploring philosophy and politics evaporated and I couldn't wrap my head around what this all meant.

Ted Johnson, our diminutive Teacher's Assistant in Comp. 101, had given us the assignment of writing a persuasive essay on any topic we wanted. In my paper, I attempted to persuade readers that 18-year-olds should be allowed to vote. I had just returned from 13 months in combat and was still too young to vote or drink alcohol. It felt like I deserved to have a say in how my country operated because of my experience. Did those in the CUB yesterday have enough life experience and concern for the world around them to have a say in how our country operates? Will they be focused on other things a few years from now? Am I alone pondering the meaning of the universe and human responsibility? I felt ambivalent when I passed it in to be graded. I got a "C." At the end of the semester, only two of my classmates got "B's." No one got an "A." I got a "C" for the semester.

I was very prepared for my next class, Biology 101. I read the first two chapters and was looking forward to a lively discussion of the variables presented. The author of the textbook, Nathan King, was the professor. I walked into the auditorium of 300 freshmen and took a seat. Mr. King's voice was a mumbly monotone. If you needed to sleep, his lectures would be a great sedative. He read us Chapter One word for word. Nothing was highlighted. Nothing was added. I left the hall after the hour-long lecture hoping it would be better tomorrow.

My next class was German 101. I decided to start with college entry-level German because my two years in high school German were conversational study. I choose this less intense class because my brain always took a while in the Fall to start working. This was three Falls later, I was struggling through my thickest molasses brain, yet. I made the same choice by taking College Algebra, instead of going straight into Calculus. Thank goodness I did it that way because despite doing all the homework I was struggling to get C's in German. I was getting B's in Math. Mathematics had always gotten me my best grades in high school.

I slowly began to realize that something was working differently in my brain.

In mid-October, while I was doing a two-page proof of an equation in Math, I couldn't remember the early parts of the proof. I turned back to the first page and had to redo the whole beginning to remind myself how I did the most important part. I got stumped again. I could barely keep in mind the critical part needed to solve the equation. This wasn't right. I solved this kind of problem on the fly in high school and never did the homework. I wondered if this thinking problem had something to do with me being in combat. I didn't have a clue what it was, yet.

The next morning I went to the payphone in the lobby on the first floor. On the government pages, I found a phone number for the Veterans Administration Medical Center. After waiting on hold for 15 minutes, a male operator asked me who I wanted to talk to. I explained that something was wrong with how my brain was working.

He said, "You will have to come to the hospital in Spokane and they will only admit you to the psychiatric floor to get checked out if you are willing to get a shot of antipsychotic medication like Thorizen." I thanked him and hung up. No way was I taking that medicine that I knew makes you a drooling zombie.

I can't blame the doctors and nurses. Veterans like me will be calling them for the next 12 years, complaining about flashbacks, strange thinking problems, uncontrollable crying, and suicidal thoughts before they even have a diagnosable condition to treat. In 1980, Post-Traumatic Stress Disorder was included in the Diagnostic and Statistical Manual of Mental Disorders for the first time. Vietnam veterans were already establishing storefront counseling centers in our country's major cities to assist fellow war veterans. The counselors were initially volunteers. Many of the women counselors had been nurses in combat hospitals. I have been a veteran readjustment counselor since 1986 and have met some of these caring, talented people. These volunteers used Rap Group therapy as the main focus of treatment. I never heard of Rap Groups or these volunteer counseling centers until a decade later. Maybe if I had come back to Seattle instead of podunk Port Angeles, someone might have steered me to their door.

18 years later, in 1986, the Seattle Vet Center asked me to apply for a contract with the Veterans Administration to provide readjustment counseling for combat veterans and their families. From 1979 to October 1, 1986, I had done thousands of hours of volunteer work with veterans on the North Olympic Peninsula. My probation officer had given me a Disabled American Veterans (DAV) pamphlet about the Vet Center program and the value of Rap Group therapy. Because of that information, and my conversations with him, I started organizing Vietnam Veteran Rap Groups in March 1980. I got the word out to the community by posting handmade 8 ½ by 11 flyers. I pedaled around town on my bike because my driver's license was suspended and put the posters up in bars, restaurants, laundromats, gyms, grocery stores, and around the college campus. My therapist at the time agreed to co-facilitate the groups with me and said we could hold them at his space in downtown Port Angeles.

By that time I had a BA degree in counseling and had worked eight-month in 1977 as a CETA supervisor of economically deprived youth. I gave talks at civic organizations such as the Rotary Club, the Elks, Peninsula College, and churches to tell people that this group met every Wednesday evening. The group slowly grew over the next seven years.

From 1977 to 1986, I was a member of Laborers Local #252, but my back was getting stiffer and stiffer each year due to injuries sustained in Vietnam. Each spring, it became more difficult to wash my face at the sink because I couldn't bend over until I had worked for a few weeks and my spine had loosened up. My back was so bad that I had to wash my face in the kitchen's taller sink in March of 1985, and I knew I needed a new job, but I did the summer of construction work anyway. In September of 1985, I applied for a position as a nighttime caseworker for Child Protection Services for the State of Washington and was hired on the spot. I felt good about assisting troubled children in after-hours crises and the agency appreciated my efforts. Throughout my time in construction and working for the state, I continued to do volunteer work with veterans.

I was thrilled when the VA contacted me. My first office was in the Lower Elwha Tribal Center for $200 rent per month. My caseload filled up within a few months and the community knew me as the combat veteran counselor. It quickly became apparent to me, as the literature supported, that survivors of adult trauma who also had troubled childhoods were more likely to have mental health problems. My clients repeatedly told me that they could hear the punitive internal voices of their parents criticizing their behavior, even though they were now in their 30s and 40s. The shame these men and women felt for how they dealt with the random chaotic violence of combat was like a megaphone inside them reinforcing the internal voice that they were no good. By helping them be realistic about the power they had and didn't have in their youth and combat, they could begin a second chance at healthy development. Short-term therapy was at least a year of weekly work. Now, 32 years later and counting, I have helped over 1000 Vietnam combat veterans feel more connected to their worlds.

Back at WSU, 6 months removed from Vietnam, I walked alone over to the campus, like every day so far. My roommate was engaged to a girl our age who lived in a sorority house where he spent every night. I was the only guy on my floor with a room to himself. I got to play Pinochle and Cribbage with some of the guys on my floor, but mostly I kept to myself studying or reading. One or two evenings a week I rolled up a towel and blocked the crack at the bottom of the door so I could smoke some of the low-grade marijuana I brought from Port Angeles. It was hard to tell if I even got high because I am so anxious about getting caught. I blew my exhales out the open window, having no idea if any of these guys knew anything about pot. They seemed more naive than I was.

In the lobby on the bulletin board, there was a notice and signup sheet for the annual two dormitory Bridge Tournament. How exciting! Only one guy on my floor played, but I had taught three of the Juniors and a couple of Freshmen how to play. Over the next couple of weeks, I organized games most evenings. I signed up on the board with Peter Overmeyer, the junior who knew how to play.

Every day I checked the board. On the morning of the tournament, Peter and I were still the only names on the board. What a disappointment. Was I a dinosaur? College and bridge seemed synonymous to me. I was told by Ken and Steve, Juniors from Room 1031, that for the last two years, the tournament had been a raucous affair. Their freshman year the tournament had been the talk of our dorm floor and in the cafeteria. Would I have survived freshman year at 18, if I had been here? Playing bridge all the time might have done me in as a grab-assed game-playing kid.

Josh and his fiance, Grace, stopped by our room later in the day the tournament was supposed to happen with their pet skunk. Although its scent glands were removed, its body odor was pure skunk. The couple wanted to leave it with me while they went on a weekend camping trip before the weather got bad. I thought, "How bad can it be?" and said, "Sure." The little critter got more active as the evening wore on. I know from childhood experiences with neighborhood dogs that animals can sense when you're afraid. The skunk, Henrietta, seemed agitated by my preoccupation with being afraid of her. When I tried to sleep I started thinking of her biting my toes. I couldn't stop thinking about it and got more afraid. She scurried around the floor more frantically. I knew I had to quit feeling afraid, but I couldn't stop imagining being bit. Finally, at 3:00 a.m., I managed to get Henrietta in Josh's open closet, which I barricaded closed with our suitcases and some boxes of books and plugged the final hole with Josh's bowling ball bag that the skunk cannot push out of its way.

Although she quit shuffling after an hour, I spent the night awake worrying that she would work her way free. It didn't work to use the mental manipulation I figured out trying to sleep at my folks' house this summer, where I would focus on something uninteresting until my mind wandered. When this works it feels like I have hoodwinked myself to sleep. But no such luck that night. At 6:30 a.m., I grabbed all my supplies, went to the dormitory cafeteria, then to the campus for the day, and stayed gone all day. Upon returning in the evening the only thing left of the skunk was the smell. I felt unimportant, unappreciated, and taken advantage of.

Chapter Twenty-Seven
I Am Alone

"By 1971, 58 percent of Americans had concluded that the war in Vietnam was not just a mistake, but immoral"
                                    Christian G. Appy, 2015.

I trudge through the compact sand to our tent, deposit my gear on the floor and inject my filthy self into the nice clean Marines at the chow hall. My sense of superiority is palatable. I have no idea if they pay any attention to me. I know the other field Marines that are already here can sense what I have been through. The REMFs couldn't possibly have a clue. This is the solidification of my feeling that I am different from everyone around me. I'm surrounded by a group of guys who have all had varying degrees of combat, but nothing like my last three weeks or the entire nine months. The vicious edge I use in combat is sharpened with a judgmental attitude. I don't have to connect. I don't need comradery, even though some of them are brothers-in-arms.

Despite feeling separated, that afternoon I find a poker game. There is a rumor about a Float Phase. I have heard the rumor a couple of times over the last few months. It sounds like the type of duty similar to a Caribbean or Mediterranean Cruise that a few lucky guys got assigned to in training. If it is true, I believe we will cruise around the South Pacific, periodically stopping at ports of call and getting Liberty (time off duty).

After a lazy morning, where I just got to chow on time, I carefully spread out and clean all my gear. The mortar and baseplate have got sand in all the non-moving nooks and crannies. The laundry goes out at 10 a.m. The office pogue who picks it up says he has been ordered to have our stuff back by 2:00 p.m. We must be heading out again. I decide it is counter-productive to wash the grime off my body.

The rear feels foreign to me. No wind is blowing. High clouds and overcast obscure the sun. Everything is dull green, gray or light tan. At the PX, I make my biggest haul yet of comic books, six. I decide to save five of them to read next time we are back so I can find a card game. But I can't resist catching up with The Fantastic Four, who are meeting the Silver Surfer, the character who really grabs my interest. I am a kid half my age for 15 minutes.

There is an Acey/Deucey game going on at one of the second platoon tents. With the cots moved out of the way, six guys sit in a circle on their butts on the plywood floor. There is a small pile of NPC in the middle. As soon as someone wins the whole pot, I throw in my two bucks. The guy to my right gets a King/Three and bets and wins $4 when he is dealt a six, leaving $10 in the pot. I get a Queen/Two, bet the pot of $10, and get a Nine. We all ante $2 again. The game breaks up two hours later with me $30 ahead.

Back at the hooch, the laundry has been returned. I pack up, as we get the word that we will be allowed into dinner early, so we can head out in the late afternoon. It is a silent meal. I am beyond shocked that we're headed to the bush. Numb and robotic, we do our duty. The same attitude prevails as we move out through the perimeter wire two hours before dusk.

The first four miles of our journey are uneventful. The pointman summons the engineer, just as the first signs of darkness appear. Mortars are positioned near the front of the double-columns. I'm not sure what kind of booby trap they clear because they don't blow anything up. It could have been a tripwire to a poison-spiked branch stretched back. We move on after 15 minutes. The booby trap informs us that the enemy is active in this area. As we begin to dig in for the night. The full moon illuminates the thick clouds, making them appear brighter than pitch black. A sniper fires three quick carbine bullets at us. As the grunts attack him, we fire four HE rounds at him. To be honest, we all direct our firepower at an area he fled from the moment his third bullet went out. As the rain begins to fall, dinner and standing guard become more difficult. A poncho liner, a new type of blanket, was given to us in the rear. It's camouflaged, lighter than my wool half blanket, and very warm. If it doesn't rain tomorrow, it will dry quickly because it is synthetic.

I'm lying on the berm of the mortar pit on perimeter the first watch, and the rain soaks everything around me for an hour. As I crawl under my tent, the dry poncho liner keeps me warm for the rest of the night. Two days later, high, thin overcast greets us in the morning. No sky is visible but it is a relief to be out from under the constant heavy clouds. The day without rain yesterday has allowed everything to dry. My last meal is Beef Stew. As I light my heat tab, three AK-47 rounds on automatic fire whiz passed us. I eat the dirt. From the sound, I can determine the direction of the shooter. I roll into the pit and jam the bipod legs straight in the enemy's direction. Joe drops an HE round in the tube. We fire 800 meters. The grunts, who saw the muzzle flashes, radio in to have us drop 200 meters and fire-for-effect. Only three shots from the enemy and we wasted a massive barrage of small arms into the dirt and trees that the enemy had deserted. There is a feeling that we act like big dumb bullies against a karate expert. We bluster, and they taunt. They taunt, and we bluster. Nine months of this dance, so far. My constant terror of close-quarters fighting gives way to a desire to hurt the enemy within arms reach.

We patrol in the late morning. Slight breezes flit and die. For the first time in weeks, I see blue sky. The wind picks up from nothing to its usual, which today is carrying heavy clouds. The wind stiffens, and the clouds move on. I hear Amtracs in the distance and we set up for resupply with a hasty perimeter. When we are packed up, we climb on top of the Traks and ride for 30 minutes. The Traks drop us off and head home. We move another three miles and dig in for the night.

It is overcast, as dark approaches. The dark lightens an hour later as the moon must be above the clouds. The wind still gusts. Heavy clouds obscure the moon, it is warm though. During first watch, it rains for an hour, and the wind blows it into my poncho tent while I try to sleep. It might have been better to sleep wrapped up in the poncho, rather than erecting a tent. With the arrival of the first edge of dawn, it is almost cold. Last watch has been heavily overcast.

The bright glow in the east, helps me see that the bushes are bushes. There hasn't been any wind for my whole watch. I keep perfectly quiet. Eminent danger pervades the cathedral feeling in the subdued light's growing magnificence. I am alone, as I survey my fields of fire, which overlap with Greg on the right and a grunt from the third platoon on the left. Below the high, thick overcast, everyone, except us on last watch, misses the beautiful sunrise. Now to the un-beautiful can of Beans and Franks. I found a handful of wild onions beside a hooch in a village we passed through yesterday and put them in my beans. I still don't like the taste of beans, but it was nice to have a vegetable. I'm guessing we will wait here for resupply. No orders have been given but no one hustles around in the CP group. That is good because I want time to clean my mortar and 45.

It is seldom that the morning allows us to wake up slowly. At any time, our survival may depend on the smooth functioning of our weapons, so it is nice to assure they function well. I am filthy again, so the flies pay almost no attention to me, nor do I to them. We have walked 10-12 miles every day for the last five days. The memory of the battle three days ago sticks with me. I hope resupply comes in by chopper so we get air support from the Hueys, but I hear the dull clang of metal far off in the distance. The Amtraks will lumber in here soon. Every Vietnamese for miles will know where we are.

The front of our line is hit by AK-47 and carbine fire. We move rapidly toward them, and, spread into assault formation as we go. This is an organic reaction that we know will be necessary to quell this amount of firepower. Most of Lima Company have several months of combat experience. We are down to 82 guys total, as no news guys have been added to us for a month. As the grunts engage Charlie, I lob three quick HE rounds, then pick up the gun and catch up with the grunts.

When we get to the area the enemy was in, we find nothing. The second platoon is in a firefight two kilometers to the east of us. The thump and then five seconds later single explosion lets me know Del is sighting in. Everything goes quiet over there. Then we walk another five miles to a sandy area to set up for the night.

My wake-up call is a carbine round that buzzes into a thicket behind me. The people on watch send out hundreds of bullets in response. The captain yells "Cease Fire" before we dropped a round in the tube. The whole ordeal is over in seconds. A quick bullet, or three, shot at us at dusk or dawn is the most common action we get. They harass us and disappear using the cover of darkness and the familiarity of the terrain. As my adrenaline flows, there is no chance to go back to sleep, but we curl back into the warmth of our sleeping situations for the last few minutes of nighttime.

We rush around as quickly as we can, in hopes to return to the relative safety of scanning in silence. Then, while the fully equipped second platoon heads north, out to our right, the rest of us strap on our packs. We take off west in a double-column formation. "Engineer up," I hear as we approach a tree line. Joe, Greg, and Cowboy, my ammo humpers and I, stay between the first and third platoons. From the CP group, the engineer works his way passed us. A half-hour later, the engineer yells, "Fire in the hole." A large explosion indicates that this was an anti-tank mine, similar to the one that killed Mo.

Anger's razor-sharp edge begs for an outlet. This entire country has irritated me. Two years after leaving Vietnam, the same rage will be directed at our politicians and businessmen who profit from the lives of 19-year-old boys and girls who work over here. I am grateful to have moved out in search of a way to release the venom within me. I'm constantly scanning, and wish I could set the gun and drop a round on someone's head, but there is no such opportunity.

Mid-afternoon we spread out into an assault sweep. I know we are attempting to roust any enemy and force them to run into the second platoon. A ChiCom hand grenade explodes in front of us with a small dull boom. Its irregular shrapnel flies through the air around me making weird sounds. The corpsman patches up Brown, one of the captain's radio operators, who had a nail embedded in his shoulder. We move on, then as we crest a hill, we halt for an hour. Heavy US artillery sails loudly over our heads from the battalion area. The barrage hits a quarter-mile away from us, softening the area we are going to assault. The second platoon must be down in the valley on the other side of the hill we are on.

We can see a mile-wide area with sandy hills plus patches of dense brush and trees. The second platoon has the same view we do of the foothill on the other side of the valley. The company radioman says the grunts see five people running away from us. The second platoon fires down from the rise on their side of the valley. We double-time towards the running enemy, then stop and I set up the mortar and fire a spotter round. The first platoon radios back to drop our rounds 100 meters further and we shoot six rounds at the running soldiers. When we set up for the night, Johnson, from the second platoon tells me that my mortar rounds got one of the VCs. Kill number six.

The rain has poured down for my entire second watch of our three-man rotation. Two hours later, I roll off my rubber whore, wrap my poncho liner around me, and hunch over my makeshift stove. I'm glad I saved a packet of cocoa. The engineer hands me a one-inch ball of C-4 explosive. I cut it in half and light it in my stove, place my canteen cup on the lit stove, and in 30 seconds I have boiling water. The can of Chicken and Noodles is placed on the stove just as the C-4's flame begins to fade. After we eat, the entire company departs.

We travel through gully after gully that each have dense foliage between bushy rolling hills. As I am crossing a shallow ditch in the tenth valley of the day, we are attacked from close by to the right. Biting the dirt on the bank of the ditch, I can sense no place to set up my mortar. The enemy fire is heavy, and it keeps us pinned down. Two of our battalion's artillery rounds whistle in and explode, to no effect on the enemy fire. The grunts must have radioed an adjustment, as the artillery fires six volleys of two rounds each, and the enemy goes quiet. We quickly form into an online assault. I am three people to the left of the guy carrying a flame thrower. When we are a hundred meters up the side of the hill, we receive fire again. Our assault continues behind our wall of bullets. The muzzle flashes of the enemy are coming from a thick tree line just a stone's throw in front of me. I hear the click of ignition and quiet hiss of the lit flame thrower. Sudden heat and a low rolling roar accompany the pointed drippy flame flowing over the enemy position. The flame thrower gunner moves the flame side to side as we continue to move forward. "Click" and the flame dies out. As we pass through the dying flames, we are running, expecting to find our attackers trying to run away. Instead, we find nothing.

While we are eating breakfast the next day, the clouds roll in and drop rain. A light breeze keeps the clouds moving. An hour later, we walk quickly in a double column, only stopping to clear two booby traps. The sound of a tank can be heard in the distance and we set up a fighting perimeter. The tank that arrives is a flame-throwing tank, and it brings us food, ammunition, and water. When everything has been packed away and the garbage has been strapped back onto the tank, we proceed in assault formation. The tank is to my right.

Three hours later, we pass through a village with no Vietnamese around. It is strange because the village is clearly lived in. We are a couple of hundred meters past the village when we are fired at from there. The tank does a quick pivot. Its right track moves forward, while the left goes backward, tearing up the dry rice paddy in the process until its barrel is pointing at the village. We get up from our prone positions. As we move across the dry paddy in front of the village the grunts pepper it with rifle fire. Just short of the village, I feel intense heat as a fire stream of Napalm flows into the village. There is ten times as big a fire spout as the handheld device, but not even close to the size of Napalm bombs from the jets. The turret traverses the whole village, as we watch for the enemy to run.

Nothing occurs. We search the hooches and the surrounding area thoroughly. Finally, we come across two tunnel entrances. Tunnel rats descend into each. Just prior one of the "rats" shambling out, two 45 rounds can be heard. The engineer rigs two blocks of C-4 with blasting caps and long primer chords, as the other rat gets out of his tunnel. Everyone gets to cover and watches for the enemy, two large thumps collapse sections of the village. The grunts dig out the ends, revealing tunnels on both sides. Two VC bodies are being extracted from the tunnel closest to me. They resemble wet noodles. Every hooch in that village is destroyed by the fire. The tank destroys much of the land, including gardens, wells, and ditches.

Pre-dawn is split by incoming rifle fire in the light rain. We pop an illumination round and the area around us brightens. The enemy keeps sporadically shooting as the parachuted candle slowly drifts down. I see two muzzle flashes a block away and 100 feet apart and drop a mortar round on each. The grunts keep pumping lead into Charlie, as I shoot another illumination round. It is again much brighter than a full moon. There is an eerie lack of color. Two Marines, Harold Douglas and Ted Simmons, from the third platoon, are wounded.

The enemy fire ceased ten minutes ago and the third platoon gets on their combat gear without packs. They start a search-and-destroy sweep. We get sighted in with the mortar on the area the enemy was in. When the third platoon surrounds the area and we pop an illumination over them. M16 fire tells us an enemy has tried to run. An hour later, in full daylight, the Marines return. George McGovern and Harry Metcalf, holding one leg each, are dragging a dead VC along the sandy ground.

Resupply/medevac comes in on a CH-34, as a Huey patrols under heavy clouds. The earlier rain keeps the sand and dust from blowing around with the chopper's wind. After the choppers leave, everything is quiet, except for occasional light breezes until midmorning when strong gusts of wind whip around.

After we eat, we break camp, pack up and head out. We probably have at least two more days in the bush, as clarified by the amount of food we carry. The long day's trek through the brush, rice paddies, sandy hills, tree lines, and creeks is halted seven times. Twice the engineers blow booby traps. We move at a steady pace, except for the pauses. We are not rushing, but cover 15 miles before dusk announces the end of this day's journey. Most of the day I am very alert inside the bubble of the music in my head from my portable radio. The wind has stayed all day and into the night. I am in my poncho on first watch, when it rains in earnest.

Rain, rain, rain. The wind ebbs and flows all morning. At its peak, the rain is blown into everything. During the calm, the slight breezes keep the temperature cool. Everything has gotten soggy.

I am hunched over my stove at 7:00 a.m. My poncho liner is snapped inside my poncho and I am "snug as a bug in a rug." The real world of the experienced combat soldier is to find new comfort in a process I may be able to use again. At 8:00 the heavy clouds stop dropping rain. We fill in our muddy holes, pack up, and move out. There are brief periods of rain and wind, so I'm thankful I decided to walk with my poncho covering me with the liner in it. With the hood of the poncho on, I scan for the enemy with a whole-body turn. My field of vision is cut in half. The rain pauses again. Over the next hour, the wind slows down. The temperature remains in the low 70's.

We trudge a couple more miles and stop. The rain and wind build again. The engineer blows a booby trap up ahead of me, then we slog on through the next two hours of rain with the wind slowly easing off to a breeze by mid-afternoon. We stop in a grassy area for night perimeter. At dusk, cooking the last meal we are carrying, the air is still warm and I dry out in the brisk wind. After full dark, we pop an illumination round, which is ignited above the clouds. The candle power lights up the tops of the low heavy clouds. Our world turns into muted daylight, then it brightens as the light parachutes down under the clouds. No enemy makes themselves known.

Curled up in my poncho, I am quite warm and fall asleep as the rain starts again. The whole night stays warm with rain coming and going. I have last watch. It is not raining. As the first hints of morning arrive, I have an intense desire to shoot someone. Once a night on watch, is the only time I have a rifle in my hands. After months of spitting fire to feel safe, I now only get to feel that immediate protection when I am not carrying the mortar. If needed, Greg's M-16 and ammunition will produce a powerful wall in front of me. I can imagine placing that wall between me and the enemy. I have a desire to reach through that wall and have a bullet strike someone who is trying to put a bullet in me.

When we wake up at sunup to a warm morning, the wind is gently blowing. Two CH-46s fly into our Landing Zone (LZ) to take us home an hour after sunrise. Back in the rear, the wet world looks much like it had when dry. Different for us, here everything that could get wet is undercover. We are a bunch of soaked rats with wet gear. I head over to battalion supply and beg a case of C-Rations, as the chow hall is closed until supper. The corporal who gives me the rations tells me there is a rumor we have been assigned to the Float Phase.

With our gear spread out on the tent floor, we use our stoves on the plywood floor. The sides of the tent are rolled down. I never once worried about the fumes of 12 heat tabs or starting the floor on fire. Sitting on my cot to cook is much nicer than being in the mud. After we eat, big farmer Del goes over to battalion supply and gets another box of C-Rats. Shortly before noon, I almost feel full. With my gear all hung up or spread out on or around my cot, I walk over to the shower. Three guys are waiting. I don't care. I just want the "nothing to do" of standing in line. The gas fire is blazing in the metal unit hanging down into the water of the 55-gallon barrel. I hand a five-gallon water can to a guy on the ladder. He gives it to another guy on the platform, who pours it in. It takes three cans to top off the barrel.

For the second time in my tour, the club has unlimited beer. The beer is in a 30-gallon garbage can full of ice. None of my cronies are drinking at 3:00 p.m. I drink seven beers, then head over to chow and stand in line until it opens at 4:30 p.m.. As soon as I finish eating, I hustle back to the unbelievable Godsend of unlimited beer to dull the edges of my blinding hatred. The cover to the garbage can is three, two-foot-long 2X8s. I plop my butt on the top of the can, as I quickly drink my first beer and do the solitary business of getting enough alcohol in my system to make my insides feel different. I want easy access to the beer and I want the REMFs to feel a little intimidated about opening the top of the garbage can. I get the last beer out of the garbage can at 8:00 p.m. I have had ten beers and go search for a Bid Whist game. I get a heartily welcome into the game by the group of African American players. I play pretty well and have a gift of gab almost like the 'me' from high school.

Chapter Twenty-Eight
After Vietnam
Tom Hayden

In November 1969, while Marjorie and I attended the Green River Community College, my creative writing teacher, John Harris, got Tom Hayden to speak to the class about the Vietnam War. John was smiling when he said, "I met Tom in March of 1965 when he was doing a teach-in on the Ann Arbor campus of the University of Michigan. His clear picture of the facts helped me understand what was really happening over there." At the time, Tom Hayden had been in the news for over a year for being arrested at the Chicago Democratic National Convention in the summer of 1968. We all knew he was one of the Chicago 7 along with Abbie Hoffman, Jerry Rubin, and others. Both he and the popular folk singer Joan Baez had been visible participants in anti-war protests for several years.

There were only 18 students enrolled in the class, but when Tom Hayden came to speak, every square inch of our classroom was filled. My assigned seat was buried in the middle of the crowd, but I had a great view of Tom standing up front. Marjorie was using my neighbor's seat who had told me he wouldn't be attending. The room was jam-packed with older, more radical-looking people standing around the edges and between the rows of desks. Tom was dressed in a flannel shirt, jeans, and a sports coat with leather patches on its elbows. He reminded me of a more refined Bob Dylan.

John cleared his throat and drew everyone's attention to him. "We are fortunate today to have one of our nations leading historians to explain how and why the USA became involved in the Vietnam War. Since the early 1960s, Tom has been teaching about the United States' involvement in Southeast Asia in communities and on college campuses. So, without further ado, here's Tom."

I had a lot of misconceptions about the economic reasons for our involvement in the war. I still believed that communists from China or Russia would use Vietnam as a base of operations to take over Laos and Cambodia. Thailand would then be the next domino to fall. According to news reports, anti-war protesters referred to the war as a capitalistic endeavor waged on the backs of teenagers who had no idea how or why they were being used. I was aware that almost all of the soldiers I slogged around with in the Vietnam jungle were under the age of 20. My classmates at Green River were young men and women, or boys and girls, who had just moved away from their parents. Despite the fact that I was the only person enrolled in this class who was over the age of 21 and married, our discussions had been lively throughout the quarter. I had been discovering that these young people knew as much, or more than I did about the world.

Tom started with the events at the end of WWII when the US government had a fateful choice between trying to coexist with Vietnam's communist-led nationalist front (the Vietminh led by Ho Chi Minh) or intervening with weapons and funds to restore white French colonial rule. In 1945 our operatives there advised cooperating with the popular Vietminh forces. The main thrust of the Vietminh was to encourage non-intervention from foreign colonial efforts. Despite the advice of our operatives in Vietnam, our government chose to finance France.

The United States' funding and weaponry were not enough to keep the nationalist movement from defeating the French military at Dienbienphu in 1954. France's government negotiated a political settlement at Geneva in 1955, including French troop withdrawals, a temporary partition of the country at the 17th parallel, and a plan that two years later there would be nationwide elections and reunification.

The US government intervened to prevent the elections and reunification of the country, and at our advise, South Vietnam adopted a permanent partition of Vietnam. Thereafter, Tom explained, the US called the Vietminh's actions toward reunification, "Aggression from the North," and justified our continued effort to block that unification by claiming that foreign powers were supplying the war machine of the North. This was a fabricated story that flew in the face of the facts. By 1962 the southern faction of the Vietminh was called the Vietcong. As I.F. Stone reported at the time, "80% of the southern Vietcong's weapons were captured from the US or Saigon militaries, and the Pentagon's own charts showed only 179 communist-made weapons were found among 15,100 weapons captured by Saigon between 1962-1964." This was just prior to the start of official involvement of the United Satates in Vietnam in 1965.

Tom continued by talking about the Americans who were making money off the war. The Michelin rubber plantation was in a Vietcong-held territory of 31,000 acres or fifty square miles of the limited dry land around Saigon. In fact, he told us that US forces were obliged to compensate Michelin for the damage they caused to the rubber trees. Michelin had many money-making tire plants in the US. More infuriating for me to learn was that the family of Lady Bird Johnson, the First Lady, owned and greatly profited from their company that made combat helicopters. Tom gave another example of the insane amount of money made by the company that produced our military shoelaces. He said, "We didn't have enough time today to go into fortunes derived from the manufacturing of weapons and munitions."

In his final statement in his heavy New England accent, he said, "One of our country's major concerns was maintaining our access to tungsten." The US wanted to keep access to this resource. We got most of ours from Canada, but we wanted Vietnam's source to not be solely dependent on our neighbor. It is an exceptionally strong metal used to increase the hardness and strength of steel and lamp filaments. China produces 80% of the world's supply. Most of the rest of the reserves are in Russia, Bolivia, Canada and Vietnam.

I was feeling like a fool as I walked out to Marjorie and my car. I had been a small-town bumpkin who thought he knew what was happening in the world. How naive. What a sucker I had been to be played by the rich people of my nation. These nuggets of information fueled the rest of my life's conversations about Vietnam and what I was doing there. I have talked with veterans who protected that Michelin Tire rubber tree plantation. Our soldiers roamed around the outer edges of the trees, but if the enemy soldiers were in amongst the valuable trees our guys were not allowed to throw hand grenades or shoot back at them because shrapnel and bullets would injure the trees.

Two obscure books helped me understand our involvement better. A novel by Morris West, *The Ambassador*, about Henry Cabot Lodge taking over in Vietnam in that job. In the book, the CIA overpowered Lodge's State Department and supported the coup in

1963 by four Catholic generals, which the largely Buddhist populace did not support. The other novel, *The Fall of Saigon,* by James Fenton, a British journalist, gave an alternative view of how the Western powers, primarily France and the United States, tried and failed to maintain control in Vietnam. I boiled reading these books. How could my government, and particularly the War Department, ignore what Lodge was advising? I felt misled and used.

Chapter Twenty-nine
Soaked to the Bone

"If the legacy of the Vietnam War is to offer any guidance, we need to complete the moral and political reckoning it awakened"
Christian G. Appy, 2015.

The morning starts with a few clouds. It gets cooler, even though the sun provides beautifully multi-hued skies. The grass is two feet tall between areas of heavy brush and trees. I almost believe Charlie isn't in this territory. All day yesterday, through last night, none of us have heard and seen any sign of enemy.

Two Amtraks roll in with resupply. Heavy overcast heralds the rise in temperature from 66° to 80° in an hour. We use the thick double walls of the Traks as part of our perimeter. Their 60 machine guns with two of our riflemen between them are a tremendous amount of firepower in a small area. Resupply goes at a slow pace, as both, we and they feel safer in each others' protection. I am ravenous and manage to secure the ham and eggs along with bread and cocoa. A meal fit for a king.

As the Amtraks return home, we begin a search-and-destroy operation at noon. The grunts poke around, moving slowly through the grass and into the thicker brush. A grunt twenty meters to my right holds his fist up to signal a halt because he has discovered something. As he carefully probes through the grass, he uncovers a punji pit by lifting a piece of woven bamboo the size of a porch mat. Natural grass grows out of the mat to camouflage it. The mat of looks like all the ground around it. The pit is a hole 12 X 14 inches wide, and 18 inches deep. There is a sharpened bamboo stake sticking straight up in the middle of the bottom and shorter ones sticking out of the sides of the hole. They are discolored with a gooey liquid on their tips. Perfect for ripping up the side of an ankle and poisoning its victim.

Two days later, I'm on last watch, with the sky bright from the hidden full moon. It's almost the same light as an artillery illumination round. There is no breeze, only heavy clouds and overcast, as sunlight takes over. We are out of food. I wonder if that means we are heading in. An hour of doing nothing is followed by word we will be picked up by helicopter. We fill in our holes and form an LZ (landing zone). Three double-propped CH-46s land with no resistance from the VC. Mortars, the CP and the first platoon cram into the birds. One at a time the birds struggle and finally get us airborne. At the battalion landing zone, we run off the birds. They take off to pick up the other 43 guys. We are too late for breakfast, so Del and I decide to head to the Marine Airwing club at MAG-16.

We do a spit and polish cleaning of our hands and face from the spigot of the Water Buffalo near the company command tent and head to the front gate.

MAG-16 base is located at the foot of Marble Mountain's east side. The base resembles our battalion area, except that some of the buildings, including the club, are made of brick. After being too young to drink in a club in the United States, this environment will become either my downfall or my salvation in the decades that follow. I am now, still, a year and a half away from reaching Washington State's legal drinking age. I had no idea that 19-year-olds in Idaho could drink, or that I would be attending college nine miles from the state line in less than a year.

Tables, chairs, couches, and a bar are available in the club. These are not folding chairs and card tables like at our club, but sturdy chairs and tables. It's 12 noon. We order a couple of beers and take a seat. There are five other guys spread across two tables. They are clearly pilots. They keep to themselves and don't appear to be impressed by us obviously being groundpounders. Wearing a badge of honor with other people who are confident in how they do their jobs without exchanging war stories was a comfortable feeling for me. I order a 25-cent Jack Daniels whisky on the rocks. Del continues to drink beer.

I drink five more whiskeys and Del has three more beers and one whiskey over the next three hours. Rain is falling as we head back five kilometers southeast to the 3/7 battalion area in time for chow. A jeep is driving south at MAG-16 gate and gives us a quick ride into our main gate. By the time we get to our tent the clouds have thinned out, and the rain stops. We both clean and hang our gear before getting a shower. This is a great time of day to have a shower because the barrel and all the five-gallon cans are warmed up to 80°.

My main duty this afternoon is getting to the PX for my comic books and cigarette supplies. In the glow of alcohol, I can feel a tiny smile in my upper cheekbones as I walk. I look hostile to everyone else. The smile contains a sense of deadliness, along with more contentment than when I am sober. I am able to treat the mess hall staff with equanimity and pleasantries. I say more words to them today than at any other time in the chow line.

Several people mention the Float Phase during breakfast at the chow hall. It still sounds a little 'pie in the sky,' so I'm not overjoyed. (Now, 51 years later, I'm sure the office pogues learned a lot more about the horrors of the Float Phase. They didn't sound excited because it wasn't going to be a South China Sea cruise.)

Igor and I head to our light pole to practice knife throwing. At ten feet, I do two flips of the knife and stick it where I want to. Afterward, I head to battalion supply. My jungle boots are completely tan, with no black leather. The canvas is frayed, ready to fall apart.

They have no boots between sizes 9 and 12. As I walk out, I notice every office pogue is wearing shining boots in perfect condition. The feeling of 'Us versus Them' gets stronger. Now all officers, career military, and REMFs are part of the danger we struggle against. I am an 'old salt' now.

I'm sitting on my cot reading Dr. Strange, when we are ordered to get to chow early. Then we mount up. With my pistol, its bullets and my mortar tube in perfect shape, two full canteens, four meals, my rubber whore, poncho liner, etc., everything but functional shoes, I will go out and control my world. This must be how the helicopter crew chiefs feel about not being able to get replacements for the parts for their choppers that are wearing out. We Old Salts make do with what we have.

We climb onto the three CH-46 helicopters that hauled the first and second platoons before us, and fly toward the mountains and south for half an hour. We disembark and run for cover, as the ground troops are returning fire at a pesky group of enemy trying to hit the chopper. Once the birds fly away, we start an assault toward Charlie's position and find no signs of them ever having been there. In a spread-out double-column, we walk until an hour past dark. We get hit three times and clear five booby traps on the way to our destination.

Last night's trip out into the field had shown us that there are a lot of enemy troops around here. In the dark of predawn, every brushy area feels like a threat. We move slowly, are highly alert, and keep as low as possible. I have the 40-pound steel tube with the 5-pound small base plate hanging off my neck, as we spread out into a search-and-destroy sweep. By mid-morning, the hushed air gives way to building winds and rising temperatures.

The first platoon breaks off to our right, west, in a double-column, as the wind gusts stronger. The rest of the company, with us mortars, moves into a double column and continues south. Like most days of patrolling for the last ten months, I am 30 feet away from the men/boys in front and back of me, and I don't say a word to anybody for the whole day.

No one talks, as we set up watches and dig our holes. Our world is to get protected, stay alert with the ever-present push-pull of wanting to be able to shoot at Charlie and not wanting them to shoot at us. Before dark, I eat my turkey loaf and the candy bar but save the cocoa for the morning. The overcast and heavy clouds lift to a few scattered high clouds.

My right eye has been closed for five minutes when our friendly neighborhood sniper rips three rounds through our perimeter. The bullets are three feet over my head, coming from the direction the first platoon headed. The heavy clouds usher in nightfall. The moon is up there somewhere making life visible. I fire three high explosive rounds where the muzzle flashes came from and the grunts give them hell. The stage has been set for our usual night of no enemy contact. The first light of morning could be a different story.

Two days and three firefights later it has rained most of the night, soaking the hard-packed dirt. As we get up to the chilly morning, there are only high scattered clouds left in the sky drifting westward. After a breakfast of the last meal in my pack, meat loaf in a B-3 unit, the thick clouds and overcast return. The cocoa and cookies do little to brighten my mood. My world is being alert to danger, with my head hunkered over my stove, I sip from the cleaned-out can that held the cookies, cocoa, and jam.

In the late afternoon, after a thorough search of a village, we set up an LZ outside of it. The choppers bring in C-rations that were boxed up in 1955. Amazingly, nothing seems wrong with them, except the crackers with my Spaghetti and Meatballs are crumbly and the Cheese Spread is hard.

It rained during first watch last night, making the ground easy to dig. Heavy clouds slowly drift in the almost motionless air. We are set up in an area of dense brush. Our perimeter holes are 20 feet apart. As we finish breakfast, heavy slow-moving fog rolls in with rainfall forcing us into ponchos. We slog out for today's movement.

The air is now tomb-like. Low visibility has us walk eight feet apart. Up and down the grass-covered hills, crossing tree-lined creeks, ducking under two-inch-thick vines, ever alert for booby traps, snipers, and ambushes, while always hoping to catch the enemy moving without them seeing us first. The fog is a blessing and a curse. They cannot see us, but we cannot see them.

The first platoon in the vanguard gets ambushed just ahead of me. They are invisible in a creek bed. I crest the low hill that leads down into the draw they went through. Up ahead, through the thick fog, I hear the pling of a grenade spoon and hit the dirt. I scan the area with my 45 pistol, and await an apparition. Where will he come from? I can't tell what the terrain is like 15 feet away from me. Finally, the grenade explodes. No Marines scream. Ak-47 fire peppers in front of us, splintering trees above the creek. I scuttle to a grassy area away from the trees, drop the base plate of the gun and send a HE round ahead of the first platoon. They can't help me adjust my fire, although they are shooting in the direction of the incoming bullets, they can't see the muzzle flashes or my exploding rounds.

As quickly as it started, the ghostly fire-fight disappears into the fog. What just happened? No one is screaming. As we mount up again and spread out, I drift in and out of being completely alone or barely able to see Greg in front of me or Joe behind me. The rain stops. The breeze dies completely by the time I finally cross the creek where the first platoon was ambushed.

We walk for another hour and the wind picks up and blows the fog away. We are spread out to reduce the attractiveness of any particular part of our line. In an open area between two tree lines, we set up a perimeter along a dirt road. The same convoy that carried us out here comes to pick us up two hours later.

When we get back to the battalion, we head straight to chow. I hear several conversations about the Float Phase. It sounds like it is going to happen. But, tonight is just another night in the rear. Clean gear, hang everything to dry, go watch a movie and find a poker game. Harwell cleans me out of all my $100 by 2:00 a.m., and I head to bed.

The battalion area is shrouded with thick mist in the foggy, placid morning. Mules move around doing the business of the office pouges. As I walk toward the chow tent, I hear "Stick." Cowboy catches up with me and says, "I heard for sure we are going on the Float Phase." More conversations in the mess tent are about what it means. I have my image of the first time I heard the idea with almost no alterations, a pleasure cruise.

My mind sees us on ships sailing from India to Hawaii, stopping at ports of call for liberty, taking showers every day, wearing clean clothes and eating hot food. When I get back to our tent, I hunker in with my comic books and reread this month's supply. These superheroes' lives are dedicated to fighting the evil that regular citizens can't handle. The sense of invincibility with which I have learned to walk around in this strange country feels similar to them. I will conquer any evil before it can get me or my fellows. Much like my super hero friends, I barely seem to make contact with the guys I work with. When we are in the line of fire, the equally invincible Marines and I have intuitive connections to route out the enemy with bullets and then we hold our perimeter from intrusions. This was never talked about in my combat tour, but as time moves forward more and more, moments of perfect coordination become evident. I ignore our chicken-shit leaders and the pouges.

As if orchestrated to highlight the building rumors about the float phase, the wind picks up at about 10:00 a.m. The fog is gone. The temperature starts its slow climb. At noon, the air goes motionless and I head to the shower. I am the third guy in line and the five-gallon cans are warmer than they were in the nighttime. At its coldest, the water is 73°. I head back to my tent and the wind gets serious. I think it is Bid Whist time, so I go over to Kilo Company and get invited into the game. My skills are on par with these guys now and it is a challenging game that Harry Carpenter and I win. The game breaks up and I walk by the second platoon's tents as the wind has faded away. I stop and go into one of the tents and watch a poker game.

The tent door opens and the company clerk's head pokes in the door following the wind and announces, "We are officially not going on the Float Phase."

The wind slowly peters out as the day wears on. Dinner is Shit-on-a-Shingle for the tenth time since February. The "Shit" is gravy made with some kind of lunch meat in it, poured over the hard toast. The movie is Madame X again, so I head back to the mortar tent and settle myself into my short cot to prepare for my last 120 days of the same old shit.

The fog lifts as I walk to chow for breakfast. Somewhat crestfallen about the loss of the dream of the Float Phase, the food is even duller than usual. There is no chance to go to China Beach today because we will probably be sent out. Back at the tent, I write a letter to my Mom for her birthday, November 30th and tell her about the weather. Then I pin my disappointment to Marjorie, filled with a million swear words about being stuck in this hellhole for another four months.

Mid-morning, the wind picks up and ushers in the rain. I have got nothing else to do. There is a commotion outside, as I sit on my cot with my back against the tent support. Our tent door is wide open and I walk down the two steps to the sand to see what's going on. Carl, from Alabama who got to Lima Company three days after I did, comes runs over to me and says, "Stick, we are going on the Float Phase."

Bud comes from the company office and tells us, "Pack up our gear, the trucks will be around to haul the gear away in a few hours." It is the closest thing I have seen to a jubilant atmosphere. I'm in disbelief, like the rest of the 19-year-old boys, it seems like we're off to a holiday.

The tents seem naked with no packs, rifles, mortars, flax gear, helmets or cartridge belts around. After I eat an early dinner, I find a nickel, dime and quarter poker game. Harwell didn't get my small bills and change last night in our game or Tonk. He will be transferred to a different battalion because he only has two months left in country and everyone with less than three months isn't going with us. It takes me about an hour to win $30. At the two-dollar ante game, I play conservatively until I crack over $100, then I play my usual, proven style of folding most poor hands or raising early to set up a bluff. I have $250 a couple of hours later, enough to get me in a big game.

I walk past a row of the four tents that had housed the second and third platoons, and find a better game than I had hoped for. All the cots in one of the second platoon's tents are moved to the sides to be out of the way. Eight guys, including Harry, Dick, and Dave from Lima Company, sit cross-legged around a large pile of money. 30 guys mill around them. Even with the wind outside, cigarette smoke fills the tent. The rain pounds the roof, and drowns out the radio in the corner. The game is Acey/Deucey with a $5 ante, so every time someone clears the pot, there's $40 put in the pot from the antes. Two of the guys appear to be nearing the end of their money. Only one grunt waits to enter the fray, a tall blond guy.

Harry has a lot of money to bet from and goes for the whole pot on a Queen-Three, only to lose when he hits a deuce. There is now $80 in the pot. Nobody bets on the next six flops of two cards in front of players. A cigar smoker with $10 in front of him is dealt a King-Deuce. Several bystanders join in on the wager, and I chip in $10. We bet the pot as a group. An Ace is dealt, and the cigar smoker is replaced by the blond. The pot is now worth $160. Small bets are won and lost until a Kilo company solier with several hundred dollars in front of him gets an Ace-Three, goes "pot," wins the whole thing and yells, "Fuckin' A, Man." Mike, the first platoon corpsman, bets his last five dollars.

I take my seat after the player to Doc Mike's left wins the pot with a five on a Jack-Deuce. I remain $250 ahead and bide my time by placing small bets. We decide that this pot with $280 in it will be the last pot. When it comes to me, I get a King-Five. I scratch my head for several seconds. The pot is unlikely to be returned to me again, so I bet the entire amount, despite the fact that the odds of getting a 6, 7, 8, 9, 10, or Jack are only 8 to 5. A "6" is dropped. In the Philippines, $560 was going to be a lot of money.

So ends my Mom's birthday.

Chapter Thirty
After Vietnam
Thanksgiving Dinner in Port Angeles

At Crescent Beach, Ken, Marjorie, and I were drinking beer. It was the first Thanksgiving, 1968, following being in the Vietnam War. I was craving intellectual connection after two months in the middle of farm country at Washington State University. The buzz from the beers loosened my lips, and our conversation shifted to Albert Camus and the peculiar way Americans consider what is important. Even the wealthy suffer from greed and misery as a result of Americans' preoccupation with material accumulation rather than relationships and honor.

"The struggle itself toward the heights is enough to fill a man's heart," Ken said, quoting Camus. "Imagine Sisyphus content. Success is about feeling useful, not about outdoing others by owning a more expensive car or home. The struggle against the status quo is what gives life meaning."

"I rebel; thus I exist," I quote.

My family's dinner was at 3:00, but our conversation kept going throughout the afternoon, so I didn't pay attention to the time. We were nice and toasty drunk as we sat on two big logs by our driftwood fire. The hours had flown by. We had finally run out of beer by 3:30, so after kicking sand onto the dying fire, we continued our conversation in Ken's car. With Marjorie in the middle of the big Ford's front seat, our thoughts had been swirling around our conviction that being aware of yourself can only be accomplished by reflecting on what is outside of you. "The meaning of my life has to be about the object that is me in its surroundings," I explained.

"Jean-Paul Sartre said, 'If subjectivity knows itself inside, it is dead,'" Marjorie said.

"White Americans believe we are so exceptional that we have forgotten the need to help others, and we are thus destined to feel free to act on greed and self-righteousness," Ken said. "The Bible even mentions it."

"Man looks on the outward appearance, but the Lord looks on the heart," I explained.

Eight beers seemed about right to deal with my parents. I had been at odds with them by the end of the summer two months ago. They made several comments about socially appropriate behavior, and I had a few of my own opinions. What they called 'socially appropriate' sounded more like 'keeping up with the Joneses' to me. Where was moral responsibility?.

I came in to the house wearing my field jacket, jeans, and a tee shirt, they were finishing turkey dinner. Brad wore a cardigan sweater and Chris wore a dress. Mom instructed me to wash my hands before eating. This had been my life mantra, so despite my resentment at being told what to do, I went into the small upstairs bathroom and washed the obvious beach dirt off my hands.

As I ate a plate of our traditional Thanksgiving fare, Chris, Brad, and I exchanged school-related stories. Brad and I were both enrolled in Composition 101. Marjorie Avalon, his professor, was a close friend of Marjorie's. During the summer, we went to her house and talked about philosophy and writing. I informed them that no one had received an 'A' on our first three essays at WSU.

"With 30 students in the class and me working harder and harder on each paper, I received one of the two Bs on the third one," I explained.

Chris expected to get straight "A's" this quarter if her Algebra final wasn't too difficult.

My parents did not say anything to me until I had finished my meal. "Go downstairs and put on some nicer clothes before the Thompsons arrive for dessert," my father said, almost commandingly.

My tone was harsh as I snapped back, "These clothes are just fine."

"Everyone else is clean and neat. You'll be out of place."

"Out of place according to you. What do my clothes have to do with whether I am a good person? I believe helping other people is what makes a person valuable."

"The Thompsons will feel disrespected if you have on grubby clothes," Dad said.

I yelled, as I headed for the door to leave, "I won't put up with you trying to control me with your ideas of responsibility. Instead of worrying about nice clothes and nice cars, while looking down your noses at people who care about our world, when are you people going to start paying attention to things that matter?"

I fumed as I drove away. I decided I was too riled up to get together with friends, so I drove into the foothills and remembered Camus and Sisyphus. The rock I push up the hill repeatedly was my attempts to educate my parents about their responsibilities for our country's war in Vietnam, for mistreating oppressed people, but mainly for looking down their noses at anyone different from them.

This scene kept repeating itself over the next eight years. As I learned more about the economics of the Vietnam War, I got increasingly confrontational with my parents. When my son Ben was born in 1975, they dearly loved him and wanted to spend as much time with him as they could, but invariably they would tell me how I should be parenting him and a fight would ensue.

I would say, "Your value system is what led to the Vietnam War. Can't you see it is your ignorance about things like child-raising that had you acting so irresponsibly?"

Over the first three years of Ben's life, they made fewer and fewer comments about my long hair, grubby clothes, parenting style and our marginal living environment. My siblings remember waiting and hoping that my little family of my partner, Holly, Ben's mother, her daughter, Allison, Ben, and I would come to dinner; at the same time, they were dreading the inevitable blow-up between Dad and me. I got quicker and quicker to pack up my family and head out the door at the first signs of criticism. Their arrogance butted heads with my arrogance and it was never resolved.

The world changed.

374 DMZ & Vicinity – Dong Ha

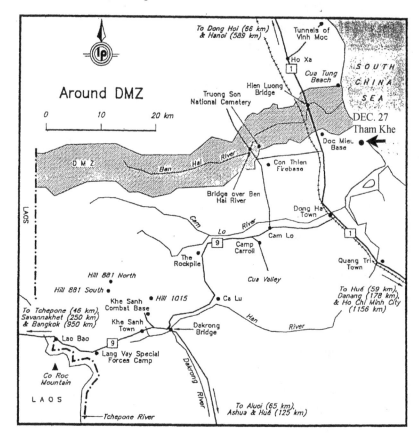

Chapter Thirty-One
Float Phase

"The past is always speaking to us, if we only listen"
Christian G. Appy, 2015.

There is a scurry of activity around the battalion area, as jeeps, mules and office pogues hustle from place to place. Gusts of wind blow around the tents with thick overcast skies. The chow line is the longest I have seen and is filled with the most noise of people talking I have heard in ten months. We walk over to the motor pool from the chow hall, as there is nothing but cots left in our tent. Looking naked with no weapons or gear, Marines pile into the 40 Six-By's.

Near the middle of the line of trucks, Lima Company climbs into five of them. 20 of our 88 company members are not present. Del and Bud are rotating to the States in the next two months, so they have been transferred, as were all the "Short-timers." We begin rolling after two hours of the usual military shambles of moving people from truck to truck for no apparent reason. I certainly feel naked leaving the gate without the protection of something that can hurl bullets at any incoming fire.

The whole remaining Lima Company fits in a four-propeller aircraft, a C-130 Troop Transport. Along the inside of the bird there are small fold-out seats with shoulder straps that we click into. The lumbering machine begins to roll toward the runway and then accelerates. As we take off, I imagine our friendly neighborhood sniper taking a few potshots at us with his little carbine. He's only two miles away from the airbase, and no one has found him yet. I may never hear from him again.

The flight becomes quiet even before we take off. We bounce around inside the gigantic flying tube. Four hours later, as we land in Manila, I can feel the increased heat even from inside the plane. Another set of trucks transport us for three hours to the Subic Bay Naval Base. The Seventh Fleet is in the harbor. We are assigned to the USS Vancouver. I feel nostalgic, as it was built in Brown's and my state, Washington.

The sleeping quarters are rows of five hammocks high attached to poles. Our five rifles are attached to a ring of clamps that sticks out from the pole at our feet. They are held by the front sights and the flash suppressors so they swing freely. I get to a top hammock and secure my rifle. We are ordered to the mess hall. Dinner is spaghetti and meatballs with french bread, salad and sautéed mixed vegetables. The dessert is ice cream with apple pie. We are told by the friendly Navy guys to stop by for snacks anytime.

The next day we get to go to the post exchange (PX) on the Navy base and I spend $125 on an Accutron Bulova watch. Our first amphibious assault training is in the afternoon when we have to climb out of an empty bay on a cargo net while in full packs and cartridge belts. I see guys struggling to get started to climb. When I try it, the robe net stretches so far that I'm flat on my back even though I reached the highest rung I could. I struggle to get a higher purchase with my hands and then pull my right foot into the next rung. My body is finally off the deck and my head is higher than my feet. The next reach has me climbing upright and fairly easily I scurry to the top and out onto the deck.

The next morning we march down the dock and load onto Landing Crafts that carry us to a beach to practice debarking through the surf. We hike into the jungle, then back to the boats, then do the whole process over three times.

After two weeks practicing amphibious assaults from Amtraks, LSTs, LSDs, and helicopters in the jungles of the Philippines, I follow Greg across the gangplank and file into the troop transport section of the USS Vancouver. The feeling of a holiday is still on us because we, and the US military command structure, have no idea how big and deadly the North Vietnamese buildup is for their coming Tet Offensive of 1968.

I climb ten feet up to the top hammock in the troop quarters. For the trip back to Vietnam the bay houses the whole, now, 120 guys of Lima Company. I picked this spot 16 days ago to be lost in the middle of the crowd, three stanchions in and on the top rack. I do not want to get picked for duty assignments or have people climbing over me at night. I am a master at staying away from duty assignments and inspections. Our rifles hang on the poles by their barrels, again. Once out to sea, you can tell how rough the seas by the degree of the swing of the rifles.

The first day and night, the slow-rolling seas have our rifles moving in ten inch arcs. It is easy to walk to the mess hall and never bump into the walls. The steps are more like ladders, which is what the Swappies call them. The breakfast is incredible. Orange juice, fried potatoes, sausage and eggs. I sit with Carl from Montgomery, AL. We have our quiet and respectful chow together. He is in the first platoon. When I finish breakfast, I notice that all of the African-American sailors are eating in the area around us. In the quiet of the afternoon, everyone is roaming the ship out of the troop area when Carl finds me on my bunk and asks to talk with me alone. He says we can't eat together anymore or he will be ostracized by the black sailors. I feel hurt but understand the dilemma he is in. From then on he and I keep our distance and the sailors accept him.

After four days at sea, Tropical Storm Ivy hit us with a vengeance. The rifles swing back and forth a couple of feet. Almost all of the Lima Company guys are puking. Most make it to the head or off the side of the ship, but our bay is building up a stench from the ones who spew in our berth. I am surprised that my stomach feels calm and I keep eating all the meals. On the third day of the typhoon, I go out on the bow of the ship. I can see the keel come out of the water when the 70-foot bow of the USS Vancouver is in the trough of the waves. As we slam into the next wave, the warm saltwater drenches me. After 15 minutes of this rough ride, my stomach begins to boil, so I head back to midships and puke over the rail.

The next day we debark in helicopters to the solid land of Vietnam. The sand is soaked from last night's rain. The cacophony of warfare sounds from near and far can be heard, but they are more numerous and intense than any I'm used to. We mount up shortly after the first light. It looks like the heavy cloud cover is going to drop rain at any time. I know from the heavy combat sounds that today is not going to be like the last 10 months, but it has some of the same feel, except that I am carrying a radio, in my new role of Weapons platoon radio operator with no one to report to. I am the only person in Lima Company with both a pistol and a rifle.

As we walk in a double-column across the sand, rice paddies, bushy hills and tangled creek valleys, I see a thing I never saw down around Da Nang. Two long lines of hundreds of villagers head south. This has been declared a free-fire zone, so anyone who is not known to be "friendly" will be shot on sight once the villagers have evacuatated. Rather than being bored at the tedium of my same pattern of walking, I am keyed up. There is a sure knowledge that we are invading enemy territory. I scan smoothly and irregular depending on the terrain with my M-16.

We walk into an abandoned village at noon, when firefights start up a half-mile to our right. I cautiously search inside a pagoda. Although its architecture is Asian, the artifacts inside are a mix of Christian and Buddhist. Bookshelves line the two sides leading to an altar that is presided over by a four foot tall statue of Christ carved out of stone with his hands outstretched in welcome. The workmanship is incredible. A peaceful look is upon his Caucasian features with long hair. As I walk back out into the war, my desire for that calmness erodes with each step and the lure of viciousness has fully returned as I look into the next hooch.

I walk at a lower crouch with my radio on the battalion net. India, Kilo, and Mike report resistance to their movements. They are far enough away that there is no expectation of hearing screams, but I know the enemy fire has to be creating casualties among the Marines by the amount of firing I hear on my radio. The rain starts amid these firefights and muffles much of the sounds. I hear a whistling scream overhead and dive for cover. Enemy artillery from above the DMZ rips over our heads. The high-pitched whistle lasts for over a second and explodes in the distance south of us. That screaming sound is like nothing I've ever heard. 15 minutes later, two F-14 jets zoom over our heads and drop bombs north of the DMZ. As the rain stops at 2:00 p.m., the nearby gunfire and mortars subside. We are spread out in a search-and-destroy sweep through a creek and then into a village. Evidence that a large enemy force had left here in a hurry includes spent cartridges, food supplies and unused ammunition. I know for sure now that I am in a different type of war.

We dig in on the north bank of the Chu Viet River and receive AK-47 fire from across the river at dusk. Three 61mm mortar rounds hit within our unfinished perimeter. Two Marines bellow in pain. For the next two minutes, the heavy fire goes both ways. Joe does a good job of traversing to hit the areas of enemy fire. The new guy, Harry, who had been in the Army previously is dropping the mortar rounds down the tube. We dug the mortar pit first and it provides us with cover as we return the incoming small arms.

Two minutes into the fight, two Hueys silence the enemy fire, as their noise guns spew heavy machine-gun fire into them. A medevac CH-34 drops into our position. The second platoon carries a stretcher with a dead guy and one new guy, who is severely wounded. One other heavily bandaged guy, who might be my friend, Mike, is assisted to climb aboard. No more activity takes place, so in the full dark, we finish digging in our defensive positions, cook our C-rations, and start watches. For the first hour of my watch, I can't see ten feet in front of me, then the cloud cover begins to lighten as a sliver of moon rises.

The overcast drifts away while we make breakfast. The high clouds capture the rising sun's rays. I am having meatloaf with bread, a cup of cocoa and cookies. Everyone keeps a low profile. Rags of mist drift out of the lowlands through the trees in our fields of fire. The high-pitched, loud whistle of enemy artillery creates an instant body movement toward the ground. In a second and a half one can move as far as 10 feet. We, in the mortar pit, simply dive to the bottom, as the round travels over us to Marines two miles south of us. If you weren't fully awake, you damn sure are now.

Two hours later, we sweep through the area the enemy had hit us from. We find evidence that a large force left quickly because of the firepower strafing them from our two Hueys with dual 50 caliber nose guns. We make a pile of all the captured supplies and set up a perimeter waiting for resupply. Mid-morning two Hueys escort a CH-34 loaded with our new food and ammo. With a sense of urgency, we quickly get our supplies. 30 guys unload the bird as 10 guys carry the captured munitions onto the bird. When the final bit of our garbage is stowed, the chopper takes off.

We continue on the sweep we started this morning. All day long we slog through rice paddies, empty villages, sandy hills and heavily brushed creek valleys. The high clouds begin to break up and we see the sky.

I think about the fact that Christmas is right around the corner. Incredible! It is such a juxtaposition. Which am I? A 19-year-old grab-assed kid, who is going to do some spiritual connecting with the family tradition of Christmas Eve Bible reading and opening one present? Or, am I a hardened killer aching to pay back someone for the horrors of the last ten months? We walk three more miles through the mounds of the vales and the rolling hills and search for tunnels of stashed gear or enemy in the empty villages. Today has the feel of "the same ole, same ole," walk in Vietnam forever, find nothing and imagine instant horrors.

As we set up watches 500 meters from the Cua Viet River, a gentle wind blows until dark when the stars come out in a mass of glory. This may be the darkest night I have experienced here. The clouds have all blown away. Stars seem to be piled on top of one another and cover the sky in all directions to each horizon. I will have the second half of the night for my watch, so I curl up on my right side, my helmet/pillow covers the back of my neck, the flash-suppressor on the tip of the barrel of my rifle near my eyeballs so that the low part of the barrel will stop an enemy knife from cutting my throat. I drop off in seconds. When Harry wakes me, the moon has brightened the sky considerably. The clouds cover the stars in the silent night.

The day starts with high clouds and no wind. Breakfast of beans and wieners is as horrible as always. Our fields of fire are obscured as a heavy fog rolls in when we finish eating. We listen for an enemy attack. The morning drags on. I break down my 45 and clean and oil it. The pistol will probably fire even if it is dirty, but it is part of my counteraction to the idea that when your time comes you just die. I constantly, every second, work to increase my odds of survival. My M-16 is truly important to baby. The slightest bit of sand in the bolt can jam it. My rifle rag shoved down the barrel needs to be carefully and slowly turned with a slight twisting motion as I pull it out. The lightly oiled rag goes through a half-inch slit in the tip of the two-foot-long rifle rod.

The fog lifts. We are told to break camp to head for the ships. The rain falls as we pile into Ch-46s. Four birds carry half of Lima Company. 15 minutes later, they return for the rest of us. The USS LST-1150, Sutter County, a Tank Landing ship, looks like a dot in the ocean as we lower toward it. The flight deck, although big enough to land four of these birds at once, looks like a crapshoot as to whether we can land on it with two birds at a time.

There is no incident and we head to the bunking area through greasy passageways. The aisleways are narrow, and the bunking area has most of us sleeping on the floor. The troop quarters are the only places that aren't greasy. The Navy dinner is way better than anything the Marine Corps ever supplied me, but not as good as the USS Vancouver.

I do the first watch. We luxuriously split the watch four ways. I wake Harry up for second watch. He seems rummy. 15 minutes later, I can see him slumped over, asleep. His shit-bird attitude would leave us exposed in the 'bush,' so I walk over and kick him hard on his tailbone with my steel-toed boot. In a low voice, so as not to wake the other Marines, I let him know in no uncertain terms that he had better get his shit together, or he is a threat to us all.

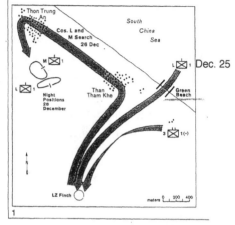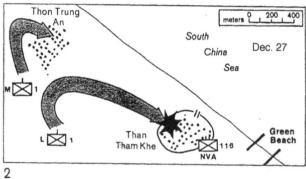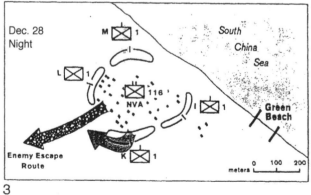

CHAPTER THIRTY-TWO
THE BEGINNING OF HELL

"Every time I say I hate officers, which I still do fairly frequently, I have to remind myself that practically none of the officers I served under survived. Christmas was in there somewhere"

Kurt Vonnegut, 1981.

Waking up on Christmas morning on the gently rolling ship after a full night of sleep seems like a fantasy. Several of us leisurely walk to the mess. Breakfast on this greasy Landing Ship Dock, a deep draft ocean-going vehicle is great, even better than on the squeaky clean Air Craft Carrier. It is steak, eggs, hashbrowns and toast. The servers give us as much as we want. Brian, the company corpsman, is sitting off by himself and I quietly join him. I'm tempted to wander over and join the African Americans, but I respect what Carl told me. I am happy to see Joe is with them. He is usually awkward but seems to fit in with this crowd.

We get our gear together after we eat and mount up in a long, slow-moving line to the bowels of the ship. At one point the line stops and I am outside in the rain for ten minutes. An hour later I can see below me the shallow drafting LSTs we'll ride in to go ashore. The seas have gotten rougher. Our small amphibious vehicles float in the water let in by the lowered door that is the entire front of the LST. We climb into eight of the boats and bob around in the hold. The wind blows rain into us. The LSTs that carry Lima Company's men are buffeted by the seas that are more of a chop from the wind than rolling waves.

The sides of the boats we're in are 10 feet high, as the Navy guys prepare to motor us out to sea, I see that, unlike the thick steel of Amtraks, the metal is not thick enough to stop bullets. I scramble up the side and see the water rush in around our boats. I have no hand or foot holds, so I slide back down. Our boat clangs into the boats around us. We head out to the open ocean. I can't resist and pull myself up for another look. The rain has stopped, but there are heavy clouds.

The official report says that we do not head to LZ Finch until tomorrow as the first company to set up for a big operation called, Badger Tooth. I clearly remember the two nights that lead up to the horrors of December 27, 1967, so I know we left on Christmas afternoon.

We emerge from the rolling surf into a half-mile-wide river mouth. I begin to feel terrified. I can imagine AK-47 rounds ripping through the boat's thin skin and me with no way to fight back. I scramble up one last time and see that the surf is still over our heads, although the beach is only 30 feet away. There's no way to know if enemy soldiers are present, but the terrain is perfect to hide a thousand NVA. We float in danger for two hours. According to the official Marine Corps report, they misjudged the tides. We're separated from the shore by a sandbar and deep water. I can't hang on the ship's side while holding a rifle, so I sit on a bench while the boat bobs on top of the water like a sitting duck at a carnival shooting gallery. My terror and inability to protect myself grow stronger by the minute.

We drive up near the beach a mile up the Cua Viet River when the tide is high enough for us to motor closer in. We run through three-foot-deep surf to reach the dry beach from the dropped-down front of the boat. A half-mile away, US artillery pounds a swath of low hills. Today's assault will be a reenactment of previous battles.

I had no idea that these two hours would be the most terrifying I had ever experienced in Vietnam until 40 years later when I was on a massage table with a therapist doing a technique he called Emotion Release. He traced a quivering muscle halfway up my right thigh, and I was suddenly back on the LST, terrified and helpless. I was barely able to keep the vomit from exploding out of my mouth. After 11 months of feeling terrified almost every day, I discovered on that massage table that another moment of terror didn't stand out at the time. The worst part was discovering 20 years later that the Navy Seals always swept the beach prior to any amphibious assault. That would have been nice for a grunt like me to know.

We quickly form an impromptu perimeter to protect the landing crafts and other Marines who disembark. Then we spread out in a double column and move further inland to the west as the Navy departs. The extreme western edge of the 'Street Without Joy' is our goal. The ground is soaked. Hard-packed dirt on flat land appears to go on forever. Half of the land is taken up by scraggly bushes. Our journey is peppered with narrow treelines devoid of leaves. The bushes are leafless.

At dark, after we walked two miles, we stop for the night. I don't have a rubber lady, so lying down in the muck is not appealing, even though I am exhausted. Luckily, I find a five-foot-in diameter circle of 2 to 4-inch stones. They are fairly flat on the surface so I curl up on my side and go to sleep. As we mill around in the morning, I see that the flat circle of rocks I slept on is a grave.

Chapter Thirty-Three
After Vietnam
Throwing Beer Bottles

Boyd and Elliott pulled into the driveway at 7:30 a.m. I hopped in the back seat and we drove the few blocks to the 400 Building of the high school that houses Peninsula Junior College while its campus was being built a mile to the east. My Dad, E. John Maier, the college president, enrolled the three of us for the summer quarter of 1968 so we could get out of the Marine Corps three months early. It was hard and wonderful to believe we weren't doing some stupid training or inspection like we were at Camp Pendleton just a week ago. Instead, we had a Philosophy class, Logic 115 at 8, Typing at 9 and Golf for Physical Education on Tuesdays and Thursdays at 10. Just enough credits to be granted an "early out" of the "crotch." It was Monday, June 10, 1968.

We managed to escape haircuts last month in the Marines, so we didn't look too weird and out of place. An officer had stopped us on the parade ground two weeks earlier and ordered us to go straight to the barbershop. We saluted and said "Yes, sir" in unison. He hadn't asked which units we were in, so we just went on about our business. We were combat veterans and probably looked different than than the 17 and 18-year-olds, and surely didn't look like career Marines. In the car, we were listening to loud rock-n-roll on Ken's Dad's 1963 Ford station wagon on the drive to school.

We sauntered across the parking lot in our field jackets carrying our books and notebooks. Jack Evans was the Logic teacher. He explained that he is on the Math faculty, but Logic can be taught by the Philosophy or Math departments. Within a few weeks, it became obvious that Ken and I had a better grasp of the philosophical concepts than Jack did. He would often let one of us explain the ideas to the class.

When we got out of typing class we drove down to the A&W and got the first of what became our weekday ritual, a hamburger with mayonnaise and pickles. Then we drove over to the little corner grocery on 6th and Cherry Street. Although we weren't 21 yet, my military ID said I was born in 1946, instead of 1948. Last Thursday, the company clerk down in Camp Pendleton asked me if I wanted him to change my date of birth on the card and I readily agreed. Being able to buy beer at 20 years old, seemed to make up for people thinking I was too old to Trick-or-Treat when I was 12. The old guy at the counter hardly looked at the ID as I bought a case of beer.

We took off driving west of town. I finished my first beer bottle when we were out in the farm country. A feeling of, "fuck these people who supported the war they knew nothing about" came over me and I threw the empty bottle straight up behind the car from the back seat. It shattered on the asphalt. There was a bitter edge to what I did, almost as if I was paying my community back for letting the Vietnam War happen. I was unconcerned with the consequences and who I might inconvenience. Elliott, riding shotgun, must have felt something similar because he followed suit and his empty shattered on the pavement. Boyd's bottle had the same result 30 seconds later.

Two weeks later as we were driving on the back roads west of PA, Ken threw a high arching bottle that hit the asphalt directly on its bottom and didn't break. What were the odds of that? We were flabbergasted. When dinner time arrived, I dropped each of them off at their parents' houses to eat. They had left me six beers and I already had more than my share, as they didn't want to be too wasted with their families.

The feeling of bitterness was growing as I drove around with nothing to do until a powerful urge to do something destructive took me over. I couldn't spray automatic weapon fire at anyone, so I parked around the block from Widsteen's Fine Men's store. Harold Widsteen was my Dad's best friend. It was 10:30 P.M. on a Monday and the streets were deserted. With a full bottle in my pocket, I walked to the front of the store on First Street and threw the bottle through the big display window. I drove away with no one the wiser.

Alone again a few nights later, the savage desire for destruction was aching for the release I felt breaking the window, so I attacked the Five and Dime store a block away from Widsteen's. Over the next two months, I broke two more big display windows in downtown Port Angeles. I never mentioned any of these outbursts to Ken and Ben.

The three of us beer bottle criminals were throwing our bottles out on the way to Crescent Beach when I threw one that again landed directly on its bottom and stayed standing. You figure about a hundred beer bottles a week for ten weeks, so two out of a thousand didn't break.

A week before the summer quarter ended, my Dad took me aside in private. He said, "Bill, I can't have you attending Peninsula College. It's not going to work for the college president's son to drink as much as you do. As a courtesy to me, Hank Terrell, the president of Washington State University was able to get you into WSU on short notice." I knew he was correct, but something about the horrors of combat made me feel entitled to go to school wherever I wanted. But I didn't argue.

The smoldering rage had been building in me and felt like it was going to burn me up, so late that night, with me almost blacked out drunk, Pat Wood drove me up to the college. He had no idea why we were up there. I said, "Park in front of the main doors." He did. I got out with my almost full bottle of beer. I threw it ruthlessly through the gigantic window beside the door. Pat and I didn't say anything as he drove me the four blocks and let me out to stumble into the safety of my bedroom in the basement. Had I lost my soul?

Chapter Thirty-Four
The Point of the Spear

"Perhaps all American wars can be described as the Civil War was: 'A rich man's war, a poor man's fight' "
Goff and Sanders, 1982

I cook my breakfast on the smooth rocks of the grave I slept on last night. The dense clouds hardly move. I eat everything in my B-1 unit's ham and eggs, fruit cocktail, crackers, peanut butter, and candy. This strange land with no leaves is filled with bushes that resemble a plant cemetery. (I had no idea Agent Orange defoliant existed 51 years ago). In the near distance, sporadic gunfire can be heard. We put our gear on at noon, spread out, and sweep back the way we came inland yesterday. We stop every few hundred meters along the line to inspect booby traps, tunnels, and enemy fighting positions. We investigate three hamlets and discover only a tattered pair of NVA pants. In the afternoon, the wind picks up significantly. The overcast has lifted to leave a smattering of high clouds that zip across the sky. The wind is up to

21 mph around 2:00 p.m. and then gradually drops to 11 mph for the rest of the day.

An hour before dark we approach Tham Khe, a large village. It is surrounded by sand and rice paddies. Just as the third platoon, which is in the vanguard, gets to the treeline 100 meters from the first hooches, my radio comes alive with reports of enemy sightings. They aren't shooting at us. I, myself, see and report on my radio, three uniformed NVA soldiers that descend into the ground ahead of me. As the first platoon on the eastern flank enters that part of the village, more radio reports come in of enemy sightings. The CP group crosses the treeline into the center of the village. The second platoon, spread to the west, also reports the enemy jumping into holes in the ground.

The official Marine Corps report says, "The infantrymen found no evidence of the presence of Communist fortifications or soldiers." This is totally inaccurate. As we sweep through this village, I listen to the radio I carry as the Weapons platoon radio operator and I hear four radiomen reporting as many as 12 NVA going underground. "This is Lima 2; There's ten NVA running into a hole to my right." "This is Lima 3; I see two uniformed, armed enemy disappearing in front of me," and so on for the other radios.

A veteran patient of mine who was stationed at Dong Ha, the area command center, told me that there were underground parties there every night. Clearly, no one recorded what we frantic radio operators reported. All of our career military personnel were at the nightly parties at the Dong Ha Base, which was five kilometers away. Obviously, no one was listening to or documenting what was being reported on the battalion net that I listened to.

We continue east after leaving Tham Khe and cross a creek. We're 2000 meters north of the village after an hour. We come to a granite hill 100 meters wide and 20 meters high and lay down for a restless night's sleep, fully aware that the enemy knew our location. We had no idea that the next day we would attack the enemy position with our meager force.

During my watch from 2-4 a.m., the sky was clear. The stars shone brightly. The sky is now overcast and cloudy. The day begins as many others in Vietnam. The temperature is a chilly 63°F, with only a slight breeze. We've already eaten and are ready to walk as the last stars fade. We spread out in a search-and-destroy sweep back toward the village where we had seen so many enemies last evening.

As we approach Tham Khe from across a dry rice paddy, my terror grows. We walk in a sweep formation, led by the second platoon. The third platoon is down by the beach on the left flank, and the first platoon is up a gentle slope in the rolling sandy hills on the right flank. We're all about 20-30 feet from each other. Behind the second platoon, I'm 10 meters to the right of the center of the CP's second wave of our assault. We mortarmen make up the right side of the second of Marines. To my right are Cowboy and a new ammo humper. A grunt from the first platoon is to their right.

The odor of human feces used as fertilizer pervades the air. The second platoon approaches a creek that is lined with trees and bushes. They cross the creek and the berm on the far bank. I'm only a stone's throw away from the creek in the dry rice paddy as the last member of the second platoon heads down the bank. Massive AK-47 fire erupts, primarily targeting the second platoon. I can see about half of the second platoon's 32 members, and to my horror, they've all been cut down like a giant scythe chopping wheat to the ground.

"A concealed enemy force opened fire with a devastating volume of fire from machine guns, rifles, RPGs, and mortars," according to the official report. 'The Streets of No Joy' became the moniker for the village.

When I hear the first bullet, I dive to the right, toward a three-foot-high hillock that will protect me. The desire to get away from all the bullets flying by causes my body to "eat dirt," but thousands of other thoughts remain etched in my mind 51 years later. I will be completely shielded from the enemy's small arms fire if I complete my dive, but I also know there are far too many bullets. This appears to be the end for all of Lima Company.

Scenarios play through my mind. My automatic first image is to get low with short bursts from my M-16. This patterned reaction always happens while heading to the dirt. No one survives in my unit unless their body learns its fastest possible movement toward the ground. If I decide to fire it will waste no milliseconds. In fact, my impact with the ground and becoming hidden will also have no delay. Following right on the heels of this image is me not firing at all. This is also a well-practiced maneuver that provides a chance of my survival by not drawing fire in my direction. Hundreds of prior firefights flash through my mind.

Then a third alternative appears to me that often provides the best of both worlds. If I access cover first and then return fire, I have several advantages. I will provide the enemy with almost no target and can stabilize my weapon, therefore will be able to put my rifle bursts directly at the muzzle flashes. I am carrying nine 20-round clips. That is a lot of firepower if it is focused from a protected position. This third alternative makes several outcomes play through my mind; if I was clairvoyant I would be running for the mortar, rather than this dive.

Now, I am halfway through the dive, and I have come to a crossroads. My three main alternatives have my pack and radio on my back when I meet the ground. Even my toenails know I need to suppress the enemy fire by instinctively firing my M-16 before I crash into the ground. Most of my previous 200 firefights required instantaneous return fire when we were ambushed. A wall of our bullets was usually our best protection. When an explosion or mortar round starts a firefight, the last guys to get to the ground are much more likely to be hit by the accompanying small arms fire. This bizarre scene is different. As I dive to the ground, 50 meters in front of me Marines are falling. The enemy firepower right now is massive enough to have cut down the second platoon.

The CP group has yet to reach the creek and are all exposed in the dry rice paddy. We only have eight rifles. The rest of the CP only carry pistols, which includes, Joe and Greg, the two mortar gunners, the two company radiomen, the aerial observer (AO), the forward observer (FO), the two company corpsmen, the Executive Officer (XO), and the Company Commander (CO). This many NVA would easily be able to overwhelm our meager firepower. The mortar squad, armed with our rifles, forms the rear guard of this 120-man online movement.

It is likely this powerful NVA force will charge us with our limited rifle firepower. I'm realizing we will all die if we are attacked in the open rice paddy. Perhaps I need to put my life in danger in order to have a better chance for some of us to survive?

I duped myself into making the moral decision to 'shoot first and ask questions later' in June 1967 by knowing that the US government thought it was my patriotic duty to keep myself alive to fight another day. Prior to that decision, the debate over whether or not to kill someone slowed my reaction time. This is significant because shooting takes less time than eating dirt. If my life depended on it, I would have pulled the trigger before my feet could move. A seasoned Marine would fire a diagonal burst of three to five rounds, which would disperse diagonally to about four feet at the target's chest.

My dive to the dirt of the knoll takes place just before the sun comes up. At dusk last night when we dug in, I knew that India, Kilo and Mike Companies were somewhere in our area. We had done three weeks of training with them during December in the Philippines to teach us varying types of amphibious assaults. Lima Company's troop strength had never been higher than 92 men, until redeploying as the adphibious brigade and were brought up to full troop strength of 120 guys. That means we had at least 60 guys with little combat experience. It is easy for me to imagine the three companies of my battalion arranged in a manner to have some overlapping protection for each other. It is a comforting thought that is completely untrue. Mike Company will come running through our position in the creek at sunrise tomorrow, December 28th with no other ground support near us until then.

My first day in the 'field' (in the countryside with no protection) on February 26, 1967, was the first time I felt as exposed as this when McCormick and I got shot at as the rest of Lima Company disappeared over a rise. Now on December 27, 1967, I have been in this position many times. Sometimes the fear of just the type of territory we travel through would start to grip me. Today the feeling is more intense and immediate. The reality of what we are doing is clear, and the scope of the task is daunting. No wonder the official record needed to say we had sighted "no enemy" in the village, they were covering their butts for having exposed so few troops to this meat grinder.

In Washington DC, a bleak, below-ground reflective black granite vertical surface, 'The Wall,' commemorates the 58,000 Americans who were Killed-In-Action in Vietnam. Their names are listed in chronological order by the date of their casualty and begin and end in the center. The 10-foot depth of those center panels represents the shame of our economic/political involvement. You see yourself reflected to clarify your culpability. Panel 32-East contains 96 names who died on December 27, 1967. Thirty-two of those men were from Lima Company. We, veterans, see our lost US brothers and sisters killed during the war behind the names etched in stones. The millions of "Farmer Soldiers" from Vietnam are intermingled with them.

If you died as a result of emotional wounds, your name did not appear on The Wall. I felt powerless to assist the family of a suicide victim attempting to get the name of their son on The Wall. During his combat tour in Vietnam, he experienced a schizophrenic episode. He remained in locked psychiatric wards until 1988 when the Veterans Administration instituted "de-institutionalization" and forced families to care for sick combat survivors. He caused his own death by taking a lethal dose of his powerful antipsychotic medicine, either accidentally or on purpose. For all intents and purposes, he died in Vietnam and deserved to be given the honor of acknowledgment of the loss of his life in 1971.

Twenty years after our country left Vietnam, more American combat veterans had officially killed themselves than the 58,000 who died in combat. It is estimated that three times that many suicided without being documented, many of whom drove their vehicle into underpass abutments.

I scan the area in front of the decimated second platoon as I dive. There are three distinct enemy fire areas, each with numerous muzzle flashes. If I complete the dive, I will be completely protected from small arms fire and will be able to keep my country's property, me, alive. Many possible scenarios end with the enemy pinning down or killing the remaining two rifle platoons. To avoid becoming a prisoner of war, I would shoot every attacker with my rifle and use all of my pistol rounds except the last magazine, which I would use to kill myself. These concepts don't strike me as particularly appealing.

While I piece together the puzzle, I keep moving toward the ground. Using the images I saw a fraction of a second ago, I realize we're all going to die if I don't risk everything to kill the enemy.

I intuitively know that heroics from me, and the other ten battle-hardened Lima Marines, like me are the only chance to survive for any of us. I know the third platoon machine gunner, Chester, senses what is necessary. He always wears a red and white bandanna around his neck. Three other dependable guys are spread out in Chester's platoon. There are another 5-10 of the new guys, who I assume, from our recent 20 firefights, might put down some effective fire. The first platoon has similar numbers without the known quality of Chester. The second platoon is completely silent between me and the heavy fire of the enemy positions. But my mind is still mostly focused on three main alternatives and how they fit with everything I know.

I need to solidify my decision. If I fly another foot toward the ground I won't be able to remove the backpack before I hit the ground. I can feel in my gut that 10 members of my company know as well as I do that in the next hundredth of a second the only chance that any of Lima Company survives is each of us acting with disregard for our own safety. So, before I smack into the ground, I get my right arm out of the pack strap, to allow me to turn my body toward the center of the CP group. This turn allows me to see Joe, with the closest mortar to me. He is just getting the two-inch web strap, which supports the mortar, off his shoulder. He has not touched the half-inch strap holding the bipod legs against the 60mm tube of heavy steel. This strap can be difficult to get open. It will take him up to half a minute to get a round fired.

You must back up the webbed section enough to pull the metal tip back through the clip, then you can free the whole strap from the bottom of the buckle.

I always complete this process while the gun is moving off my shoulder under its own weight. I use the spreading of the bipod legs to release the bottom part of the strap. Any hesitation in this process allows the webbing to hang up in the buckle. It requires no concern with the possibility it might not work. In many life-and-death situations, I had learned that if I barged through the process I was still faster, even if something hung up. My fastest time from shoulder to ground and round fired was seven seconds. Things don't go wrong when you are aggressive and sure of yourself.

I know from our practice, that Joe's fastest time to get a round shot had been 35 seconds. I am never slower than nine seconds, and I hit my targets. He is still seconds away from setting the base plate on the ground when I hit the hillock. He is then going to have to tackle the strap until it is undone before spreading the bipod legs. The slide that holds the legs to the barrel still needs to be unloosened and moved to the correct position. For Joe the correct angle of the gun would have been trial and error, then several readjustments until he could get the gun level on the bubble setting.

I know exactly where the slide needs to be to have the least need to adjust the leg length to get the proper angle. I also have the experience, before Joe got to

Vietnam four months ago, of being on a listening post with 12 of us, when a double column of enemy soldiers was moving down a draw straight at us. When we opened fire with a mortar, machine gun, rocket and seven rifles, the enemy fired a burst from their 75 soldiers and ran away. From the mortar pit during this June firefight, I could see the tall grass moving around me from the incoming bullets. It looked like the wind was blowing, but there was no wind. Little did those NVA know we weren't at least 30 guys.

Now, six months later, I know these NVA will think twice each time they stick their heads up or consider advancing on a group of Marines while mortars land on them. There is steady massive fire at us and no protection. Our mortar rounds must hit those muzzle flashes fast. I have no etched patterns of images in my memory from the middle of my dive until I arrive at Joe's mortar two seconds later.

Decision made, a new process takes me over. This is a deeply internal, procedural process. Each movement wastes no time. The two seconds to get to the gun are dramatically different from the clearly recognizable, seemingly infinite thoughts in the last tenth of a second. I manage to remove the radio and backpack before I hit the ground and keep hold of my rifle.

Smack! And I am up. Only my rifle and right forearm meet the ground and I push off, careful to not let the trigger mechanism get dirt in it. Then, I run in a low crouch. Twice, my left-hand hits hard-pack dirt between the tufts of dry rice plants to keep my forward movement toward Joe. He has just set the base plate of the mortar on the ground as I zoom along the ten meters to his exposed position in the dead center of our assault.

While I run across the middle of the dry rice paddy, I know exactly where the enemy positions are. Joe moves aside, and I grab the bipod legs, unbuckle the canvas belt, expand them to the hardpan, slide the collar to almost vertical, and yell for no increments (the small plastic warped explosives clipped between each fin around the shotgun shell in the tail section of the high explosive (HE) 60mm round). I look through the sight as I traverse to the middle area where I see the enemy muzzle flashes.

My first round blows up 10 feet behind the flashes, so I adjust and fire three rounds right on top of them. I traverse to the left and drop the barrel enough to reach the area I want to hit next, drop four rounds, traverse back to the center position fire two more rounds, and traverse to the right and drop our last three rounds of HE. I then fire two White Phosphorus (WP) rounds at each position.

The rest of the CP group has scrambled up to the creek. I scurry back over to my radio and pack, and with the rest of the mortarmen move as fast and low as I can up to the creek bed. All 20 of the CP are packed into an area only 30 feet wide, but we are protected from the enemy fire by a berm on the south side of the creek. Moans, calls, and yells for help are coming from the second platoon, on the other side of the berm. Enemy bullets constantly slam into the berm. Twice, enemy mortar rounds land on the other side of the berm, and shower dirt on us.

The 20 ARVN who travel with us are huddled in a tight, terrified, scrunched-down mob between me and the captain. Many of our M16s jam from all the firing, sand and mud. Mine does too. I quickly clear my jammed rifle with a strike on the exact point of the 22.62 mm round with my rifle rod. That knocks the spent cartridge out of the open chamber. Ten Marines, mostly the mortar ammo humpers, lean their rifles against the huddled-up ARVN, so I can easily reach them and get them clear. On the fifth rifle, I miss the exact point of the round and make the rifle jam worse. The other rifles I clear.

Capt. Homer sends the mortar squad toward the third platoon to the east. I only make it 50 feet from the captain and the group of ARVN, enough distance that we mortarmen are 5-10 feet apart when I hear the "pling" of a hand grenade spoon pop off a thrown grenade. We hit the deck in the shallow water of the creek. My legs are in two inches of water and I try to push my chest deeper into the berm. Dirt from the exploding grenade rains over us. There is a new level of terror with the enemy so close. I thought we were being attacked from the treeline 100 meters away with mortars. But no, these NVA are hidden only a grenade throw from me. With our chests pressed to the berm, we blindly fire a few rifle rounds toward the enemy every few minutes. We remain pinned down and two more hand grenades throw dirt on me.

Harry, on the other side of Joe, is further down the creek toward the beach. I see him crawl up the side of the berm on his haunches and stupidly hold his head and chest above its protection, a perfect target practice silhouette. What an idiot. I guess that kicking him in the ass wasn't enough to wake him up to the danger we are all in. His head abruptly snaps back, then flops to his chest, and he drops face-first onto the berm.

I pray to God to get me out of this mess. I promise to read the Bible every day, pray and go to church regularly if I survive. Brian bravely comes walking past me at a crouch. He gets to Harry without being shot at. He rolls the limp body over, then heads back the way he came. He says, "Harry was shot through the right eye and died immediately." Ten minutes later, Joe starts thrashing around, kicking his leg up in the air. He is just 10 feet from me lying almost completely in the shallow water. His jungle pants aren't tucked in his socks, and a leech four inches long is stuck to his right ankle. Barely managing to keep from laughing, I go back to waiting to die.

When this firefight ended 24 hours later, we found a tail section of the WP round inside the doorway of the central bunker. Joe would have shot his first round shortly after I had used up all our ammunition.

With the mortars stretched out toward the ocean, the CP group is filled with officers, radio operators and forward observers. Although they total 11 guys, they only have one rifle without the mortar squad. The captain leads them on a fatal assault toward the enemy bunkers. Each of us along the berm tries to help them with cover fire at the enemy. They are cut down by enemy fire and only five of them make it back into the creek with only two of the wounded from the second platoon. The corpsman tends to the two injured. The captain is dead and still out in No Man's Land. Jack Brown and the aerial observer, Johnson, are alive, but both have severe-looking shoulder wounds.

Over the next two hours, we sneak over the berm with heavy coordinated cover fire and get a total of 10 more wounded to our relative safety. Back 200 meters out into the dry rice paddy, is a small mountain of granite, 30 feet high and 100 feet wide. A Sea Knight CH-262 lands there as the medevac chopper. I hoist a guy shot in the leg over my shoulder and start the harrowing run over the exposed territory to the protected bird.

Behind the block of granite, I head up the ramp and deposit my Marine on one of the seats along the sides. I grab a box of rifle ammo and head back to carry another wounded out of this hell. My next guy is Jack, the company radio operator who I walked with up to the company office on February 24, 1967. He is covered in blood from a big right shoulder wound. I run with his left arm over my shoulder and carefully set him in a seat and strap him down. My third and last trip is another very bloody Marine, Mike. He is draped over my shoulder. When I get on the bird all the seats have wounded Marines in them except two near the rear entry. In the front of the aircraft, four helicopter corpsmen work frantically to save the lives of a couple of Marines.

No one is watching me.

As I strap Mike in, I realize I can strap myself in and look like all the rest of the bloodied Marines. They would take me away from here to the hospital ship where they would discover I had deserted the battle scene and I would be court-martialed. Not willing to spend the rest of my life in prison, I scramble back to the fighting.

All day long the fight continues. The helicopters and jets are hardly noticeable to me, nor do they affect the enemy. For some unknown reason, the NVA has decided not to overrun us.

As dark falls, there is a decrease in the enemy fire. We still have not connected to the third platoon on the beach. The first platoon is stretched from what is left of the CP group inland up away from the fortified enemy stronghold. All of us in Lima Company remain on hyper-alert throughout the night. A couple of times an hour we fire at the enemy and at about that same frequency they fire at us. When we've been lying in this creek bed pinned down for 24 hours, Mike Company charges through our position at a full run with their rifles over their heads. They meet no resistance and our horror abruptly ends. Am I part of some WWII movie? It feels unreal to have survived. The dreaded enemy force that has killed a third of my company has been chased away.

The Executive Officer, 1st Lieutenant Foster, directs Lima and Mike Companies to search the village. I make my way to the center bunker of three hills, where the grenades were thrown from. The three hills are seven feet tall and twenty feet wide, with old hardwood trees growing out of them and look like natural hills. As I descend the two dirt steps into the center bunker to a trench three feet below ground level, I notice a tail section of a white phosphorus round. I can only imagine the mayhem that WP caused as it threw fire from the bottom step. The first four or five NVA must have been flailing away from the rapidly burning, burrowing chemical that ignites when it comes into contact with air, searing through their clothes and skin. Patching up these NVA and getting them out of the prime shooting positions may have saved our asses, as we rushed up to the creek.

Maybe I made a difference.

The NVA had been firing through a gun slit, made by two wooden planks 12-foot long and a foot wide. I had to stoop a little to walk the length of the bunker. Later I found out that Chester, the machine gunner from the third platoon in the rice paddies next to the beach, had completely exposed himself, as I did. In order to get a higher angle of fire to make his bullets go into these gun slits, he had jumped onto a two-foot high paddy dike with his M60 machine gun, firing from the hip and got shot several times in the gut. I imagine he killed several people in the bunker that faced the beach. His intuition, like mine and 10 other hardened combatants, helped him see exactly what he needed to do if any of us were to survive.

The gun slit is a six inches opening running the length of each bunker. An incoming bullet would need to be shot at the right angle and enter the opening between the bottom edge and the top to hit the NVA. Even an artillery round landing on the bunker would not have hurt the people inside under six feet of dirt. They had full fields of fire and little danger of being hit. They probably bounced around a lot from the bombing runs of the jets, but no bomb craters were on the actual bunkers. The hand grenades thrown from this doorway had clarified that we were not being shot at from the treeline yesterday, but instead from these positions and the trenches that connect them. Tunnels were everywhere, connected back to the village and spider-webbing throughout the area.

We finally sit down to eat two hours after Mike Company has provided us with a complete 360° perimeter. Only three of the 20 hooches I saw coming through this typical-looking village the night before last are still standing. The rest were destroyed by our bombs and artillery. Bamboo sticks lie strewn about from the mats that had covered the hooch walls. The enemy would have been in big trouble if they had been above ground. Heavy black diesel smoke fills the air as Tanks, Amtraks, and Antos join our search. The sulphurous, metallic odor of all the spent munitions from both sides creates an olfactory environment that I will continue to smell in my memory for the next 17 years whenever I am afraid I am going insane.

It wasn't until I was working as a grade checker behind a road grader in 1984 that I connected the smell of its diesel exhaust to the horrors of my time in Vietnam, rather than my belief that the Devil was slowly enslaving me. I had been in treatment for Post-traumatic Stress Disorder for four years at that point, and many of my anxiety symptoms had significantly subsided, or I may not have got this clarifying insight.

Just 20 feet from me, two Mike Company guys drag an elderly man out of a tunnel. Feeling terror, my rage rises. Where are all those NVA? He was with the people who decimated my company. The man is so frail that it's difficult to believe he can walk. He couldn't possibly have been fighting us, but he might know where all the enemy are. He is dressed in shorts. His skin appears to be stretched over the bones of his lower legs, chest, and arms. His thighs have little flesh on them. He resembles a walking skeleton.

Mack, our interpreter, and I are ordered by the officer-in-charge, OIC, to find out from him where the NVA are hiding. The old man says nothing in response to Mack's questions. I coldly shoot a hole in the little bit of flesh on his left thigh with my 45 pistol. This is the weapon that I used 4 months ago to drop a charging 2-ton water buffalo with one shot. The old man screams but still refuses to tell us who the enemy were and where they have gone.

Slats from blown-apart wall mats of a hooch are strewn around the dry ride paddy. I grab one of the thin bamboo sticks, and think, "Ah...this will do". I coldly swat the bloodless jagged wound with the slat. The elderly Vietnamese man looks me in the eye and appears in disbelief that I will continue this brutal act. I feel vicious and determined to find out if we are in danger. I swat him again. He sees my resolve and hatred and starts jabbering. I don't know what he is saying but glee bubbles in me. Every time he goes quiet and Mack wants more information, I swat him. This happens four more times until Mack says he has told everything.

We are no longer in imminent danger because we feel convinced that the enemy have deserted their stronghold. In the dark of last night, 1000 soldiers of the 116 NVA Battalion had used an escape tunnel to the beach between the CP and the third platoon to leave in a flotilla of hidden boats.

Mack tells the OIC that he has told us everything. As the officer walks away, he turns around and looks at us as if in answer to our unspoken question of what to do. He nods his head affirmatively. One of us shoots the old man in the head.

Chapter Thirty-Five
Cap Memory

"It was an expensive education and Vietnam bore by far its greatest cost"

Christian G. Appy, 2015.

The official Marine Corps history says this intel came from a dying NVA soldier, instead of the truth, that an old villager had refused to leave his village because he probably would never have survived the journey south.

While several hundred other Marines scour the village, Lima Company moves out in a double column toward the west. Adrenaline fuels my body for the three hours we walk. We dig the mortar pit and fighting holes, which is always hairy, but now it seems impossible that we aren't picked off. We dig frantically, and even with two guys with rifles watching in two directions, I feel like a beacon for enemy fire, especially when we first break ground. Then, I am secure in the pit. Later in the night, I am on the last watch. The temperature gets cooler. It drops from 72° to 57°

by first light at 7:00. Fog obscures the world around me.

My thirst for revenge is strange. It barely holds at bay my moral repugnance to the atrocity of yesterday. I try to eat as I sit in the mud at the bottom of the mortar pit. I worry, where are those thousand enemy? To add to my frustration, the air is getting colder and the rain is a downpour. I huddle in my poncho trying to eat, when suddenly the scream of an enemy artillery round tears through the fog and rain. I dive deeper into the mud. The round explodes 10 feet away and arches dirt over me. This is the closest an artillery attack from North Vietnam came to me, so far. It takes 20 long minutes of terror to wait for the jets to bomb the NVA artillery. It takes the enemy about the same amount of time to reload and shoot a second volley. As the life-or-death race for us between the jets and the enemy guns begins, I find myself thinking about playing football in mud like this at North Kitsap High School.

My reflections are pierced by a second volley of high explosives, followed by the screams of two wounded Marines. We walked until nightfall yesterday. In the morning, all the radio operators are summoned to the acting captain's tent. For the first time in two days, the rain stops and the fog lifts. Everything is wet, and the air is chilly. In this brief respite from the fog and rain, the wind whips even harder. On my walk to the company command post (CP). I see a North Vietnamese Army boot two feet to my left as I pass through an opening in a tall thin line of bamboo. The boot contains the bottom half of the right leg and foot of a soldier. The shattered bone protrudes eight inches above the boot, and jagged flesh dangles from it. A pile of about 100 NVA bodies is to my right. A 'Crispy Critter' faces me halfway up the side of the heap of bodies. He is a completely burned soldier in a crawling posture. I don't feel morbid curiosity, and I have a tendency to look away. I avert my gaze on my way back a half-hour later while the rain pours down in the dense fog.

I had no idea that 51 years later, I would still see that 'Crispy Critter' more than any of the other horrific memories I carry. This is referred to as a 'Cap Memory' by trauma counselors. It's a memory that, while gross and disturbing, isn't as frightening as many others.

"One hundred bodies from the 116th NVA Battalion were abandoned in the sand dunes," according to the official record. "The enemy force apparently had evacuated its casualties through the gap between Lima and Kilo Companies during the night."

As the rain finally stops the next morning, it is even chillier. We're not going to be able to dry out in this soaking wet heavy fog. This terrified man/child's cold-killing efficiency increases. A 19-year-old boy or a ruthless killer? I manage to light a cigarette and a heat tab. The hot food warms the oblivion of doing nothing in the freezing cold. We are on high alert.

The visibility is approximately 50 feet. Someone could throw a hand grenade from inside the fog and we'd only hear the explosion.

We, the radio operators, are summoned to the CP once more. Before I see the boot and its now pale yellow flesh, I smell the bodies as I go back through the bamboo again. The heap of bodies appears to be frozen in time. Only the scent indicates that something has changed. The wind continues to howl.

When we wake up the next day, the fog and rain don't hide the stench of rotting flesh. Everything is soaked and puddled. The leafless trees and bushes drip all the time. Because I have a Zippo, I can smoke and eat hot food. If I could unwrap my mind from the horrors of the last ten days, I might be able to enjoy my cup of cocoa. Dave Martin, a new corporal, has been assigned to the mortar squad. He arrived with another E-4 who was assigned as a squad leader to the second platoon. They both appear to be relaxed and amicable. Pops is grousing about his back. I can tell he's lying. I'll be relieved if he escapes because anyone who doesn't carry their weight is a liability to the rest of us. Good riddance to Pops, as he gets sent to the hospital ship to get checked out.

I go to the company command post for the third day in a row. The leg in the boot has turned black today. Above the stinking pile of bodies, a CH-46 with a lowered cargo net on a cable, hovers. Two Marines are standing on the pile. They swing each body onto the net. That chopper departs with a net full of dead bodies, and the next bird arrives and lowers another net. What a grisly enterprise. Will they still be able to smell death and decay after their first shower on the ships tomorrow? Can they still smell death after 51 years?

I am unaware that the rain has stopped.
Back on the ship, I shower for the first time since Christmas. The blood and dirt of six days ago, December 27th, are still ground into my skin. The smell of the pile of bodies can't be washed out of my memory. The hot seawater is pumped through the ship for various purposes, including showers. I don't have to hoard it, as I have had to hoard water in the field for the last 300 days. When I go to dinner a few hours later, I can still see dark stains on my hands, under my fingernails, and up my arms.

The record reads, "On January 2, 1968, the BLT, (Battalion Landing Team) had left the 'Street Without Joy.' In fierce fighting at Tham Khe, the Marines suffered 48 killed and 86 wounded. Lima Company incurred the largest amount of these casualties."

Chapter Thirty-Six
Tyrannosaurus Rex

"With the possible exception of the Civil War, no event in U.S. history has demanded more soul-searching than the war in war in Vietnam"
Christian G. Appy, 2015.

Over the next three weeks, we attack against well-dug-in enemy soldiers five more times. Our artillery slams into the village we are assualting today, with the third platoon as our vanguard. Massive small-arms fire cuts through us from the village. The enemy AK-47 rounds are thick as locus. I hear bloodcurdling screams on either side of me. Two Hueys arrive in 90 seconds. For 20 minutes it is touch-and-go. Again I fear we may get overrun. There are 10 times more of them than us. The Marine F-14 jets scream over our heads for a bombing run. The NVA go quiet as the jets do four more runs. We rapid-assault the village as the jets circle nearby. No NVA are anywhere to be found, but we capture two Amtracks full of weapons and ammunition. On the north side of the village, a recoilless rifle is set up in a small dry rice paddy. It looks forlorn. Two more Lima Company Marines are dead and six are hauled away wounded.

Back at the Dong Ha base three days later, I buy a case of Hamm's beer and walk out into an open area. The rest of my company take showers. The nearest bunkers to me are 100 feet away. I pull out a beer, chug it fast, open another one, and sit down on the case while I pour through the booze. After drinking 18 beers I must have passed out. When I wake up heavy clouds cover the sky.

Yesterday we had walked into Dong Ha on a zigzag path between three consecutively taller rows of concertina wire on the south side of the base. The closest in coils of wire are a pyramid ten coils high, the next is six coils, then three, with the farthest out being a single coil, like around our battalion area near Da Nang. Today, we head out of the north side on a familiar zigzag path through the wire. As we leave the final opening in the single coil of wire, we enter what looks like a village, except it has no evidence of cultivation. There is an emaciated Vietnamese man standing in the doorway of the first hooch. His face is rotted. I can see his teeth on the left side of his jaw. We walk wearily through a Leper Colony. Our miserable condition seems like a Greek Isles vacation compared to the lives of these lepers.

The DMZ looms ominously to our right. We head back near the last abandoned village that we kicked the NVA out of ten days ago. At dusk, we set up a perimeter on a gently sloping hill. The area is sandy with patches of dirt and bushes. I feel strange with the leper colony and the secure base two miles away, but I know my job. We are in the land I am familiar with. Be as instantly violent as possible, shoot first, and ask questions later. Those other two communities have different safety rules. Both communities could sense our values and left us alone when we were around them. One is safe because no one wants their disease, and the other is safe under piles of sand and behind the wire.

Lima Company is flying toward the west after a day on the ship. There is fog where Vietnam waits, snarling with Tyrannosaurus Rex ferocity. It wants our souls. The devil orders us to sacrifice ourselves. But I know it is my duty to my country to survive and that no power greater than me has any idea what I need to do today to do my job. I have the impression that the enemy wishes to be linked to the muzzle of my M-16. The Brass or the NVA are the adversaries. In my viciousness, they alternate and intertwine. Will today be a stupid gamble or a ruthless killing?

We swoop down into an area where two other CH-46s have landed. This is the village where we saw the Christian pagoda a few weeks ago. Gunshots can be seen in the trees to the east. The Hueys fire back, and the Marines fire as they dismount and form a perimeter. New light shafts appear in the skin of our helicopter. Six feet away, a bullet passes through the floor and ceiling. We run out of the back as quickly as possible and fire our M-16s as we go. The last two birds give birth to violent Marine fangs. The second platoon, consisting of mostly guys freshly here from the States, runs toward the enemy fire. The first platoon sweeps online toward the treeline's left edge. The third platoon circles to the other side. We haven't yet fired our mortars. Pre-sighted artillery from Dong Ha slams into our objective as soon as the birds have flown away. Two minutes later, I receive a radio order to take cover, and the village is decimated by heavy artillery fire.

Remnants of the pagoda are strewn around its former location. The head of the Christ statue is lying on its ear in the mud. Although it weighs five pounds, I decide to carry it in my backpack to bring to the States. I also pick up two. four-inch tall brass sphinxes with wingnuts on the bolts in their bases. I can imagine them fastening onto bookends for a shelf of memorabilia, if I ever get out of this place.

A week later as we assault another village, a Marine shrieks in agony. A 61mm explodes 100 feet to my left. Johnson, from the first platoon, is thrown five feet through the air. His odds aren't good. After the jets stop the enemy fire, our futile search of this fourth village along the Cau Viet river lasts a couple of hours. We blow up three empty tunnels. At 2:00 p.m., over the ocean, on the way to a Vehicle Transport Ship, I am numb, my deeply hidden fury has no place to vent itself.

At the time I had no idea the Tet Offensive of 1968 was going to begin on January 31 but I knew I was facing a very different opponent. They harass us only with artillery and mortars. We discover and attack a thousand of them at a time. They run away. Unbeknownst to me, the troops we are running into are preparing to hit every major American base and all of South Vietnam's cities in the next few weeks. Hue City is to be hit hard. Hue is just south of us. These NVA soldiers are most likely heading there.

On the Cua Viet River's north side, we circle back east to a large village directly across the river from this morning's assault. A well-protected enemy fires at us as we find protection in and around the village to fire back. Our artillery rounds slam into the enemy. They go quiet for five seconds. The day goes on like this with the wind building, as artillery barrages hit the enemy-held village at least every 15 minutes.

SSgt Steve, Cpl Dave and I find a Vietnamese bomb shelter for our place to sleep when not on watch. It is a four-foot-high mound of dirt 15 feet long. The bomb shelter is built out of 2-inch in diameter, 5 feet long bamboo, leaned into each other at 45°, that are notched and packed tightly together, leaving an opening five feet wide and eight feet long that Steve and Dave will sleep in. The entryway is one step down into an eight-foot by two-foot wide area, under more bamboo and dirt, where I decide set up to sleep.

After full dark, I work my way over to the mortar pit. The enemy isn't shooting at us. Our artillery continues to hit them. There is an eight-foot-high natural rise along the north side of the Cua Viet River. The cloudy night moves on with no exchange of small arms fire. I have my radio and hear a grunt report that he can see groups of NVA walking around with candles between our artillery barrages.

It feels anything but neighborly, to be so close to the enemy. Whenever I crawl out of the dark bomb shelter I am in immense danger. The enemy vastly outnumbers Lima Company, but in mid-morning I venture out to stretch my legs. My back has been aching since I fell and strained it several months ago while carrying the heavy mortar tube. Now, after a day scrunched underground, I am only slowly able to straighten it out.

Cpl Dave and I walk over to the second platoon's area of responsibility and find Joe's bunker. The inside of his is identical to ours. Dave ducks down and crawls past Joe into the A-framed depths to my right. Joe is sitting with his legs stretched out and his back against the three-foot-deep north wall of the entryway, where I sleep in our shelter. I sit on the second step so that I have the mound of the bomb shelter between me and the now-silent enemy riflemen across the river. Then the shrill whistle of enemy artillery fire has me dive in by Dave. Joe is flat on the ground and we are all safe. Two mortar rounds explode just a few meters outside the thick walls of the bunker.

Joe says, "That's a fuckin' powerful housewarming gift you brought with you." We all crack up laughing.

The ground shakes the next morning, as two F-14s drop four bombs across the river. The crescent moon flits in and out of the clouds. One of the smoke clouds from our constant artillery looks like a bright pink mastodon. Out of the beautiful sky, death rains down on us. I don't hear the swish of the five 61mm mortar rounds, but I see the explosions near the river. Cpl Joe has been killed! Dave is slack-jawed. I tell him I am going over to the second platoon and he follows. The hole from the 61mm explosion is a foot deep in the entrance step I sat on yesterday while we talked with Joe. I remember seeing him sitting there. His flak jacket was not buttoned up. He was protected on all sides from any type of incoming, except something landing in that doorway. If that round had swished out of the sky yesterday while Dave and I were there, it would have landed on my head and killed me while leaving Joe safe in the bunker. Tiredness overshadows my rage.

Dave heads back to our bomb shelter and I go over to the XO as a spokesperson for the exhaustion and raw nerves of our whole outfit. The second platoon commander, Harrison, a tough-looking six-foot-tall sandy-haired guy with big shoulders and an athletic, muscled body, who is crying as he talks to the XO. I tell the XO we can't take this anymore. We have seen too much death. We all have injured friends out on the hospital ship. He has to do something to get us someplace where we can get a night's sleep. He is clearly powerless and our day goes on. Nothing changes. Another 61mm mortar round explodes on the other side of our perimeter. No one screams. When I am back in the bomb shelter the scream of NVA artillery precedes the ground-shaking explosion inside our perimeter.

CHAPTER THIRTY-SEVEN
FORTY DAYS AND FORTY NIGHTS

"But George's faith in America's global goodness was forever destroyed in Vietnam"
                                          Christian G. Appy, 2015.

Joe is no longer alive. One man out of 120 is killed while sitting in the most secure position possible. The other two guys in the bunker were unharmed. The environment is ruled by random, chaotic violence. I am reminded of the fancy sleeping hole I built in the garden months ago, when the hand grenade bounced off my poncho tent and blew a hole a foot from me without even waking me up.

When Steve, Dave and I are back in the relative safety of our bomb shelter Steve sings *Ain't Nothin' but a Hound Dog*. Dave and I sing along after a few verses. We sing popular Rock-N-Roll songs or play Rummy in the afternoon and evening. I leave to go out into the clearing fog to pee at 2:00 p.m. The sound of enemy artillery pierces the air just as I return to the shelter's roof. As it approaches, I dive to the dirt floor of our bunker.

Another dull morning surrounded by thousands of enemy and barrage after barrage of artillery and mortar fire, my radio informs me that everyone should remain in their shelters, bunkers, or fighting holes with their heads down. Massive explosions rock the ground at 10:32. I see Dave and Steve bounce between the roof and the ground three times, just as I do. We are told an hour later that this was a TPQ, a Radar Controlled Bombing run, with B-52s flying silently at 32,000 feet and dropping eight, 500# bombs on the enemy position across the river. When it is over, we go outside and discover a piece of a bomb shell casing stuck into the side of our shelter. It's a one-foot-diameter, half-inch-thick curved metal plate, like a big, flat bowl. It has penetrated eight inches into the hard-packed dirt.

Finally, a week later we move to the village across the river. The sensation of being in a post-apocalyptic world has taken hold of me. The enemy is not attacking, and I am not stationed on the perimeter. Cpl Dave and I are five feet apart, our faces glum. I say I can't take any more of this intense combat. He nods, a sad expression on his face. Wisps of fog drift across the landscape. We find what's left of their blown apart, smoking fortifications, and dig in our perimeter to search in depth tomorrow.

As I clean my rifle, in the middle of the afternoon the next day, the wind picks up, blows away the fog, and ushers in the heat, as Dave approaches me. He asks me to assist him to break his trigger finger with a wooden hammer he discovered in an abandoned hooch. He has his right index finger wrapped in a sock and requests that I hit it with the hammer while he holds it on top of a chopping block. He claims that this is just a test to see how bad the pain would be. It's difficult for me to force myself to hurt my friend, but I'm in the same never-ending state of desperation. The sock absorbs the first blow. He claims that the next one will be less painful. "One more, twice as fucking hard. Tomorrow I'll fuckin' take the pain." he says.

I decide that I should injure myself, too. It only has to be enough to get out of the dangerous incompetence of my commanders and the brilliance of the enemy's strategies. Unlike Dave, who needs an injury that will keep him out of combat forever, if I get sent to the hospital ship I am too short (only 50 days left) to be sent back out here. This reminds me of a grade school incident that might help me now. In fifth grade, I sprained my ankle in a very funny manner. Kerry Garbie, the guy I walked to school with every day, had peed on his shirt at the urinal. At recess, I was teasing him about it so he was chasing me around the playground. On the baseball diamond, I climbed up the backside of the backstop to get away from Kerry. He grabbed a bat from the front side and tried to hit my feet. I jumped down eight feet, landed on my right ankle, and twisted it. He kept chasing me and I ran on my throbbing ankle. When the bell rang and we went back to the classroom, my ankle swelled up. When the pain got to be too much, I told Mrs. Stapleton and she sent me to the nurse's station. The nurse called my Mom, who called Dad at work to come to take me to the doctor's office. For two weeks I couldn't walk on it. I soaked it twice a day in a pan of ice water and alternated with a hot pad.

Here in Vietnam, I try to sprain my left ankle because I think the once-injured one will be more vulnerable, but I picked the wrong ankle. We're in an odd void in this northern territory. There are major battles going on in every direction, but nothing comes at us. Dave claims he is ready to break his trigger finger today. I'm determined to sprain my ankle. We make our way over to our secret location. He places his sock-wrapped finger on the chopping block and asks me to hit twice as hard as I did the day before. He manages not to scream in pain, but it doesn't break. I cram my left toes into my hole and leap violently into it, my weight smashes into my left foot. It doesn't even hurt. (Now that I think about it, I realize how tough all of my tissues had become after 11 months of hard walking.) My feet have an eighth-inch thick callus around the bottoms of them, and the soles are a solid callus. My filthy skin doesn't scratch on the thorny bushes. It's no surprise that the hardest-working part of my body isn't injured. I retreat deeper into my hostile and hopeless shell.

I decide to see how deep the dirt is on the palm of my hand. With my K-bar I start scraping an area one-inch square on my left palm. One hour later, I have a nice patch of skin showing. I guess that proves I am a human being, not a dark, cold, dirty, vicious killing demon. What is real? The covering of my whole body or the tiny patch of skin. Both. Those thoughts only last a few minutes. As my situation demands, I allow focused, vicious alertness to take me over. The concept of being like a human is way too complicated and distracting. My filthy self knows exactly what to do in every situation. No hesitation. Shoot first or die. I am my most base instincts; fight, flight, flop or freeze, with no concern for the thoughts and feelings of others.

Two days of walking in terror, four times burrowing into the earth for a second and a half waiting for an artillery round to land, have made me brittle with an intense desire to shoot someone. Our only brief firefight yesterday lasted until the jets patrolling nearby ripped into the NVA with 40mm miniguns. Steve returns from the second platoon and informs me that he and I are going to Da Nang to get new glasses tomorrow.

The next morning, I dig out my toothbrush and thoroughly clean my mouth. Today, I am going to be in the presence of human beings in a few hours. These people around me now are either vicious fighting machines like me or terrified new guys trying to get their bearings. I know the Da Nang Navy hospital territory well, but I have no image of the character I have become to be able to be around REMFs. Lima Company and I walk for three miles and spread out around a dry rice paddy for resupply. The two CH-34s disgorge their supplies and Ssgt Steve and I hop on board. Steve also lost his glasses in one of our heavy battles.

On the ride, we see Marble Mountain through the fog and rain, and familiar terrain begins to appear. Shortly before dark, we land at the SeaBees' base next to the Navy hospital. Lima Company had walked through this base in June to set up our week-long mortar watch. We are escorted to a tent, where we deposit our gear on the cots and are taken to the club. We sit at one of the five tables. I order vodka and grapefruit juice, the same as Steve's. The drinks are almost a clear color, like a full water glass of vodka with a splash of juice. The bartender says they are "on the house." The vodka, though harsh, feels like it is cleaning my dirty insides. Seabees are beginning to gather around us. They look like me, however, in real life, they are clean as a whistle with gentle, efficient looks.

Under the dirt, Steve and I are barely visible. Our clothes are browner than their original green, and the harsh expressions on our faces have them approach us with caution. The most daring of them buy us more drinks. At the end of the night, we have five full drinks in front of us. Steve challenges me to a chugging contest. He and I grab a glass and pour the whole contents down. I get half of the second one down and I can't do it anymore. Steve finishes that one and one more.

We stagger out of the club, loudly sing rock-n-roll and move across the base. For the first time in my drinking career, there is a gap in my memory of events. I remember that we interrupted a basketball game on a hillside, then nothing until I am rolling down the court laughing. Then I remember someone guided us to our cots. My blackout turns into sleep.

As I wake up, I wonder where the heck I am and why I am in a puddle of water. As the tent comes into focus, I realize everything else is dry. I see Steve lying on the floor in a big puddle of puke. He is snoring and blowing bubbles as he exhales in it. Then, it dawns on me that I am lying in a massive amount of my own pee. Two Seabees come and get us up and to the showers. They take our clothes as we shower and we sit around naked for two hours. My dark green baggy clothing feels comforting when it's returned.

The next day Steve and I get on a CH-34 and head back to the bush. Over the next two weeks, Lima Company is in three pitched battles, then we finally set up in an abandoned village. I am starving and terrified with nothing to do all morning. This is the drudgery of combat with no resupply yesterday because we had firefights throughout the day. With only the last vestiges of our ammo, it is a relief near noon, when two Amtraks clang in and seem to scare the fog away. We reload our bellies and ammo belts, as the Amtraks chug out.

Seven of us gather for a card game just outside one of the hooches that didn't get burnt down. My deck of cards has swollen to four inches thick. Truly it is amazing these Bicycle cards are still functional. Doc Faust is playing with us for the first time out in the bush when massive AK-47 fire slams into our game. Somehow, I don't get hit. We return fire with everything we have. In controlled terror, I low-crawl to a mound 15 feet away. The incoming rounds come from three different directions. With cold efficiency, I use my first magazine in four to five-round bursts into the center group of muzzle flashes, change magazines, expend it on the muzzle flashes on the right, change magazines again, and expend that where the muzzle flashes on the left had come from. Our LAW rockets, 60 machine guns, mortars, M-79s, and 100 M-16s silence the NVA before the Hueys even streak overhead with their machinegun fire.

What a bloody mess. Thank goodness Doc is right here. He rapidly patches up the four wounded Marines. He tries to stop the squirting of blood from a major artery in the right thigh of Mark Johnson from the second platoon. I am not sure he can save him, but I know he would die for sure unless one of us stops that blood flow. We all knew how to administer a tourniquet, but none of us, non-corpsman, had ever put one on. After the tourniquet is on, Doc patches Kellogg, the third platoon machine gunner, around his gut. These two are going nowhere without a medevac. The bullets keep flying. I efficiently hit areas of incoming muzzle flashes with rifle fire.

As quickly as it started, there is suddenly no incoming fire. In the middle of silent chaos, I feel no relief. Death feels imminent. My deck of cards is spread around in the bloody dirt. No use trying to salvage them. 15 of the cards are completely covered in blood and half of the rest have been splattered enough to make them difficult to clean and use. I think about building a deck out of paper but never do. Planning the construction of the cards distracts me from the tedium and horror I am feeling.

Ten days later, I crest a low sandy hill. angrily thinking of Mo blowing up in front of me when another company of Marines comes at us from the right diagonal. It is rare to see another company in the bush. It happened only three other times here near the DMZ. This bunch of Marines looks more bedraggled and seasoned than my comrades and me. My part of the assault line intersects with the oncoming Marines as our two groups walk through each other. The dirtiest guy I have ever seen spots me and turns in my direction. He seems drawn to me like a moth to a flame. I see he has a necklace of dark brown things flopping around his neck. He grins ghoulishly as he walks right up to me and says, "Fuckin' A, brother, look at the ears I cut off the gooks I've killed." I don't say anything back to him. He stares intently at me as if evaluating his next disclosure. When he senses brotherhood in me, he reaches into his right breast pocket for a leather drawstring pouch and shows me 20 teeth with gold fillings he cut from the enemy and says, "I'll melt these fuckers down back in The World and get some fucking dough."

I wonder, could I ever become as bloodthirsty as this guy? I feel a similar attitude. I guess, something about my hostility and isolation had him single me out. Have I changed so much that I might completely lose myself to my anger and act outside my moral bounds? This doesn't particularly scare me. I only have a few more weeks to stay burrowed in my viciousness.

When my dentist asked me if I wanted a gold filling in my molar five years later, I told him that having gold in my mouth scared me because I had seen this guy who collected gold fillings in Vietnam. I trusted my dentist and I wanted him to know me, so we could plan together how to take care of my mouth.

At 7:07, before the sun rises, my radio squeaks. It is the new company radio operator, Craig, telling me to come over to the command tent. What do they want me for? I have never been singled out by company command. The Executive Officer, 1st Lieutenant Foster, tells me I am heading to the ships when the resupply comes in this afternoon. To myself, I think, "What? Gone from here?" It is all too matter-of-fact. I hardly notice any change in my feelings. It seems unreal. When I get back over to the mortar pit I tell

Greg and Cowboy. The mortar squad members all come over and congratulate me. I begin to feel a little excited, which feels scary. I still have to make it through today.

The morning ticks on, second by second. I wonder what it would feel like to me as a 19-year-old sophomore in college to be pulled out of class and suddenly be in my shoes and dirty body for the next eight hours? The grime, the terror and the aloneness would be crazy-making. An eight-hour nightmare of waiting. We move out in a long double column. Now a new awful feeling grows. Dread. Survival. How am I going to be the safest today? I do not know how to think this way. No more kill or be killed. There are good odds we will not be overrun today. I will not draw attention to myself by firing if I can get any kind of protection. At our first stop, I decide to dig a foxhole, which I never have done during a movement. I take off my pack, remove my entrenching tool and feverishly dig for ten minutes. When the hole is deep enough to keep my body safe from incoming fire, we move out. I am aware I have lost the battle to stay present with no expectations. My only hope is action to protect myself.

The temperature is 74°. We stop for the second platoon to explore a tunnel. Again, I dig like crazy. During the minutes of my digging, I realize I am the most noticeable target in our line, although I know the new guys probably also make themselves targets. For the next 50 minutes, I am thankful I risked digging this nice deep hole. I feel safer. We would have to be overrun or an artillery round would have to hit me in the head for me to die. As we move out, I keep my E-tool open in my left hand. With only one hand on my M-16, I won't be as effective at suppressing fire, but I know my skill at eating dirt is more likely to get me through a few hours than looking tough. If rotation out of here was still nine days away, then aggression toward the enemy would still be my first line of defense. Now, I imagine what it will be like to not be here, so I can't trust my killer instinct to protect me. The power of the stronger feelings of fear of not making it out of here has overpowered the well-honed instincts to kill, that we all have deep in us. As usual, I have no idea what we will be doing between now and when I am transported out of here.

After 30 minutes of walking, an artillery round rips through the air. Once again, my biting-the-dirt skills are perfectly successful. The round explodes in the No-Man's-Land 25 feet from anyone in Lima Company and 100 feet from me. Before I begin to dig, I pause for a full second to see if we are going to start moving. We stay hunkered down. As I finish digging my third hole of the day, we move out again. I am up, feeling exposed, with a puny 22 caliber rifle to hopefully scare the enemy from picking me as a target. The feeling of invincibility is there, but now more fragile. I no longer have a duty to Uncle Sam to fight another day. Today, my only duty is solely to myself. This change of focus confuses me. "Shoot first, ask questions later" was based on exuding power and control.

I imagine I look like "Fear" personified every time we stop.

The second platoon, in the vanguard, reports on the radio that they are suspicious of a tree line and want to investigate it. I dig hole number four. This dirt is more sandy as I dig like a madman. Compared to all my brothers who rest in as low a profile as possible, I feel exposed. I haven't scooped out enough dirt to be fully protected. None of my brothers are within 30 feet of me. They are smart, they keep their distance from me, as I am much more of a target during the 15 minutes I dig. Then, I'm safe for 30 minutes, until we move out again. I think I'm traveling to the Pot-of-Gold with my company.

I just begin hole number five, when we move out after a five minutes stop. I climb up a slight rise as we make our sixth stop of the day. I dig the Taj Mahal of foxholes. The dirt is perfect, solid but not hard. I leave the safety of hole number six, as we head out again.

Lima Company is walking on a 6-foot-high causeway toward a tall bamboo tree line. The rice paddies on each side of us are bigger than aircraft carriers. We, mortarmen, are toward the front of our double column. Two reinforced squads of the third platoon, 20 guys, are in front of me. The rest of the mortars are behind me with the 100 other guys of Lima Company following them. On our right, the paddy is filled with greenish-brown water. The paddy on the left is dry, with row upon row of tufts of rice plants waiting for moisture. I walk in a crouch on the right side of the eight-foot-wide causeway, which has been hard-packed from 2000 years of use as a road for carts pulled by water buffalo.

Eventually, the first few guys in our company line enter the tree line. A hand-raised signal to halt passes down the line. I am close enough to throw a baseball into the tall bamboo tree line. This is really exposed! What the hell do I do? I can't find protection by climbing down the steep sides of the causeway because I would be completely exposed to that side. We are in this rice paddy, up on a pedestal, like ducks in a shooting gallery. So, I do my new survival habit, and I start to dig. There is no chance for a straightened shovel to be pushed into this compacted dirt with my boot, so I unscrew the handle and change the shovel-head angle to 90°. I swing down the shovel blade as hard as I can. The tip of my sharpened E-tool sinks in two inches. I pry my little bit of hard-earned dirt out and stack it on the side of my hole. On and on I dig. How long will it take me to get my torso underground? The world seems supernaturally quiet. My comrades are stretched out, flat on their bellies, rifles trained on their sides but towards the treeline.

When hole number seven of the day is 3 feet long, 8 inches wide and 8 inches deep, the world explodes with gunfire around me. Hundreds of AK-47s fire at us from the tree line. I get my torso with head and balls underground. This time my dream about my legs being in harm's way, while my vitals are protected might come true. This is a perfect position. Have I inadvertently provided the NVA with a way to send me home with just hours left on my tour? But, thankfully, my skinny legs don't make enough of a target and I don't get hit. Four Hueys streak over my shoulder and their machine gun rounds rip into the tree line. Despite all the rockets and lead the choppers are throwing at them, there is a steady stream of bullets from the treeline that pours at us.

Two white F-4 Phantoms finally come roaring in, lighting up the enemy treeline with thousands of small explosions from their miniguns. Flying straight along the causeway, one of the jets zooms extremely low right over my buried head. I could easily throw a rock up and hit it as it still heads down. Two bombs spiral off his wings just as the jet passes me. Is it too big and fast-moving to pull up before reaching the tall trees? At the same instant that he let the bombs go, his rear engine fires and pulls his nose abruptly up, thereby, powering upward just soon enough that his undercarriage scrapes the top of the bamboo. The bombs explode, rocking the ground, but the enemy soldiers keep firing.

The NVA must be in trenches that are along the tree line. Three more bombing runs and the jets change their approach to come in along the enemy trenches. The first jet flies in above the trench line. As it approaches the area of enemy fire, the pilot fires his afterburners, which pulls the nose of the jet dramatically up. The engine, in the back end of the tail section, is now pointed almost straight toward the ground. The momentum of the jet has it streaking above the ground with a tail of fire scorching along the ground for the whole trench. Shrieks and yells erupt, as burning soldiers roll in the dirt trying to put out their burning clothes, exposing them to our fire. The next jet follows with the same maneuver and our battle is over. Everything is deathly hushed, except the patrolling Hueys and the distant thunder from Khe Sanh to the west. I find myself thinking my part of these battles is almost over.

Now in the late afternoon, we move out and head south toward the Qua Viet River. Amtraks come rolling in from the direction of Dong Ha. A CH-34 medevac chopper comes in as two Hueys patrol up above for the enemy. This may be my salvation. The Amtraks are then filled and covered with Lima Company Marines going from this "frying pan" into the hellfire of Khe Sanh, 10 miles east in the highlands.

The snaking path of the river becomes more and more picturesque from the doorway of the chopper. The blue ocean beckons at the edge of the greens and tans of the land of terror. I see sunlight streaming through nine bullet holes in the fuselage. I feel and imagine projectiles of varying sizes ripping through this helicopter. The urge for revenge and aggression sneaks back into my being. I can't act on these feelings up here, but it is again safe to let them dominate me.

With only the ocean below me, we head toward an Aircraft Carrier. I see "USS Enterprise" in big letters on the side of the gray hull. My Nirvana. We land on the flight deck and Lima company clerk, Mark, is waiting to escort me deep into the bowels of the ship. I dump my radio, backpack, and all my gear on my rack and head for the first shower in 40 days. I soap and scrub ten times but the mire continues to pour off me on the final rinse. Three weeks from now at my folk's house, after two showers or baths every day, I still leave a black ring of sludge around the tub, and my rage is deep and untouched.

Chapter Thirty-eight
USS Enterprise

"Thank you for your sweetly faked attention"
Kurt Vonnegut, 1981.

Only six of the hundred single bunks in the deserted troop bay are in use. Stan, who arrived in Vietnam a week before I did, works here as our company supply clerk, and is across the birthing quarters near the hatch. My personal gear is in a willy peter bag, and it includes my stone head of Christ, brass sphinxes, 45 pistol, a Chi-Com hand grenade, and a C-ration packet, all of which I intend to bring home.

I make my way down to the mess deck for a full breakfast of hash browns, sausage, eggs, and orange juice. I'm alone in a city of 5000 Navy personnel and a few Marines. I exude 'Don't Tread On Me' with my scowl and the dirt still visible on my face, my tired body carriage, and the fact that I chose a seat far from anyone else. If they take any of the seats in my buffer zone, I want them to feel as if they have invaded my space.

I wander the ship and one floor below the flight deck, I discover a group of guys shooting hoops in one of the gigantic bays. Part of the flight deck moves down with a jet on it to be worked on. I get a basketball and take a shot that is far off the target. I move toward the basket and think I will make a layup to look a little more coordinated. As I attempt to go up in the air a surprise happens. I don't even get an inch off the ground and the shot bangs off the bottom of the rim. I never was a good jumper like my little brother, but my layups were usually ok. I sense that my body has forgotten how to jump after 13 months of walking with heavy loads. I walk away and roam the ship.

No one pays any attention to me, as they all seem to be going to and from tasks. On an upper deck, I hear radio transmissions that have combat sounds in the background. I stand near the door listening and hear, "Lima Six, this Lima One. We are receiving incoming fire from 199327." "Roger that, Lima One. Over and Out." Then I listened as the company commander radioed our artillery in Dong Ha and adjusted the fire with the help of Lima One (The first platoon). They must be out on a patrol a few klicks, (kilometers), from the base at Khe Sanh. Most of the radio traffic for the rest of the day is from India, Kilo and Mike companies, as they are still roaming around the Cau Viet River in the bush. Here I am completely safe, unable to make the simplest shot in basketball, while Lima Company is in Khe Sanh where the equivalent of five Hiroshimas of bombs got dropped during this time.

I wake feeling compelled to get up and listen to the radios again, but Stan tells me there is going to be an inspection this morning after chow. I have skipped out on every inspection since getting to Vietnam. I know what to do about inspections. Get everything ready and make yourself scarce. So before going to breakfast, I neatly and securely pack all of my treasures in a C-ration box. All the individual parts of my 45 pistol are wrapped in separate hiding places. The head of Christ and the brass sphinxes rest on the bottom. I carefully wrap up my Poladroid with all my pictures of the DMZ and put it in the box. I cover the top of everything with a brand-new, empty, plastic sandbag before sealing it closed with masking tape. Looking back on this, of course, the pre-inspection crew could not leave a C-ration box on a bunk, no matter how well it was packed.

I proceed directly to the radio room after breakfast and, as I walk through the hatch, hear one of the hundred radios say "Lima Six, this is Lima Two, come in." In the three seconds that Lima Two's microphone transmits, gunfire and explosions can be heard. "Lima Six to Lima Two, please report." "100 NVA soldiers are attempting to move onto a knoll 500 meters east of Khe Sanh." I can picture the dense fog of late morning, as well as the exhausted terror and rage that comes from being in this type of combat almost every day for six weeks. I also imagine our battalion colonel in his safe command bunker on that hill, smugly knowing he'd make general because he forced his men to fight like this. One of the grunt radios reports that the battalion commander had been shot at from within the base that afternoon. In the 11 days I listened to these radios, the colonel got shot at eight more times by the Marines under his command.

Knowing the inspection will be over, I head back to my berth. My rack is just like I left it, except there is no box on it. I question the Marines in the bay and no one has seen my box. I finally find Stan, who says they probably threw it in the incinerator so the inspecting officers wouldn't flunk them for non-issued gear. Two months of carrying extra weight and no memorabilia. Worse, the Polaroid camera I purchased in the Philippines was included, along with 50 priceless photos from this stage of my combat tour. I have nothing to prove the surreal nature of the last three months. I feel alone and in shock. Well, I still have a Chinese hand grenade stashed in the white phosphorous bag of my clothes and shaving kit. I managed to smuggle this dangerous device home and finally got afraid of it 30 years later and had it disposed of by my county's Hazardous Waste team.

At chow the third morning a Swabby sits down next to me. I resurrect a social demeanor and nod hello to him without saying a word. My discomfort gets stronger as two talking sailors sit across the table from us and include my neighbor in their conversation. As I pass the shortened chow line on my way back to my berth, I see Stan with a less serious look on his face. He says "Stick, I'm fuckin' out of here today." I congratulate him. This means I leave in a week. Nothing registers in my psyche other than being here waiting to go back to combat. I tell him I will come up to the flight deck at 11:00 a.m. to see him take off. Combat is all I know, everything else feels so unreal.

I go up to the flight deck at 10:00 a.m. It's a beautiful, sunny day. People scurry around the deck in all directions. There are only a few areas where it's safe to walk. To stay out of the way, I move to the right side deck, where 50 CH-46 helicopters are strapped down. The rotors are spinning on one of them. A line of 10 Marines with their gear appears at a hatch at the top of a ladder that heads down into the bowels of the ship. The Marines run at a crouch, spread out in a line and go up the waiting ramp into the rear of the bird. Stan sees me and we both wave. His chopper has been liberated. It gradually rises straight up. When it is 20 feet up, it banks slightly to the right and heads for the carrier's edge. The bird battles strong wind gusts. Once the chopper clears the cable railing around the flight deck, a downdraft pulls it down to 10 feet above the deck of the massive ship. Straining, its rotors stay clear of the ship's side. What a rush that must have been for Stan. Nine months of fighting, four months on the ships, and then imagining yourself drowning on the way out of hell. That would have been a terrible way for Stan to die.

I take my 13th shower in nine days and the muck is thinner but still pours down the drain. I head straight up to the radio room to listen and live in my most familiar environment for one more day. At 9:37 the colonel gets shot at again. I go up to the flight deck and watch the CH-46 load troops headed for rotation to the States. This time there are too many guys for a safe flight. I have been in birds that were too heavily loaded and could just barely get airborne. 16 guys and their gear are crammed in this one. Three times the bird lifts and moves to the side, but the wind currents whip around and the weight is too much. Finally, as engines roar with strain, the bird's wheels get off the deck and it pulls sharply left in hopes to get airborne. It gets sucked into the downdraft as it goes by the edge of the ship. I can't see it anymore and the straining noise of its engines is lost in the cacophony of sounds around me as it descends along the skyscraper side of the ship.

I rush down to the radio room to find out what happened. The bird and everyone in it are in the ocean with no trace. What a way for those grunts to end their 13 months of surviving. While they sat helplessly on their butts, with no fucking way to fight back against the enemy of incompetent fellow Marines. I feel a mixture of sadness and disgust for the helicopter crew who were too easy on the grunts who desperately wanted to go home today. You have to know your job or people die. They needed to indiscriminately disappoint some of those guys, so the rest could survive. If I was leaving, I'm sure I would be trying to force the pilots to take me out of here if they tried to exclude me. And yet, it is critical to know your job when survival is at stake.

I lie awake almost the whole night, thinking about flying out of here and the danger of the bird going down. Will I survive to be in the US in a few days? There is a vague realness to the feeling. I have kept that hope buried deep away from my awareness. I still can't imagine Seattle, Port Angeles, Mary Dyar or my family, but the powerful image of leaving Vietnam dominates.

I stay away from the radio room and wait for the order to go to the flight deck. Who knows what Lima Company is up to these days? As my world changes, I learn less and less about them every day. At 10:00 a.m. the speaker in the troop deck says the thing I have waited to hear for 385 days, "Corporal Maier to the flight deck." It's real. No one says "boo" to me as I grab my pack and walk with my head bent down up to the waiting helicopter. It looks just like yesterday's dead bird, an old, beat-up CH-46 Chinook. 12 of us, instead of yesterday's 16, wait for the rear door to drop open. At 11:00 a.m. we are loaded up. I am only aware of the wind and motor noise.

The bird lifts off the deck on its first try, but the wind pushes it abruptly toward the center of the deck. The engine works harder and we move toward the ship's edge, just above the deck. We have the maximum weight this bird can handle with these wind currents. As we clear the side of the aircraft carrier, a powerful downdraft pulls us halfway down toward the ocean. I am staring at the gray paint of the side of the USS Enterprise, impotent, and thinking this is the end.

Will it be just like yesterday? The pilot gives more fuel, which forces the engine to make the rotors go faster and our descent slows to a stop. After two seconds suspended, we begin to drift up and away from the ship and break free of the downdraft. Our helicopter circles the carrier and heads south.

As we fly over the ocean, I see a battleship to our left with its broad side toward the land. Our flight path is halfway between the ship and the shore. One of the eight-inch guns produces flames and smoke out of its barrel. Three seconds after the muzzle flash, the round explodes on a hillside. We turn left and fly far around the back of the battleship and then resume our route south again.

We have an uneventful landing at Da Nang Airport and are guided to the transit tent. There is my friend, McCormick. He and I head over to the club and hammer down beers and forget all about dinner. When we stagger back to the tent all of the cots except one are occupied. Ferrell, a guy from Texas that I was in boot camp with, offers us a toke off a joint he is smoking. I take four tokes as it travels among the five of us. This being my second time using marijuana I can tell that I am stoned this time. My awareness drifts around the tent. One instant I listen intently to a conversation at the other end of the tent. Then I am focused on two guys talking 15' away. Then I am vaguely engaged with the four guys near me.

McCormick and I agree to share the only available cot. He takes the position at the head, his legs draped on either side. I'm at the bottom, my buttocks supported and my legs dangling from the end. We haven't considered the oddity of my head being right in his crotch. I'm drunk, stoned, and 11 nights away from mosquitoes, and forget to tuck my pants into my socks and my shirt isn't buttoned up. When I wake up in the morning I have 100 mosquito bites around my ankles and up the center of my stomach and chest. The tiny Vietnamese Air Force bugs have launched their final harassment campaign against me.

Through the acute itching of the mosquito bites, I think how quickly I forgot last night about survival behavior in the tropical heat and the protection of the rear. With my body scrubbed for 11 days, fattened on prepared food and aromatic from soap, I was easy pickins for the blood-sucking insects. Boy, am I going to regret this lapse of judgment for the next week or so. But now, I am back in the sands of Vietnam. There is no wind at all. It is overcast and cloudy. Distance gunfire and explosions are interspersed with the noise of vehicles and aircraft as they move around the airfield. Chow is some kind of Marine Corps slop-like oatmeal.

Four guys from my boot camp platoon are here in the barracks at Okinawa, freshly back from the bush in Vietnam. I remember that hole in the fence where I snuck out to go to the bars, but I don't know my schedule for heading to the airport, so I stay put. After the usual dull Marine Corps breakfast, we wait in line to call home. I am one of the last guys that get to use one of the eight phones. My mom answers the phone in tears of excitement. It is Friday, March 15th, 1968 there at 9:00 a.m. and 1:00 p.m. Saturday here. I will fly into Seattle via Travis Air Force Base on the 16th at 5:00 p.m. My three minutes on the phone are up in a second.

The 15-hour flight across the Pacific is interrupted for an hour to refuel in Hawaii. We land at Travis Air Force base in time to stow our gear and head to chow, which makes the delicious Navy food seem tasteless. The sauteed vegetables, split pea soup, baked potatoes with butter and pork chops are all perfectly cooked. I wonder if Air Force people always eat like this?

It is an unfamiliar feeling to wake up on a mattress with sheets and a pillow in the comfort of a brick building with windows. Breakfast is waffles and ham. The rest of the morning is spent waiting in lines to finish all the paperwork and be transferred to our new units. I am assigned to the Hotel Company, Second Battalion, 27th Marine Regiment of the Fifth Marine Division in Camp Pendleton, CA. My 30 days of leave will start as soon as we get done with the paperwork.

At noon, I head to the airfield and get on a plane loaded with guys I have never seen before. It is the plane to SeaTac International Airport. After an eternity, we taxi down the runway. I am a little nervous as

I remember how the helicopter struggled to get airborne two days ago. The 707 takes off easily. We are above the clouds in no time. The rest of the trip could be flying over any part of the world. Two hours later when we dip under the low clouds north of Seattle, Mount Rainier is beautifully visible in front and to the left. The Puget Sound and downtown Seattle drift by underneath us. The landing stops at an elevated passenger walkway. There is no climbing down the steps and walking across the runway. Other than being in uniform, we are like regular people.

I do not know who is going to be here to greet me. As I emerge from the tunnel I see my little sister Chris first. How different she looks from age 12 to almost 14 years old. She still looks like a little girl, except taller and way more physically mature. What has she been doing since I last saw her in December 1966? Big sister Barbara runs over and hugs me with tears in her eyes. Mary Dyar waits with my parents for me to reconnect. My Mom is crying. Dad and Mary have big smiles. Dad tells me that Brad is in the State Regional Basketball Tournament this evening and couldn't be here. This seems impossible to me. I am not mad, but it is hard to relate to the idea that my coming back to my family could be less important than anything else.

Inside me, the magnitude of the transition is enormous. My expression and reactions are stoic. I wait with them at baggage claim, awkwardly unsure what to say. They tell me about my cousins and friends. I'm not sure which part of the last few days to bring up. I begin to drift away. Everything around me vanishes. My impulses are dominated by all the blood and gore I have kept from them. I smell gunpowder and diesel smoke, see the debris-strewn rice paddy, and imagine the old man we interrogated. When I see the crispy critter playing in my mind's eye between me and the airport environment, my panic subsides. These horrible ghost stories mingle with me, my family, and the baggage claim area. I re-bury the memories of the nine-year-old girl I shot in the shoulder, Clint's murder, and the old man's death, but they follow me. I'm ready to leave Vietnam.

My old self was never at a loss for words. Now my new character is off to a life with almost no concern for social niceties. I am alert. I walk slowly, aware of each step as we walk toward the car. Treading lightly in this "safe" reality versus explosions awaiting my footfalls. My face and reactions remain stern.

Acknowledgements

The evolution of my fear and those who helped me.

For fear that my horrific combat memories would all come flooding back into my awareness at once, I delayed the task of writing this book for decades. Then, as I finally began, my confidence grew and excitement began to overshadow my trepidation. By March 2019, when I finished the rough draft, I had developed a belief that the world would condemn my actions as a teenager, but I knew I wouldn't be taken over by all the blood and gore of the events I had forgotten.

By reading the entire raw document, Mark Pesola, my friend since seventh grade, entered the story of my writing and still called me his friend. Then, I wanted to know what the rest of you in the world thought of me. I am so thankful for Mark's hand-written notes, of which I included almost all, for they lent me the courage to pursue more input.

In 1990, Jim Stapleton helped me write about my

sole-proprietorship combat veteran counseling business, but the book became a memoir of my time in Vietnam, leading to the above-mentioned fear. So, we shelved it, but over the next 28 years, we discussed my theory of practice helping combat veterans. He and his wife, Diana Bigelow, critiqued the preface of this book. Thank you, Jim and Diana.

I would like to thank my partner, Lois Colton, for being there for me all through the process of writing, editing, querying, and publishing. I met her just before I started writing every morning at 5:38 a.m. on February 23, 2018. She held me emotionally, physically, and socially while I was doing the task I knew I needed to complete. She listened to word choices, sentence structure, paragraph organization, and the overall ideas of my project with sensitive and imaginative commentary. She consistently encouraged my writing style while being my most loving and ardent critic. I'm biased, but I think she is a wonderful writer and coach.

I also want to express my gratitude toward my later readers. Michael Stevens, a fellow Vietnam vet and combat veteran counselor, deserves special thanks for his artistic ability to see how the details of my writing could be improved to enhance the message of my work. George Jackson, Lois's brother, did a read-through looking for redundancy and thankfully found them, although if they remain it is probably that I missed his comments. Jonathan Lurie and Angus Colton, Lois's son, read portions of the manuscript to help me get across the combat value of having been a rebellious, trouble-making boy.

Sandi Scheinberg, of Scheinberg Consulting Inc., moved me toward a narrative style. My stories seemed to be separate balls of yarn that she wanted me to knit into a blanket. Jennifer Springsteen, of PDXWriters, did the yeoman's work of a structural edit of the whole piece. She brought my work into the present moment. Thanks to her, I better saw my intent and therefore, I highlighted the climactic scenes. Moueen A. @QualityHub, from Freelancer.com, provided my line editing.

If any of the book's design graphics catch your eye, credit goes to Karl Moeller. His publishing knowledge and creativity helped to evoke the underlying themes of this challenging time in my life. He has been a joy to work with.

I am grateful for all of my family, who have been encouraging, curious, and patient with how much time I have been preoccupied with the production of this memoir/novel. And thanks to my many colleagues and friends who were tremendously helpful.

Author End Note

A half-century after returning from Vietnam in 1968, I got up 90 minutes early every morning and documented what I could remember of the coinciding dates of the 13 months of my combat tour of duty as an enlisted Marine. I wanted to write down as much as I could remember in order to come to terms with the moral implications of the day-to-day compromises I made during the war. For decades I resisted this job out of fear of re-activating the vicious persona that took me over in combat. However, instead, the writing awakened a sense of duty toward the 1000 Vietnam veterans I had treated for PTSD. The courage those men and women demonstrated in telling their stories helped them heal and lent me strength.

That sense of duty expanded in the 13 months of daily writing to include the men and women who survived combat but were still suffering and hadn't yet sought mental health services. Many of these combat veterans could see no way out of their memories and longingly hoped that suicide would give them relief.

This highly addictive belief grew and grew in their private hells. All of the suicidal patients I treated believed their emotional suffering would end with their death. Could reading about facing my own demons and my recovery, help veterans seek help? By 1990, more American combat veterans had officially died by their own hands, than were killed in action.

I had the added incentive that these disclosures might be sobering to young people with glamourized images of warfare. The inside look at the vast amount of time in "the bush" where nothing happened, many times for hours, even days, and sometimes for weeks, interspersed with moments of random, chaotic violence, might illuminate the realities of how young recruits would spend their combat time. The irrevocable moral injury of killing is an intimate truth for me, and this book contains important insights for people thinking about participating in or advocating for war as a solution to conflict.

Some of my memories were fleshed out as I wrote and became like live-action movies and soon evolved into this book about how my war experiences changed me. I could remember how afraid and in shock I was at the beginning of my tour. I could feel the morning mist on my skin and the smell of the gunpowder and diesel that often surrounded us. With the writing, I learned the reality that all those years ago, my survival instincts had grown with each day in the pressure cooker of combat.

I tried to show the war's psychological and moral cost to me, as well as the cost to America, with over 300,000 wounded and 58,000 killed. Despite our country's friendship with Ho Chi Minh, the president of North Vietnam, we attempted to control this fertile country against the wishes of its people. Over three million Vietnamese died as a result of our war.

Bill Maier

Printed in the USA
CPSIA information can be obtained
at www.ICGtesting.com
BVHW070755170823
668636BV00001B/2